Leading School Renewal

Leading School Renewal explores how school principal leadership behaviour impacts on school change endeavours, and in particular *pedagogic renewal*, which is a form of educational improvement that is primarily concerned with the growing of the knowledge, skills and beliefs of education in a manner that optimises students' life options. The authors identify attributes of principals who have engaged in school renewal and examine the influences on their leadership behaviours and disposition towards renewing their schools while also acknowledging the influence of site-specific contextual variables. The authors propose that certain leadership behaviours exhibited by school principals are integral with renewing a school's pedagogic focus. They argue renewal is a preferred form of sustainable educational change because it relates to deep-seated cultural changes in approaches to pedagogy, curriculum and school structures. Whilst also maintaining that leadership is at the heart of school improvement and principal leadership practices which are based on a clear sense of purpose, values and beliefs about learning and teaching can transform a school into a learning organisation.

Including a foreword by Professor John Hattie, this book is appropriate for all school leaders and educators who want to learn more about school leadership behaviours and highly effective school change.

Steffan Silcox has had an eclectic career in education including roles as both a primary and secondary school principal, district superintendent and Director of schools. He was a lecturer and coordinator of Curtin University's education degree practicum programme. Silcox gained his PhD from Curtin University with ground-breaking research in the area of school pedagogic leadership.

Neil MacNeill is a high-performing school principal, and has been a school superintendent, principal consultant, and lecturer in university Master of Education courses. A prolific writer, Neil constantly looks for better ways to promote teaching and learning, and he encourages younger teachers to write by offering co-authoring opportunities. Neil is currently a principal of a large primary school in Western Australia.

Leading School Renewal
A Guide for Educational Ground Breakers

Steffan Silcox and Neil MacNeill

LONDON AND NEW YORK

First published 2021
by Routledge
2 Park Square, Milton Park, Abingdon, Oxon OX14 4RN

and by Routledge
52 Vanderbilt Avenue, New York, NY 10017

Routledge is an imprint of the Taylor & Francis Group, an informa business

© 2021 Steffan Silcox and Neil MacNeill

The right of Steffan Silcox and Neil MacNeill to be identified as the authors of this work has been asserted in accordance with sections 77 and 78 of the Copyright, Designs and Patents Act 1988.

All rights reserved. No part of this book may be reprinted or reproduced or utilised in any form or by any electronic, mechanical, or other means, now known or hereafter invented, including photocopying and recording, or in any information storage or retrieval system, without permission in writing from the publishers.

Trademark notice: Product or corporate names may be trademarks or registered trademarks, and are used only for identification and explanation without intent to infringe.

British Library Cataloguing-in-Publication Data
A catalogue record for this book is available from the British Library

Library of Congress Cataloging-in-Publication Data
A catalog record has been requested for this book

ISBN: 978-0-367-68988-9 (hbk)
ISBN: 978-0-367-68986-5 (pbk)
ISBN: 978-1-003-13993-5 (ebk)

Typeset in Times New Roman
by Taylor & Francis Books

Contents

List of illustrations xii
Foreword xiv
Introduction xvi

1 Defining concepts associated with school leadership and change: Renewing school renewal   1

OUR BELIEF 1 1
Differentiating school renewal from school reform 2
Leadership of school renewal 10
OUR BELIEF 2 11
Concluding remarks on chapter 12

2 School leader leadership and the processes of leading a school renewal agenda   15

School renewal 15
School leadership in framing the school renewal agenda 17
School leaders' behaviours influencing the teaching and learning enterprise 26
Building a sense of cohesion and Team in the school 28
OUR BELIEF 3 29

3 School leader efficacy and change   31

OUR BELIEF 4 31
School leader and teacher pedagogic efficacy 34
Teachers' pedagogic knowledge bases 36
Student learning and teachers' efficacy 37
Working with teacher self-efficacy instruments 39

vi Contents

    Teacher efficacy and change 39
    Putting it all together: Collective efficacy 40
    Concluding comments on chapter 42

4 Moral leadership guiding school change and vision setting   44

    OUR BELIEF 5 44
    The mission and vision as the starting point for change 46
    The purpose statement and pedagogy 48
    OUR BELIEF 6 51
    The impact of a school leader's personal motivation and flow on their change predisposition 54
    School leader leadership and flow 56
    The importance of moral leadership in school vision setting 57
    Moral purpose and shared leadership 57
    What is a shared moral purpose? 58
    Shared leadership 59
    Moral leadership and authentic learning 60

5 System reforms as catalysts for school renewal   63

    OUR BELIEF 7 64
    The system reform: Moving towards greater local empowerment 64
    Advantages of a devolved system of education 66
    OUR BELIEF 8 68
    Building classroom relationships 69
    OUR BELIEF 9 69
    The external factors influencing classroom culture 69
    Pedagogy: A better way to go 70
    Supporting teachers 71
    The failure to recognise that business models give us a better understanding of what is happening in some education change models 73
    The illusion of autonomy 73

6 Situational factors and their impact on school leadership and change   76

    OUR BELIEF 10 76
    Barriers to change 77

Staff resistance 77
Staff union resistance 78
Parents 79
System level barriers 80
Piggy in the middle (keep away). 81
Toxic management: A culture devouring its future! 81
Toxic management 82
OUR BELIEF 11 83
Toxic school culture 83
Toxic, reluctant managers and toxic, self-promoting managers 84
Toxic culture survey 87
A culture of sycophantocracy is a barrier to change initiatives 88
OUR BELIEF 12 89
Leaders' Achilles' heels 89
Sycophantocracy in school systems 90
Developing a field guide for identifying the sycophantocracy 91
What to do 92
General comment on chapter 93

7 Pedagogic leadership: A view of what real school leaders do   95

   OUR BELIEF 13 95
   Towards an understanding of pedagogic leadership 95
   Pedagogy and curriculum 97
   *Pedagogic obsolescence: School leaders as the endangered species
     in education 98*
   *The Public Management Movement and its implications for school
     leadership 98*
   Pedagogic leadership and Public Management policy 100
   OUR BELIEF 14 100
   Role discontinuity: Killing school leaders softly 103
   *The way forward: The school leader as a significant and credible
     "other" in the work of teachers 104*
   Staff resilience and work practices 105
   OUR BELIEF 15 105

8 The pedagogic wars: A challenge for school leaders   108

   The "pedagogic wars": Deskilling teachers 111
   *Using a full repertoire of teaching strategies: Tiger Woods's golf
     bag 111*

Audit of teachers' pedagogic skills 112
Performance management is a conversation with a purpose 113
OUR BELIEF 16 114
Coaching 114
Mentoring and/or peer observation 115
OUR BELIEF 17 116
Pedagogic profile and performance management 116
Rationale behind the Pedagogic Profile 117
General comment on chapter 117

9 Distributed leadership in modern schooling contexts: Delegation is not distributed leadership   119

OUR BELIEF 18 119
Revisiting distributed leadership: All hands to the lifeboats 120
High-stakes testing and the concept of good in education 120
OUR BELIEF 19 121
School leadership: The importance of a school leader's beliefs 122
Distributed leadership 123
OUR BELIEF 20 123
One external education agency view of school leadership 125
Distributed leadership and our take on it. 125

10 Schools as learning organisations: Growing organisational, professional and personal capital   127

Defining a learning organisation 129
What learning organisations look like 130
Leadership in a learning organisation 130
Schools as learning organisations 131
OUR BELIEF 21 131
OUR BELIEF 22 132
Implementing practices that characterise the learning organisation at the school level 132
OUR BELIEF 23 134
General comments on chapter 134

11 New school leadership: Jettisoning the comfortable present   136

The wild, non-conformist characteristics of entrepreneurial school leadership 136

OUR BELIEF 24 137
Formal performance management of the principal 138
OUR BELIEF 25 141
Concluding remarks on chapter 142

12 Value-adding and student voice   143

OUR BELIEF 26 144
Measuring value-added 145
OUR BELIEF 27 145
Assumptions underpinning value-adding in an educational
  context 146
OUR BELIEF 28 147
General comments on chapter 147

13 Profiling school leaders' leadership standards   149

OUR BELIEF 29 150
OUR BELIEF 30 153
Self-assessment issues in profiling leadership behaviours 154
OUR BELIEF 31 155
Profiling professional growth using the Professional Standards for
  Educational Leaders (PSEL) 156
General comments on chapter 156

14 School leaders and psychological resilience and mental health   160

OUR BELIEF 32 161
Lessons on resilience from a military context 161
The lessons for education 162
OUR BELIEF 33 164
OUR BELIEF 34 165
School leaders dealing with a range of mental health issues
  presenting in schools 166
OUR BELIEF 35 167
OUR BELIEF 36 168
The growth of mental health problems in schools 170
The American case of Adam Lanza 171
The Australian case of Martin Bryant 172
Systemic early identification and risk management 173
General comments on chapter 174

15 Catalytic teachers and the X factor of teaching and learning   178

OUR BELIEF 37 179
How teachers learn and accept changes to their practice 179
Catalytic teachers and teacher leadership 179
OUR BELIEF 38 181
OUR BELIEF 39 182
The characteristics of a catalytic teacher 183
Build the capacity 184
Catalytic teachers and the X factor of teaching and learning 185

16 Accountability and public confidence   186

OUR BELIEF 40 186
The tightening "loose coupling" relationships in schools 188
OUR BELIEF 41 189
OUR BELIEF 42 191
OUR BELIEF 43 195
Venomous accountability 197
General comments on chapter 198

17 Introducing the universal five key steps to sustainable school renewal   200

Leadership and change 200
OUR BELIEF 44 201
Distributing the leadership 202
OUR BELIEF 45 202
OUR BELIEF 46 202
A vision with a thirteen-year horizon 203
Pedagogic leadership 204
The accountability context 205
Introducing the planning for school renewal 207
The human aspect of the Five Phase Change Model 208
Sequencing of planning development 208
Adaptable, multi-skilled leadership 210

18 Conclusion: Positioning the future-oriented school   213

Sustainable school renewal – An ongoing, continuous improvement orientation 217

A summary of our beliefs about educational renewal and change and school leader pedagogic leadership 220

Appendix 224
Index 227

Illustrations

Figures

2.1	Influences on school renewal	18
2.2	A developed model of principal leadership and renewal	24
4.1	School leader leadership style accommodating staff behavioural dispositions	53
5.1	A typical teaching and learning cycle	70
9.1	The distributed leadership – delegation dichotomy	124
13.1	Principal leadership styles and change and risk willingness	155
14.1	Efficiency as a factor of days in combat	163
14.2	Confidence, credibility, resilience and receptiveness to renewal	166
15.1	Critical mass of staff required for change to be initiated	182
16.1	Level of accountability versus public trust	187
17.1	Human Agency Hierarchy of Sustainable School Renewal	209
18.1	Sustainable school renewal schema	218

Tables

1.1	The principles of learning, teaching and assessment	5
1.2	Characteristics of school renewal and school reform	7
2.1	Characteristics of school renewal and school reform – The locus of control	16
3.1	The knowledge bases of teaching	36
5.1	Comparisons between Franchising Model and Independent/Charter type schools	74
6.1	Understanding moral intent and staff efficacy in organisations	85
7.1	Themes and components of The Public Management policy push	99
10.1	The locus of control dichotomy in organisations	128
10.2	Environmental changes as the learning organisation evolves	134
11.1	The phases of development of independent schools	138
13.1	Principal Profile sub-dimension behaviours (Begley & Murray, 1993)	151

13.2	The Administrator as a Visionary Leader (Principal's Profile, Begley, 1990)	151
13.3	Profile Dimensions (Drake Predictive Profiling Instrument, 2001)	152
13.4	The Components of Emotional Intelligence (Adapted from Lanyon & Goodstein, 1998)	153
13.5	Fullan Leadership Behaviour Domains (Fullan, 2001)	154
13.6	Dimensions of Pedagogic Profile of Principal Leadership (Silcox & MacNeill, 2007)	157
13.7	The Creation of a Professional Profile using the PSEL Metric (Structure) Part 1	158
13.8	The creation of a Professional Profile Using the PSEL Metric (Content) Part 2	158
17.1	Pedagogic leadership and instructional leadership	205
17.2	Kohlberg's stages of moral development and external accountability	207
17.3	The universal phases of school and project developments	208
17.4	The five universal stages of sustainable renewal and the leaders' roles	209
18.1	Renewal and innovation differences in school settings	219
18.2	Our personal beliefs about education, leadership and school change	220

Case Studies

CASE STUDY 1	2
CASE STUDY 2	4
CASE STUDY 3	9
CASE STUDY 4	65
CASE STUDY 5	67
CASE STUDY 6	108
CASE STUDY 7	169
CASE STUDY 8	191
CASE STUDY 9	193
CASE STUDY 10	206

Foreword

Esperance is a small town in the south of West Australia, just over 700 km from Perth, almost in the middle of nowhere. It has great beaches, and should be world famous for fining NASA for littering, after parts of the Skylab space station crashed onto the area in 1979. Steffan was the school superintendent and we had some great times running professional learning, meeting the school leaders, and exploring the parks (and both narrowly missing standing on a venomous western brown snake!). Both Steffan and Neil started as principals in rural schools and then rose to be senior government officials, both making major improvements to all aspects of schooling that they touched. This commitment to education shows throughout this book: the experiences of being a school leader, systems leader, researcher (both have doctorates in education), being creative, great listeners, and of course avoiding those snakes that are often around to trip us up.

This book is about focusing all stakeholders in the school in a common narrative, mission, evidence-based and relentless focus on the learning lives of the students; it is about putting the impact of teaching at the forefront; and it is about not being distracted but attending efficiently to all the management, human relation and systems demands on school leaders to ensure this narrative is realized, reliably identified, esteemed and valued. It highlights the deep power of attending to the culture of the school, and the way a narrative by the leaders empowers all in the school to lift this narrative into action and thence into the culture and life of the school.

Viviane Robinson (2017) has implored that we have debates about improvement and not about change (too much change can stifle improvement) and the school renewal focus echoes this claim. It is not imposition from outside or within, it recognizes and builds on the excellence that already is in the school, it capitalizes on a strengths-based approach, but it is not blind to the areas where major improvement may be needed. A major starting point is understanding the expectations of the staff – what do they mean by having a major impact on the learning lives of students, what do they mean by sufficient growth, what do they mean by leading from the middle within a school?

As Rubie-Davies (2015) has convincingly argued, teachers who have high expectations tend to have them for all the students, and sadly those who have low expectations tend to have them for all the students they teach as well. I also note that the average effect-size of student expectation is two to three times more than teacher expectations, so school renewal also means understanding the missions, motives and beliefs of all the students in a school – what a powerful alignment if the leaders, teachers and students (and perhaps also parents) have high expectations, and a purpose of schooling is to realize these high expectations.

As we have demonstrated, those teachers we recall as adults who had major positive impacts on us either aimed to turn us onto their passion and/or they see something in us we do not see in ourselves – hence the purpose of schooling is to raise the expectations that students may have about their aspirations and school performance and not merely accept their own beliefs. It is turning students onto what we value we want them to learn, teaching them the strategies that make the difference when they move towards appropriately challenging goals, making sure that the success criteria are challenging, transparent, and shared, and often smelling the roses of this sweet success of attainment so as to encourage them to keep investing in this place called school. The case study about Outcomes Based Education (OBE) as outlined in this book is fascinating in this respect. OBE focused too much on learning and not enough also on learning about what? It is both the skills and passion of learning and the breadth and depth of precious knowledge that matters in schools. Hence, the anchoring in the beliefs, values and attitudes of the staff, a clear and agreed understanding of what is important for students to know, comprehend and care about, and ensuring these are in "the water" for the narrative, the vision and the daily life of all in the school. And all means ALL. This book is an illustration of collective efficacy in action.

Professor John Hattie
Laureate Professor
Melbourne Graduate School of Education
Melbourne University

References

Robinson, V.M.J. (2017). *Reduce change to increase improvement.* Thousand Oaks, CA: Corwin.

Rubie-Davies, C. (2015). *Becoming a high expectation teacher: Raising the bar.* London: Routledge.

Introduction

> It is better to be a leader among leaders, than a leader of followers.

The intent of this book is our desire to present an insight into significant aspects of school leadership behaviours, and efficacious, effective school change. To some extent our interest in the topics presented in this book have developed as a consequence of our joint, close involvement with schools and school administrators in a variety of contexts over the past 40 plus years, and the direct links that we have had with subsequent periods of significant educational change and personal school renewal endeavours during this time.

It is our determination to explore how school leadership behaviours impact on school change endeavours, and in particular pedagogic renewal, which is a form of educational change that is primarily concerned with the growing of the knowledge, skills and beliefs of education and learning in a manner that optimises students' life options.

We identify the attributes of leaders who have engaged in school renewal and examine the influences on their leadership behaviours and disposition towards renewing their schools, while also acknowledging the influence of site-specific contextual variables on both leadership and leadership outcomes.

Major beliefs about leadership and leading change processes in schools along with associated theoretical constructs that leaders can employ along with challenges they are likely to encounter will be further explored and developed throughout the book.

We propose that certain leadership behaviours exhibited by school leaders are integral with renewing a school's pedagogic focus. Consequently, a fundamental assumption we make in this work is that renewal is a preferred form of sustainable educational change because it relates to deep-seated cultural changes in approaches to pedagogy, curriculum and school structures. We also maintain that leadership is at the very heart of school improvement and so it follows that school leader leadership practices which are based on a clear sense of purpose, values and beliefs about learning and teaching can transform a school into a learning organisation.

Our premise is that while there is a significant body of knowledge that has evolved over time about school leadership, there is in fact an identified paucity of literature on the role that school leadership plays in bringing about a school's pedagogic renewal from practising school leaders' perspectives. Further, we believe that the full impact of school leader leadership behaviours on a school's pedagogic renewal endeavours along with the likely challenges and potential barriers that may be encountered have not been adequately explored in the literature.

Importantly, we have identified a five-phase model of school renewal, and these phases give guidance to school leaders about their courses of action. We argue that the moral imperative of sustainable school renewal is such that the model cannot be ignored.

Join us as we leap into a better future for our students, our staff and our school communities.

1 Defining concepts associated with school leadership and change

Renewing school renewal

Change is exciting when it's done by us; threatening when it's done to us.

It is important to note that in the opening chapters of this book we will differentiate between the concepts of school change, school renewal and school reform and then further, examine the extant bewilderment between the concepts of school leadership, pedagogic leadership and school management. We acknowledge Professor Hattie's timely warning that we need to focus on school improvement, not just the mechanics of change.

Initially, it is important that the concept of school renewal is a term that is differentiated from other forms of school change because the concept of renewal creatively acknowledges what is *in situ* and then inclusively builds on the physical, cultural, personal and spiritual components of the resurrected creation.

So, what do we mean when we speak of school renewal? Renewal is defined and categorised within more recent historical conceptions of large-scale change where the locus of control resides within the school community. Therefore, we begin in Chapter 1 by differentiating between school reform as a change paradigm and school renewal. The relationship between school change propensity and school leader efficacy is also discussed at this time.

OUR BELIEF 1

The sustainable re-culturing of a school requires a proven renewal paradigm of improvement that can be driven by the school leaders.

We have adopted the definition of school renewal as being a continuous process, and a focus on learning and reflection within, and across the school. It is a focus on a school's shared covenant of teaching and learning, and trust in its inclusive processes rather than addressing short-term problems and solutions; and although we acknowledge these must be responded to, a renewing school doesn't lose sight of the big picture. We maintain that school renewal is a moral form of educational improvement that is well suited to thinking school communities. Furthermore, the school renewal process fits seamlessly into the development of sustainability in schools, taking the roots of this concept back to its origins in the renewal of slums and ghettoes in decaying urban sites.

Change for improvement in schools has developed a predictable, cyclic predictability, and as Jukes (2001, p. v) observed: "... there appears to be a furious, top-down, heavy handed, test-driven approach to schooling that is 'primarily being promoted by politicians, corporate officials, and others with mainly political agendas,' not by educators". As a result, we argue that this leads to a great deal of staff and community frustration with the growing perception of the lack of change adeptness of schools.

School renewal is seen as a quantum leap – a paradigm breakthrough – in how we think about and act in relation to change. Low-order change looks at improvement in the efficiency and effectiveness of what was currently done, without really changing or disturbing the basic organisational features of a school. Therefore, school leadership in such a paradigm is very much involved in tinkering at the margins. School renewal as a change process on the other hand seeks to alter fundamentally the way in which a school operates, inclusive of its teaching culture and the goals it pursues, and the structures and the roles of individual groups involved.

At its bottom line, school renewal is seen as an activity aimed at re-culturing the school community to improve students' learning.

Differentiating school renewal from school reform

Educational reform typically seeks to ensure that the functioning and outcomes of education will be in accord with prevailing expectations of education and it assumes that policies, structures and programmes can be modified or realigned to realise this intention. Typically, educational reform focusses on structural change and curriculum modification. Organisational considerations are the dominant force in educational reform and have been often viewed as detrimental to the educative purpose of schools.

CASE STUDY 1

Architectural determinism: Open-area classrooms

Teachers are by nature adaptive, and they can be seen to change their teaching methods to fit the environments in which they find themselves. However, there is another hidden force at work when teachers make changes, and that is they constantly make adjustments between the change and the pedagogic style in which they feel most comfortable. So, while architects have flights of fancy about what they think *modern teaching* will look like, the practitioners are often the greatest resistors to un-negotiated architectural determinism. Such was the case with the Open Area Classroom fad of the 1960s, 1970s and 1980s.

> Larry Cuban (2004, p. 69) pointed out that the Plowden report in the United Kingdom first promoted the idea of open-area classrooms after World War 2, and then because of the severe criticisms of American education following the Sputnik launch, the Americans were attracted to this idea: "Open classrooms focus on students' *learning by doing* resonated with those who believed that America's formal, teacher-led classrooms were crushing students' creativity."
>
> Architects designing new schools in the 1970s were asked to give teachers large open spaces in which to deposit their captive audiences in a way that gave them pedagogic flexibility. Soon. *Berlin Walls* of pinup boards and white boards broke these spaces into traditional four-walled classrooms. And, teachers agreed not to teach near the dividing walls because of the noise intruding into neighbouring teaching spaces.
>
> It was our experience in hundreds of schools that the *open-area classrooms* experiment failed because its pedagogic prerequisites didn't match teachers' capabilities at that time; or, for that matter, the students' requirements for effective learning.

The notion of renewal is grounded in assumptions about the maturation of individuals and society. It speaks of a process of self-renewal through self-criticism with the learning process in mind. Paradigms of educational change, educational reform and educational renewal, result from views as to how the world, human nature and human behaviour are perceived. The renewal paradigm concerns questioning and redefining values about social structure, democracy and freedom, whereas the reform and improvement paradigms, assume compliance with ordained values. Renewal is characterised by teacher responsibility concerning a moral obligation to create and nurture learning environments for their students, as well as themselves.

The renewal approach creates schools that are intrinsically self-renewing in contrast to being reformed or being improved by imposition of externally prescribed and pre-determined goals. The press for renewal is driven by the educational needs of individual students in conjunction with the need for ongoing teacher learning. Thus, renewal is recognised as a *bottom-up* change process that assumes sustainable change emanates from the classroom and school, but it can still be supported at the district and educational system levels. The challenge in implementing school renewal is to change role expectations with respect to how the school leadership views their work and what they value in it. It is seen as a process of building new cultures of teaching as well as of teacher and student learning.

The adoption of a school renewal approach as both a rationale and process for enabling sustained and clearly directed educational change is proposed as a more viable and morally defendable alternative to the existing reform and improvement approaches.

At its most fundamental therefore, school renewal is viewed as an ethical process of change or reform. However, as indicated, there is a recognised difference between educational reform and school renewal. The paradigms of educational reform and educational renewal result from how the learning and teaching enterprise is viewed. The renewal paradigm requires questioning and redefining values about social structure, democracy and freedom. Educational reform on the other hand, assumes compliance with prevailing values. The reform approach seeks to ensure that the functioning and outcomes of education are in accord with the prevailing values and it assumes that policies, structures and programmes can be modified or realigned to realise this intention. Transforming schools, whether directed towards school reform or school renewal, is inextricably linked to the exercise of school leadership.

It is important to differentiate between the term school renewal as an improvement paradigm as opposed to that of school reform with the most significant difference identified between reform and renewal being the locus of control. School reform refers to a top-down, system initiated, temporally defined processes that needs to be done because something is perceived not to be operating efficiently. School renewal, on the other hand, is characterised by a bottom-up, ongoing school community driven approach to educational improvement. As such, the latter suggests that successful school change of a renewal type dimension depends on the school leader building and maintaining collaborative cultures among teachers while simultaneously engaging the wider school community stakeholders in the process.

Educational reform typically seeks to ensure that the functioning and outcomes of education will be in accord with prevailing expectations of education and it assumes that policies, structures and programmes can be modified or realigned to realise this intention. While educational reform is primarily focused upon structural change and curriculum modification this is often accompanied by a corresponding neglect of the learning and teaching process. Political-system level considerations tend to be the dominant force behind most educational reforms, and they are often seen as being detrimental to the educative purpose of schools.

CASE STUDY 2

Failed reform: Outcome based education in Australia

Change, improvement, development, renewal and reform are all types of change in schools and school systems, and because they are a major public cost there is always a multitude of experts who think that can make schooling more efficient, more purposeful, cheaper, and smaller. Not unnaturally, schools are sitting ducks for cyclic reform as the newly appointed levels of government mark their political and socio-economic territory. Such was the case in the late 1990s when state governments across Australia developed their home-grown versions of Spady's (1994) Outcome Based Education (OBE).

In broad terms, Spady's two-part framework was to define what students had to learn, and then redesign the system to give students a maximum opportunity to learn the material (Simonds, 1994, p. iii). This mantra unleashed a reformist trend that was intent on changing the *how* of teaching and learning in schools, with the undisclosed aim of redefining future societal relationships in Australia. The seven Principles of Learning, Teaching and Assessment (Curriculum Council 1998, pp. 33–36) gave instructions to teachers about how to guide the OBE learning process (Table 1.1).

Table 1.1 The principles of learning, teaching and assessment

---

P1. Opportunity to learn. Learning experiences should enable students to observe and practise the actual processes, products, skills and values which are expected of them.
  Pointers:

   1.1 Students engage fully with the concept/s.
   1.2 Students can observe people modelling learning behaviours.
   1.3 Students can view high-quality products of learning processes.
   1.4 The learning situation should be authentic.

P2. Connection and challenge. Learning experiences should connect to the students' existing knowledge, skills and values while extending and challenging their current ways of thinking and acting.

   2.1 Learning should be based on the zone of proximal development.
   2.2 Learners need to be able to connect to new experiences.
   2.3 Students are challenges to go beyond the familiar.

P3. Action and reflection. Learning experiences should be meaningful and encourage both action and reflection on the part of the learner.

   3.1 Learning is enhanced when the student is actively engaged in the task.
   3.2 Learning is an active process (do, imitate, plan, discuss, experiment).
   3.3 Language is a tool for learning.
   3.4 Knowledge and skills are interconnected.

P4. Motivation and purpose. Learning experiences should be motivating and their purpose clear to students.

   4.1 Students should be provided with a purpose for the learning activity.
   4.2 Learning is a rewarding experience.
   4.3 Long-term learning goals need to be developed.

P5. Inclusivity and difference. Learning experiences should respect and accommodate differences between learners.

   5.1 The teaching programme must accommodate children's diverse experiences.
   5.2 Students develop at different speeds.
   5.3 The learning experience should extend beyond the school grounds.

Table 1.1 (Cont.)

P6. Independence and collaboration. Learning experiences should encourage students to learn both independently and from, and with others.

    6.1 Students must become responsible, autonomous learners.
    6.2 Learning experiences should be structured to include access to the community.
        6.3 Classroom practices should recognise that there can be more than one way to do anything.

P7. Supportive environment. The school and classroom setting should be safe and conducive to effective learning.

    7.1 Conditions in the class support the learning environment t.
    7.2 Students should be challenged but never put down.
    7.3 The classroom must be supportive and free from harassment.

The detailed prescription of *how* to teach students meant teachers using the words "teaching and learning" were immediately corrected: "We say, learning and teaching now". School teachers negotiated the curriculum with students, practised cooperative learning, and the teachers became the *guides on the side*. Schools were all required to convert to a student-centred learning paradigm.

Schools quickly made the necessary changes, and implemented Kagan's and Barrie Bennett's student-centred strategies in their classrooms.

By 2003, our schools were high-performing models of cooperative learning, and we show-cased our classrooms in a project called *The Pedagogic Walk*. In this programme five schools opened their classes to hundreds of visiting school administrators and teachers. The feedback was excellent, and we received voluminous confirmation that we were doing the right thing for our students.

However, in 2007, state-wide testing, the precursor to the national testing programme (NAPLAN), was launched and some schools' results were dismal, but there was still a commitment to OBE. That dream was finally ended when system representatives informed school leaders that unless literacy and numeracy results were improved their schools would be punitively reviewed, and put under administrative control.

So ended an ideological experiment that failed to deliver essential learning to students, and as a result the disadvantaged students became even more disadvantaged.

School renewal on the other hand must result in a systematic, sustained effort aimed at change in learning conditions and other related internal cultural conditions in schools, with the ultimate aim of accomplishing educational goals more effectively. The notion of renewal is grounded in assumptions about the maturation of individuals and society, a process more akin to sustainable self-renewal. Paradigms of educational change, educational reform and educational renewal, result from how the world, human nature and human behaviour are viewed.

The renewal approach to change intends to create schools that are intrinsically self-renewing in contrast to being reformed or being improved by imposition of externally prescribed pre-determined goals. The press for this renewal is driven by the educational needs of individual students in conjunction with an associated professional dialogue and ongoing teacher learning. The challenge in both encouraging and supporting the implementation of school renewal is to change role expectations throughout the educational system, particularly how teachers and school leaders view their work and what they value in their work. It is a process of building new cultures of teaching and of teacher and student learning.

Educational reforms are typically episodic and non-continuous, and where specific outcomes are identified, programmes are then developed and implemented to achieve these outcomes. New outcomes are identified, new programmes are developed and implemented and so the cycle continues. The episodic nature of educational reform to result from ephemeral political fashions and result on a new lexicon of *buzz-words*. The persistence of episodic educational change is due to the absence of an agreed strong sense of the purpose of education based on fundamental and enduring values about the future of schools and society.

A significant difference between reform and renewal is that where the former is designed to correct organisational, school or system behaviours or circumstances by external sources, the latter is self-initiated, involving learning from experience and adding to the effectiveness of a school's learning and teaching activity.

There are very clear distinctions between the language of educational renewal and that of education reform. The language of reform carries with it

Table 1.2 Characteristics of school renewal and school reform

... *School renewal*	... *School reform*
• Is a process – general sense of direction	• Is a programme with specific outcomes
• Not specifically time-related	• Has published, short-term timelines
• About personal growth	• Organisational development
• Ecological and serendipitous	• Planned roll-out
• Values the individual	• Values the system
• Learns from failure	• Avoids failure
• Values complexity	• Avoids complexity
• Ethically driven	• Politically driven
• Continuous, critical reflection	• Accountability and evaluation
• A spiritual component	• Managerial goals
• Personal and school growth	• Episodic improvement

the traditional connotations of things gone wrong that need to be corrected, usually by some top-down edict. Consequently, the language of reform is not uplifting. School renewal is a much different game and in terms of approach, multidimensional. The language and the ethos of renewal centres on educators in and around schools improving their practice and developing the collaborative mechanisms necessary to improve the outcomes of their schools. Goodlad (1996) argued that the language of renewal is the language of the self and reflects a supportive and caring learning and teaching ethos. Nothing was found to be comparable in the language of school reform. However, it is also noted that in a renewal context, for desired changes to eventuate, all stakeholders involved need to share the vision as articulated for the proposed change by a school's leader.

School reform, on the other hand, is a largely system initiated and more technically oriented process. As such the approach assumes that school improvement is primarily a problem that can be solved through policy development, resource provision or redistribution or professional development with associated accountability, monitoring and evaluating processes attached (Smith & Fenstermacher, 1999).

Conversely renewal literature discussions tend to relate to a process of teacher and school change, and involve nurturing the spiritual, affective and intellectual. Sirotnik (1999) confirmed this distinction between reform and renewal:

> Reform was about whatever was politically fashionable, pendulum-like in popularity, and usually under-funded, lacking in professional development, and short-lived. Renewal was about the process of individual and organizational change, about nurturing the spiritual, affective, and intellectual connections in the lives of educators working together to understand and improve their practice. Renewal was not about a point in time; it was about all points in time – it was about continuous, critical inquiry into current practices and principled innovation that might improve education. (p. 607)

Renewal as a change paradigm is the ongoing process of *critical inquiry* and problem solving, and so becomes a dichotomy where the professional/organisational life in schools versus some new implementation of whatever seems fashionable or politically expedient for teaching, learning and evaluation. This form of critical inquiry requires continual and informed reflection about what the school is doing now in terms of its learning and teaching approaches, how it came to be that way, what values, beliefs, human interests are at work (and at stake), what further information is needed, and what action is taken, and cycling through this whole process over time. Such a view also sits comfortably with the concept of a learning organisation. The concept of a school as a learning organisation is more fully developed in Chapter 10. Learning organisations are characterised as having an ability to adapt by being change-adept, foster staff learning and experimentation, rather than being stuck in unproductive routines. School renewal recreates the organisation from within, through changes that are encouraged and supported by continuous reflection and improvement of the education process at every level.

> **CASE STUDY 3**
>
> *The impetus for change*
>
> Three principals share their perspectives on the underlying reason that they were going to address curriculum and cultural change in their school by employing a renewal paradigm of change.
> The first principal interviewed indicated that:
>
>> In terms of personnel and school operations the school was a basket case. When I was first appointed to the school the teaching was didactic, threatening for students. The parents and the teachers were at war. It was a toxic environment for learning and teaching to occur.
>
> Similar concerns were expressed by a secondary principal who indicated that:
>
>> The school change culture was best described as resistant and reluctant, slow on uptake of system imperatives, lack of knowledge and currency, some keen to learn, others fearful. Teamwork could best be described as dysfunctional due to lack of teacher leaders, undermining by original staff towards new staff, newly appointed staff created cooperative minority. However, there was at least a willingness to explore working together if given the time to do so.
>
> Another principal remarked:
>
>> A group of traditional parents was very influential with the past principal in determining changes within the school. They became obstructive and divisive when they did not agree with decisions made or changes planned, bullying tactics applied to other parents and towards me. They had a strong commitment to maintaining status quo and openly argued an anti-change disposition.

Peter Senge (1995) proposed that the essence of the learning organisation was a deep learning cycle with the development of new capacities with individual and collective shifts of mind. This results from a developmental process in which new skills, capabilities, awareness, sensibilities and attitudes and beliefs evolve. From an educational change perspective, school renewal necessitates teachers themselves to be actively engaged in learning (an anagram of renewal is "we learn").

Leadership of school renewal

The school renewal paradigm we have outlined is one associated with transformative change that brings about multi-levelled structural, social, pedagogic and educational changes through the actions of school leadership and staff. The role of the transformative (in the adjectival sense) leadership in the school renewal process can be conceptualised as multi-faceted, but significantly underpinned by an understanding of how students learn, and pedagogy specifically.

We have indicated that at the school level the school leader is charged with establishing a community of professionals working towards a vision of teaching and learning, so consequently this implies that a goal of leadership in a renewal context is to get all stakeholders heading in the same direction.

School leaders can achieve this goal by being *change-adept* and *risk-willing*, establishing a common perspective of the desired future state (achieved by engaging and collaborating with staff) and by making explicit the connections between successful informed pedagogical theory and practice.

However, while effective leadership is identified as a prerequisite for school renewal, in itself it is not enough. As indicated, it also requires the presence of a clearly articulated and compelling vision for the school, grounded in a reality that describes what the organisation will look like when operating in its future state. Too often school staff have a tendency to overly depend on strong school leaders for direction and guidance to encourage and facilitate the renewal changes momentum, energy and ongoing stakeholder commitment to the cultural outcomes being sought.

We acknowledge that it is often difficult for some school leaders to change their leadership styles after operating within a given school culture for some time, and consequently perhaps an ideal opportunity for a school to engage in renewal occurs when there is a leadership change within the school context. Such a change creates an opportunity for the school community to explore – through processes of visioning – school renewal, in conjunction with the incoming school leader. However, while this presents an ideal opportunity to address underpinning cultural and pedagogical change, it is in no way a prerequisite for a school renewal approach to be initiated and fostered. The necessity for the school leader to facilitate, motivate and show leadership throughout the changes proposed are of course identified as essential prerequisites for successful renewal outcomes to be maintained. Therefore, the school leader occupies a crucial role in facilitating change processes, balancing the demands of the various stakeholders within the school with those external to it.

According to Rust and Freidus (2001), to be effective as a change agent within a renewal context, school leadership needs to adopt four critical roles. These are the negotiator, the nurturer, the learner (i.e. learn the delicate balance of guiding and letting go) and the pedagogic-curriculum developer. Leadership within a renewal paradigm, therefore, would necessitate school leaders possessing behavioural attributes that enable them to rethink, reshape and revision schools and schooling. The skilful school leader will be able to establish an empowering atmosphere in a school such that teachers see themselves as working cooperatively for their mutual benefit and for that of their students.

Those leadership factors or characteristics likely to be found in schools which are seen to be most effective in achieving excellence in student outcome attainment or whose performance is continually improving over time are readily distilled from education literature available on this topic. Among those factors identified in extant literature and our practice include: adept and credible leadership from the school leader; a shared vision and goals clearly articulated by the school leader that underpin the school's operations; the school leader ensuring a school environment that is focused on its core business of learning and teaching; strong school leader and school community expectations for student learning; the school leader engaging and encouraging parent participation in the governance of the school with clear communication processes fostered by the school's leadership and, a learning organisation ethos being fostered in the school.

School improvement, the result of a school's decision to initiate action in the light of an internal or external assessment against determined school effectiveness considerations, requires a fundamental change in the culture of the school. Consequently, school improvement activity will by necessity impact upon the beliefs, values and attitudes of the school leadership and the community about the school and, in particular, about learning and teaching practices employed by staff. We argue that pedagogic and curriculum restructuring does not lead to improvement unless there is a corresponding change in school culture to accompany it.

OUR BELIEF 2

> The improvement of students' learning outcomes often requires a significant change in a school's pedagogic culture.

The concept of re-culturing is critical in understanding school leadership and school renewal and its relationship to organisational efficacy and effectiveness. To be sustainable, school renewal requires a holistic pedagogically focused leadership approach guided by clarity of vision, a commitment to mission and with attention given to every aspect of a school's learning and teaching programme.

A word of warning to principals getting ready to undertake a renewal journey from a fellow principal:

> One step at a time. Don't bite off too much at once. You don't have to be on top of one change agenda before you start another. Knowing staff

capacity for change and your resource limitations are essential considerations when renewing a school's learning environment.

Effective school leader leadership can both ignite and initiate action amongst staff, guide their learning and teaching endeavours in a given direction, maintain the efficacy and effectiveness of the processes, and unify efforts towards a common goal. Leadership is seen as the purposeful intent of influencing others to contribute to commonly agreed goals and begins initially by describing the journey's destination. In this way, it becomes a consensual task through which the leader devises and articulates a vision, establishes a road map or strategy for achieving it, then through motivation, builds a significant mass of people who agree with and can accomplish the vision.

Concluding remarks on chapter

Any school's efforts at improvement will necessarily impact upon the beliefs, values and attitudes of its staff and the community that it serves, in particular those relating to the learning and teaching practices employed by staff, approaches to curriculum delivery and subsequently on the learning and teaching culture itself. School change can often be the result of a collective decision to initiate action in the light of either an internal or external assessment against determined school outcome considerations or the easing of constraints through system level reforms, and consequently it can be expected that this will result in a change in the culture of the school.

Pedagogy, curriculum and organisational restructures do not lead to improvement unless they result in a very real change in school culture with a resulting gain in student outcome achievement. Such re-culturing may involve going from a situation of limited attention to pedagogy and assessment to a situation in which teachers and others routinely focus on these matters on a daily basis in their classrooms.

When the locus of this re-culturing grows within the school itself, the term school renewal is often applied. Sustainable school renewal requires school leader leadership and a holistic teaching approach guided by clarity of vision, a commitment to the school's stated mission and with attention given to every aspect of a school's learning and teaching programme. Re-culturing is the process of developing professional learning communities in the school. When this happens, deeper changes in both culture and structure can be accomplished.

Improvement and change in a school's learning and teaching culture requires of all its staff a commitment to contribute to commonly agreed goals, whether it be for the benefit of the individuals as well or for the organisation or common good. Any major change effort must begin initially by describing the journey's destination which in itself is a consensual task through which teachers devise and articulate a vision for the learning and teaching enterprise of which they are part, set a strategy for achieving it, build a network among their colleagues who agree with and can accomplish the vision, and motivate these people to work hard to realise the vision.

Cultural change is always difficult where teachers' pedagogic behaviour is based on deep beliefs, values and assumptions that they hold and which may have been shaped over considerable time and through a multitude of varied life experiences, and further it relies on an unwavering ethic of continuous and lasting change that will enhance student engagement with their learning. "The main problem in public education is not resistance to change but the presence of too many innovations mandated or adopted uncritically and superficially on an ad hoc fragmented basis" (Michael Fullan, 1993). Fullan's words point out that within our schools we are what we do.

Teaching is recognised as a complex task and this complexity is evidenced in the many issues and responsibilities that are dealt with by both the school's leadership and staff, on a daily basis. Therefore, any press for change must be tempered by contiguous whole-school accountability and compliance with prevailing legislation and system regulations and policies concerning management of finances and resources, and staff. The school leader's role encompasses both *leadership* of student learning and contribution to the *management* of the school as an organisation, and while the latter is important, it must never have the primacy over our role as leaders of learning.

Quality teaching is still the key to success in our schools. What school leaders do in their schools and their stewardship of both teaching and learning impacts on student outcomes.

Pedagogic school leaders along with their staff make a real difference to their students' life prospects.

References

Cuban, L. (2004). Whatever happened to ...? the open classroom. *Education Next*, 4 (2), 69–71.
Curriculum Council of Western Australia (1998). *The curriculum framework for kindergarten to year 12 education in Western Australia*. Osborne Park, Western Australia: author.
Fullan, M. (1993). *Change forces probing the depths of educational reform*. London: The Falmer Press.
Goodlad, J.I. (1996). *Educational renewal: Better teachers, better schools*. San Francisco: Jossey-Bass.
Jukes, I. (2001). Foreword. In W. Spady, *Beyond counterfeit reforms* (pp. i–iii). Lanham, MD: The Scarecrow Press.
Rust, F.O., & Freidus, H. (2001). *Guiding school change: The role and work of change agents*. New York: Teachers College Press.
Senge, P.M. (1995). *The fifth discipline: The art and practice of the learning organization*. New York: Doubleday.

Simonds, R.L. (1994). Comments from the field. In W.G. Spady, *Outcome Based Education: Critical issues and answers*, (pp. iii–v). Arlington, VA: American Association of School Administrators.

Sirotnik, K.A. (1999). Making sense of educational transformation. *Phi Delta Kappan*, 80(8), 606–610.

Smith, W.F., & Fenstermacher, G.P. (Eds.) (1999). *Leadership for educational renewal*. San Francisco: Jossey-Bass.

Spady, WG (1994). *Outcome Based Education: Critical issues and answers*. Arlington, VA: American Association of School Administrators.

2 School leader leadership and the processes of leading a school renewal agenda

This chapter specifically examines the role the school leadership plays in a type of whole-school change called school renewal. If addressed systematically, school renewal can engage and excite the school community to promote, accept and embed the changes intended to improve student learning outcomes. We believe the school leader's leadership qualities play a critical role in bringing about effective school renewal.

School renewal

Change in schools is both topical and problematic. Understandably, school staff are tired of the episodic, politically driven waves of reform that last as long as those in power persist. An alternative to reform, school renewal, is a change process that has an almost spiritual, and certainly an ethical motivation that re-excites the motivation of the many teachers who entered the profession of teaching as a calling to do good for others. The challenge for the school leader is to create a learning context that will operationalise the visionary components of the whole-school changes that are being proposed. The resurrection of urban slum areas is termed *community renewal* and the renewal of religious beliefs is called *spiritual renewal*. School renewal elicits the positive connotations of both of these processes, and it has the ability to change forever people's beliefs about learning, teaching and schools.

We believe that a word of caution is necessary at this juncture, however. Reformers who wish to disguise their top-down political intentions sometimes access the positive connotations of the term school renewal. In Table 2.1 we have outlined a basic dichotomy that demonstrates the difference between reform and renewal. The comprehensive characteristics of school renewal presented will serve as a working definition for this chapter.

The contextual power of a cultural framework to create a reality for an educationally defined construct such as renewal lies within the lived experiences of both the framers and the framed. For the initiators of a renewal agenda, the knowledge and implementation processes, they have devised and enacted are perceived to be moral, plausible, coherent and right.

Table 2.1 Characteristics of school renewal and school reform – The locus of control

	School renewal (Locus of control in the school community)	School reform (Locus of control is external to the school)
Participatory leadership	Initially reflective and pedagogically and curriculum focused and led by the principal. A collaborative and participative approach evolves as staff embrace changes. The principal initially establishes the boundaries and vision for the change and facilitates staff professional learning.	Principal acts as a motivator for centrally determined curriculum, policy or structural change. Teacher involvement in leadership roles and decision-making as required. Teachers as change agents.
Shared vision and goals	Principal initially articulates a sense of purpose and direction for renewal. A shared vision evolves with time along with staff ownership of the change that is characterised by a sense of unity of purpose. Pedagogically focused. Consistent practice sought.	Vision developed within parameters established external to the school Accountability and outcome-driven. Changes sold as being for the whole school's good. Strong structural and curriculum elements to change.
Teamwork	Collegial and collaborative.	Teacher involvement and empowerment. Opportunities for collaboration and collegiality are contrived.
Learning environment focus	A safe supportive and inclusive student-centred and focused atmosphere. A staff culture that values informed practice in learning and teaching. Strong parent involvement and participation in governance. Experimentation and risk-taking encouraged.	An effective school orientation with an orderly and secure environment. A positive ethos. Risk-taking is facilitated with associated monitoring processes.
Learning and teaching focus	A focus central to student needs. Varied and appropriate repertoire evident in teaching practice. Teachers encouraged to learn and new strategies.	Outcomes emphasis. Achievement focus. Efficient and effective organisation. Clarity of purpose. Adaptive practice.
High expectations	High expectations held for all by the school community. Aspirations and success criteria shared communicated and celebrated. Intellectual challenge.	High expectations about and for student learning.

Table 2.1 (Cont.)

	School renewal (Locus of control in the school community)	School reform (Locus of control is external to the school)
Monitoring and enquiry	Setting, monitoring and evaluating success criteria. Classroom research techniques used by teachers. Ongoing review and necessary adaptation of curriculum and teaching approaches.	Emphasis on monitoring student performance. Evaluating school performance in line with external measures.
Students' rights and responsibilities	Teachers as facilitators and negotiators of student learning. High pupil self-esteem. Students have responsibility for their learning.	Eliciting students' views about the approach to learning. Control of work in line with outcomes orientation.
Learning for all	Teachers seen as continuing learners. Coaching and mentoring by leadership and peers. Peer observation and feedback. "Critical friendships". School-based and initiated staff development.	System-based staff development.t
Partnerships and support	Parental involvement, participation and governance.	Schemes to involve parents and community. External support. Developing networks and clusters.

School leadership in framing the school renewal agenda

The four predominant influences on the framing of a school renewal agenda associated with whole-of-school educational change are:

- the attributes and disposition of the school leaders, including their moral, efficacy and ethical beliefs;
- school contextual influences relating to stakeholder perceptions of the leader's credibility and integrity;
- the perception of school staff perpetuated through previous experiences in respect to educational change (intrinsic and extrinsic); and,
- the leader's leadership disposition and engagement in renewal.

The impact of and interrelationships among these idiographic and nomothetic framing influences on the creation and enactment of school renewal processes associated with the eclectically defined construct are illustrated diagrammatically below in Figure 2.1.

18   *School leader leadership*

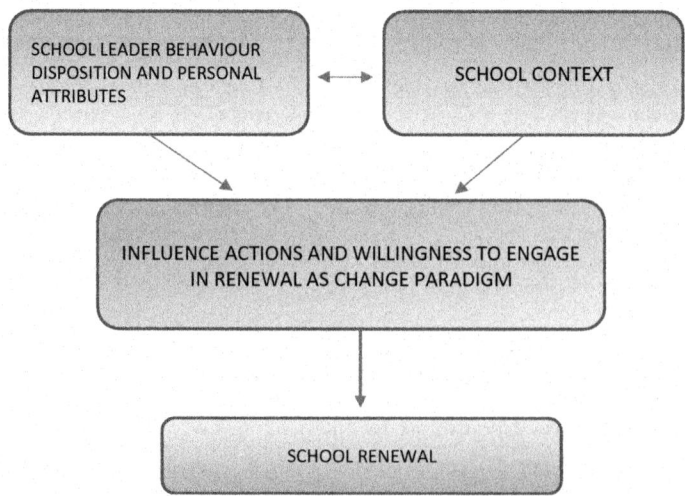

Figure 2.1. Influences on school renewal.

The three influences on school renewal were seen in a dialectic sense, both of the construct and in the framing itself. All three combine to create the framework through which an interpretation of the construct of school renewal can be understood and analysed. In the model presented in Figure 2.1, school environmental factors and, in particular, staff, and, or, community disposition towards renewal, are seen to influence the rate of adoption of change. The orientation of the wider school environment, whether positive or negative, has a direct impact on the leadership approach adopted by the school leader in respect to the way they engage stakeholders in the renewal process. Communication strategies employed, coaching and training styles, relationship building activities, flexibility and team building (relationships) approaches are influenced by stakeholders' attitudes. Likewise, the school leader's own disposition and personal attributes (proactivity and risk orientation) are identified in the model as influencing their attitude towards initiating and implementing change in a school. The combined influence of the school context (including stakeholder dispositions) and school leader behaviours will together influence whether or not the school leader is predisposed to adopting an approach that leads to initiating a renewal agenda in a school.

The model proposes that by a school community engaging in renewal there is a corresponding reciprocal influence on the school context and disposition, and likewise on school leaders' behaviours. This is because, as the renewal agenda progresses, staff and community attitudes alter as the changes are adopted and gain general broad acceptance with them. A change agenda therefore, requires different behavioural emphases at various stages of implementation. The literature in the area of educational change indicates that in the initial phases of change behaviours associated with motivating and stimulating stakeholder interest are required from the school leader (namely, visioning, change agency, communication). These leader behaviours alter as the renewal agenda becomes embedded in the school to encompass an orientation of more relationship building (coaching, team building) and nurturing in nature.

It is realised that renewal needs to be grounded in the realignment of the school's pedagogic and curriculum practices. School leaders are required to assume a key pedagogic leadership role in the renewal process. The evidence provided through a detailed school-district study has indicated that school renewal progresses through a common frame of action that incorporates:

- a personal predisposition to making changes in the school's existing pedagogic and curriculum approach;
- a stage of contemplation during which time the vision for renewal is developed, strategic alliances and networks formed and, collaborative teams developed;
- expectations for renewal are negotiated with informed practice identified, boundaries established, line-management informed;
- a stage of action during which time existing practices are challenged, creating experiences and professional learning opportunities. It is at this point that the use of catalytic staff is identified; and,
- a period of consolidation where staff members are engaged in renewal and pedagogic practices become routine and gain widespread accepted.

The response to change of this form is not uniform, however, as this school leader's statement to the authors expressing her frustration at staff attitudes to school renewal indicated:

> There was a general hostility, indifference and reluctance to renewal from staff. Traditional teacher-directed strategies and thinking was dominated by a lack of a genuine commitment to teaching and knowledge of current pedagogies. Unfortunately, strategies were very teacher-directed; traditional, with excessive use of dated teaching methods. I worked with staff who had shown some interest in their learning and teaching practices in order to get them on side with the changes I proposed.

And another response from a secondary school leader regarding the task of initiating and maintaining a change agenda in her school:

> In terms of culture, I knew from my own professional readings and study that a collaborative culture, based on open and honest reflection, could be helpful in bringing about improved student learning. During the first part of my appointment to the school, I was quite didactic in what I wanted from teachers, but I think the results of this were to take teachers away from their old ways of thinking and doing their work, to being much more receptive to new ways.

A leader's decision to renew or maintain the pre-existing school culture will be influenced by both school context and extraneous influences (staff and community disposition to the renewal agenda) and the behaviour disposition and personal attributes of the school leader. In terms of the school context and associated influences, staff and community disposition towards change impacts on the rate at which the school leader can implement the desired renewal agenda. The rate at which the renewal agenda can be progressed is further affected by the rate at which staff members are willing to accept and adopt desired practices as articulated by the school leader as part of the renewal agenda.

Staff progress through a number of phases in their acceptance of the renewal agenda:

- Firstly, they gain knowledge and experience with and about the changes proposed and/or required of them in terms of pedagogic and curriculum practices. These desired changes are articulated by the school leader, usually in the form of a sense of direction or personal vision for learning and teaching in the school.
- Secondly, staff form an attitude towards the renewal agenda (positive or negative) based on their personal perceptions of the effect and impact of that change on their personal teaching endeavour and comfort.

The leadership approach adopted by the school leader is a crucial consideration as the degree of persuasion and influence exerted, along with the coaching and mentoring of staff are seen to impact on the teachers' decision to adopt the changes proposed. Once staff have decided to implement the change agenda at the classroom level, they then seek confirmation from leadership about their choice and relevant credible feedback on their endeavours. In summary, the process can be presented as:

- staff exposure to the pedagogic and curriculum changes required;
- an attitude towards the renewal agenda, either positive or negative, is formed by staff;
- engagement or resistance is exhibited;
- staff employ desired practices in their teaching endeavours within the classroom and at a whole-of-school level; and,
- teachers seek reinforcement for the practices they have adopted and acknowledgement of their efforts.

A school leader undergoing a re-culturation process in her school remarked:

> As the school was a merit-select school I was able to introduce a critical mass of staff who exhibited the pedagogical approaches and curriculum

understanding needed to bring about change. I guess I used a divide and conquer approach.

School renewal requires pedagogic leadership from the school leader. Such a proposition would support the contention that leadership and management are not mutually exclusive, but that school leaders have a disposition towards a certain approach that is either more leadership or management focused. The corresponding impact of the approach they adopt will influence whether or not the school will be likely to undertake a renewal experience or continue in a maintenance mode with little likelihood of significant changes occurring to its existing culture and interactions.

School renewal requires a disposition towards behaviours associated with change agency, visioning, issue discovery, proactivity, coaching, team building, risk-willingness and improvement, whereas maintenance of the existing school culture requires behaviours that are associated more with management type behaviours. Within a school renewal context, leadership is seen as the exercise of high-level conceptual skills and decisiveness, and is about articulating a vision for the organisation, developing an orientation for the change agenda proposed, inspiring staff and stakeholders with cultural change the product.

Leadership of renewal is about conceiving new ways to promote professional discourse among teachers about their pedagogic practices to enhance learning and teaching outcomes. In order for this discourse to eventuate, the school leader's understanding and credibility in terms of pedagogic practice is an essential ingredient in the process. From our experience we note that such leadership can be very demanding personally on the school leaders, requiring them to lead and not to be caught up in the day-to-day milieu of administration associated with school management.

Implementation of a renewal agenda in the school incorporates wholeschool cultural change. By implication the change in school culture, in turn, influences existing staff and community attitudes and disposition towards learning and teaching. Such a change also influences reciprocally the school leader's behaviour within the school context, further enhancing or otherwise their sense of efficacy and credibility with respect to initiating and leading whole-of-school change endeavours. The disposition of staff and community towards change influence the rate of implementation of the proposed change and, further, the behaviours of the school leader. This further impacts on the way the school leader goes about implementing change, communicating the expectations for the change agenda to stakeholders and how professional learning experiences are created and facilitated for staff to encourage different pedagogic approaches to learning and teaching. In Chapter 15 we explore the potential use of what we term *Catalytic Teachers* by school leaders that can help facilitate the cultural change processes.

The model represented in Figure 2.2 recognises that the school leader's leadership orientation towards school renewal is influenced by both a specific set of individual leader's behaviour attributes and disposition and, the rate of renewal by school community attitudes towards the change agenda proposed.

It is acknowledged that leadership within a renewal context is concerned with deeply embedding change, particularly when shifts in underlying assumptions and beliefs are required. Achieving ongoing cultural change through organisational renewal is a challenge of school leadership. The differentiation of school renewal from school reform is important in this respect as renewal is very much concerned with whole-school cultural change, particularly in terms of the school's approach and attitudes towards the learning and teaching function. School renewal is facilitated when the school-based change has staff reflecting upon, and where appropriate, renewing their fundamental beliefs and enthusiasm about teaching and learning.

Whole-of-school cultural change is always difficult to initiate and achieve, particularly in cases as described by renewal where existing behaviour and dispositions are based on a staff and community's deep-seated beliefs and assumptions about learning and teaching that may have been shaped over prolonged periods of time.

Fostering learning at the individual level is not just a matter of supporting and coaching people in acquiring new skills and knowledge. The leadership challenge in a renewal context implies such aspects as working with people to assist them to become more self-aware about how students learn, to clarify and to challenge if necessary their assumptions about learning and teaching, and to identify realistic strategies for moving forward in a collaborative and collegial way in the school. School leaders' roles in renewal, at this level, are about creating and facilitating the conditions under which the staff and community can reflect upon existing learning and teaching practices with an eye to improvement. It is clear, therefore, that in performing the tasks associated with the role of leader, the school leader becomes the context setter for school renewal and the designer of learning experiences for the school community. The connections between school leader behaviours and leadership orientation towards renewal within the model, as represented in Figure 2.2, capture this relationship.

A process perspective on leadership suggests that the leader of renewal needs first to reflect on assumptions about what is implied in the changes proposed, particularly in terms of attitudes and beliefs about learning and teaching and whether resistance is likely to occur and why. Identifying the resisters and what specifically is causing the resistance will influence both the leadership approach and strategies that are eventually adopted. The prevailing school culture and disposition towards renewal is identified as a most significant consideration expressed by school leaders. The rate at which changes proposed could be introduced was determined, largely, by the disposition of the school staff and wider community towards what was being proposed. The model presented captures this relationship and the influence that such a community disposition has on the leadership's willingness to engage in renewal.

A perceived danger is that the school leader, in articulating a vision for school renewal, will focus on doing what is already being done in terms of learning and teaching practice, although perhaps with an eye to fine-tuning and continuous improvement of what already exists. Building capacity for achieving effective implementation of a school renewal agenda, for dealing with contentious issues and for achieving desired change, however, often requires that school leaders do some quite different things equally as well, particularly in terms of introducing changes in the way to make staff think about their teaching and build shared ownership in the process.

A comment by a primary school leader interviewed about the process they were employing in re-culturing their school captures the intent of the process of renewal:

> Curriculum and pedagogy issues drove my decision-making agenda in the school. Priorities for school renewal fell out from this process. For every change the question was asked – how will this decision or change improve the quality of teaching and learning across the school? In initiating a pedagogically focused whole-school change initiative in the school I first determined the number of staff who had orientation to learning and teaching required. They were used to help develop the understanding of other staff.

And the comment of a secondary school leader along similar lines is likewise insightful:

> I was willing to engage them (staff) in a direct way because I was confident that they would derive benefit and enjoyment from the experiences offered in renewing the schools learning and teaching program.
>
> During the first part of my appointment I was quite explicit in what I wanted from teachers, but I think the results of this were to take teachers away from their old ways of thinking and doing their work, to being much more receptive to new ways.

Leadership of school renewal, with its focus on major curriculum and cultural change, necessarily involves both risk and threat. Leadership also implies a need to deal with emotional factors – including the fear of one's own response to the reactions of others. The leader's personal sense of efficacy is identified as an important consideration in this regard. Leaders who have a strong belief in their personal and professional capabilities think, feel and behave differently from those who have doubts about their capabilities. Those who doubt their capabilities shy away from difficult tasks and problems and have low aspirations and weak commitment to the goals they choose to pursue. To those with a strong

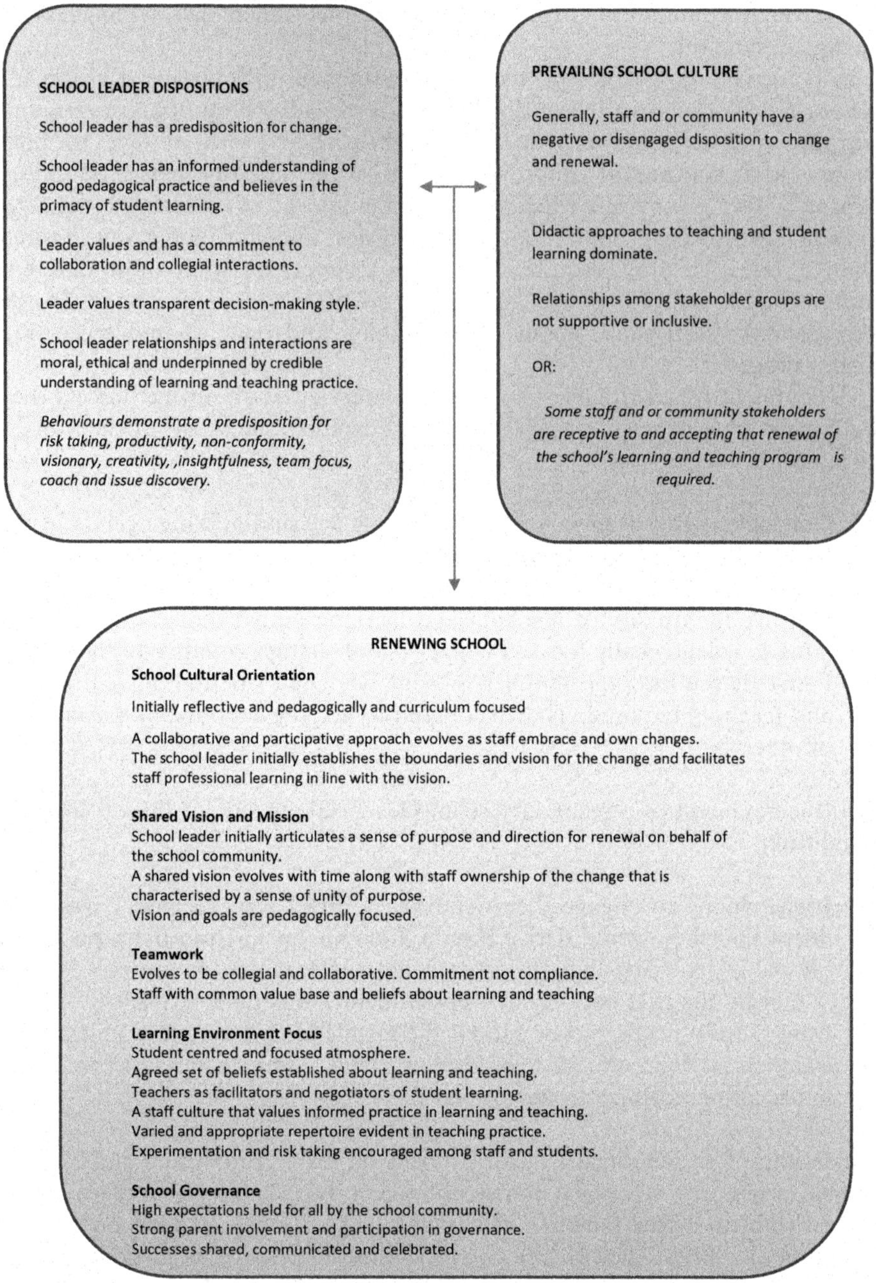

24 *School leader leadership*

SCHOOL LEADER DISPOSITIONS

School leader has a predisposition for change.

School leader has an informed understanding of good pedagogical practice and believes in the primacy of student learning.

Leader values and has a commitment to collaboration and collegial interactions.

Leader values transparent decision-making style.

School leader relationships and interactions are moral, ethical and underpinned by credible understanding of learning and teaching practice.

Behaviours demonstrate a predisposition for risk taking, productivity, non-conformity, visionary, creativity, ,insightfulness, team focus, coach and issue discovery.

PREVAILING SCHOOL CULTURE

Generally, staff and or community have a negative or disengaged disposition to change and renewal.

Didactic approaches to teaching and student learning dominate.

Relationships among stakeholder groups are not supportive or inclusive.

OR:

Some staff and or community stakeholders are receptive to and accepting that renewal of the school's learning and teaching program is required.

RENEWING SCHOOL

School Cultural Orientation

Initially reflective and pedagogically and curriculum focused

A collaborative and participative approach evolves as staff embrace and own changes.
The school leader initially establishes the boundaries and vision for the change and facilitates staff professional learning in line with the vision.

Shared Vision and Mission
School leader initially articulates a sense of purpose and direction for renewal on behalf of the school community.
A shared vision evolves with time along with staff ownership of the change that is characterised by a sense of unity of purpose.
Vision and goals are pedagogically focused.

Teamwork
Evolves to be collegial and collaborative. Commitment not compliance.
Staff with common value base and beliefs about learning and teaching

Learning Environment Focus
Student centred and focused atmosphere.
Agreed set of beliefs established about learning and teaching.
Teachers as facilitators and negotiators of student learning.
A staff culture that values informed practice in learning and teaching.
Varied and appropriate repertoire evident in teaching practice.
Experimentation and risk taking encouraged among staff and students.

School Governance
High expectations held for all by the school community.
Strong parent involvement and participation in governance.
Successes shared, communicated and celebrated.

Figure 2.2. A developed model of principal leadership and renewal.

bias to rational analysis this can be a frightening prospect, resulting in procrastination or complete avoidance or risk-averse behaviours. As such, it differentiates, to some degree, leadership and management behaviour orientations of school leaders.

Differentiating factors identified within the context of school renewal is not recognised as visionary leadership in itself, but a commitment to a clear purpose as articulated in outcome terms relating to core values held in respect to learning and teaching practice.

Next it is important for us to differentiate between leadership activities, and those more in the realm of a management role before focusing more closely on pedagogical leadership of the process.

Leadership and management may be perceived as distinct, albeit complementary processes which led to different outcomes, however, it is acknowledged that management tasks may detract from leadership functions. School management is concerned with responsibility for routine organisational operations through established decision-making procedures. In contrast, leadership requires dealing with uncertainty and finding solutions to new problems. Reacting to existing circumstances and situations essentially maintains the status quo and tends to fall significantly in the purview of the more managerial inclined role. At another level, proactive leadership will entail elements of experimentation and risk-taking; however, both are essential for effective school development.

Whenever successful change or reform occurs, usually it is possible to identify certain key individuals who are crucial for its implementation. These individuals usually have stimulated the change, supported the change process or provided leadership at various points in time.

At this point we have challenged and confirmed aspects of school renewal. Firstly, the school leader is the key player in facilitating school renewal. Secondly, the school leader typically exhibits these behaviours in fostering school renewal: risk-willingness; proactivity, non-conformity, a change disposition; and visionary qualities – creative, insightful and team-focused coaching. Thirdly, school renewal is culture building that promotes and encourages distributed leadership approaches across the school. A further elaboration on the topic of distributed leadership in schools is outlined in Chapter 9. Fourthly, in choosing to adopt school renewal the members of the school community are influenced by a personal and complex equation that balances effort against benefits. Finally, school renewal is an ongoing, dialectic change process that results in improvement.

It is acknowledged that leaders of renewal are often engaged simultaneously in handling reform agendas while initiating and developing a renewal agenda in a school.

School leader comment:

> I have consciously adopted a renewal approach in my school. However, I do acknowledge that while the renewal program is in place I am still implementing systemic reforms at the same time. Systemic reforms,

mainly relating to curriculum requirements would not have been possible to implement in the school without some addressing of fundamental pedagogic and structural issues in the first instance.

We believe that pedagogic change requires a renewal paradigm as it is centred on relationships, primarily based on how a teacher relates to a student, but also how teachers relate to each other and the parents in the school's community. Further, it is our contention that it is these relationships that are enhanced and developed through a leader continuing focus on the school's pedagogy. Consequently, the schools' pedagogic orientation and successes will inform and determine its culture and the structures necessary to implement desired curriculum initiatives will flow from this.

Achieving ongoing cultural change through renewal is the very real challenge of school leadership and is perhaps best summed up by a school leader's remark:

> I was happy to work toward achieving school goals, but felt they were primarily administrative goals, so I took the high moral ground by focusing on kids' learning and looking at the quality of the teachers' pedagogy.

School leaders' behaviours influencing the teaching and learning enterprise

Research focused on the interrelatedness of school leadership and school renewal as a change paradigm is also closely interrogated the corresponding school influences on their leadership behaviours and disposition towards renewing their schools. Particular emphasis in the extant literature was given to the school leader's role in establishing a vision, a sense of direction and purpose for change in schools.

We have canvassed literature pertaining to leadership behaviours, particularly that which underpinned a leaders' involvement in implementing a successful change paradigm within a school context. Clearly, of prime importance in such an enterprise is the gaining a commitment by expecting high standards from staff and students.

Gaining a commitment by expecting high standards from staff and students has been well documented in the schools' effectiveness research. The expectation of high standards sets value on students' learning and teachers' pedagogic practices. The effective schools' literature described the need for high standards of student learning. By way of comparison in competitive sport, athletes win approval and a personal sense of achievement by improving their performance. In a school scenario this aspect is slightly different, it is about gaining commitment from stakeholders through achieving high standards and success. There is a saying that nothing succeeds like success and this dimension posits that success and high standards generate commitment that produces success and higher standards.

In our time we have seen a growing awareness of the importance of the school leader' roles in influencing students' learning. The Coleman Report (1966) was a massive dampener on educational thinking on effect-size when the authors claimed to have shown:

> ... schools bring little influence to bear on a child's achievement that is independent of his background and general social context; and that this very lack of an independent effect means that the inequalities imposed on children by their home, neighbourhood, and per environment are carried along to become the inequalities with which they confront adult life at the end of school. (p. 325)

In the post-war period when tertiary education became more attainable, and educational achievement was then seen as a ticket for social and economic advancement. And, the Coleman Report was in direct conflict with what teachers believed and saw in their classrooms every day.

However, such was the weight of the Coleman Report there were very few authoritative challenges to its basic finding for almost thirty years until testing procedures and statistics managed to catch up. So, while measures could be attributed to classroom teacher. The school leader effect was difficult to quantify. Many claimed that the school leader is second only to the classroom teacher in influencing student achievement, but the problem was the indirect measure of school leaders' influence on student learning. The 2013 RAND paper (Burkhauser et al., 2013) restated the supportive nature of school leaders' influence on students' learning:

> Through their roles as school leaders, principals can influence student achievement in a number of ways — monitoring instruction; evaluating teachers; hiring, developing, and retaining school staff; maintaining student discipline; managing the school budget; establishing a school culture; and engaging with the community. (p. 1)

Herein lay the research problem of directly measuring the influence of school leaders, while matching teacher inputs.

School leaders owe a massive debt of gratitude to the development of the statistical methodology of meta-analysis; and Robert Marzano, Tim Waters, and Brian McNulty who wrote:

> After examining 59 studies involving 2802 schools, approximately 1.4 million students, and 14,000 teachers, we computed the correlation between the leadership behaviour of the school leader in the school and the average academic achievement of students in the school to be 0.25. (2005, p. 10)

At last school leaders had an evidence-based number demonstrating their effectiveness.

School leaders committed to improving the education of students are often described as pedagogic or instructional leaders as they have an identified and credible understanding of the teaching and learning process. These leaders display a credible knowledge of pedagogy and become actively involved in the school's instructional programme and student learning. However, exercise of curriculum and instructional leadership is often tempered by the demand for attention to non-instructional, management-oriented demands and issues arising within the school and also externally from the educational system itself.

Building a sense of cohesion and Team in the school

Team building in an educational setting is predicated on the belief that an improvement in teacher motivation and performance will result in an improvement in students' motivation, engagement and learning outcomes.

An element of school leader leadership in an effective school is the expectation by the school's leadership and staff that all students would be engaged in their learning. As a consequence, students are expected to learn well and to achieve and demonstrate improvement in the achievement of learning outcomes. The school's leader mirrors these beliefs through their actions by creating a team focus on learning and teaching and by encouraging experimentation, innovation and risk-taking in terms of teacher pedagogical approaches and school structures. Therefore, the school leader, in an effective school scenario, ensures goals are well defined and constantly evaluated. There is an expectation also that student outcomes will be monitored regularly.

As a school leader's attitudes are perceived to influence teachers' attitudes to the teaching and learning function, this has important, relevant implications for students' attitudes towards learning. It stands to reason, therefore, that in order for a school to achieve a degree of effectiveness and the desired improvement orientation, it is of vital importance that the school leader, as the pedagogic or instructional leader, be motivated by a strong sense of self-efficacy. These self-efficacy beliefs are seen to have behavioural correlates. In particular, these are identified as being associated with a proclivity towards leading change, fostering relationships, team and coalition building and providing a sense of direction for the organisation.

The development of high expectations for academic and social behaviour and the clear communication of those expectations to the school community by the school leader are consistently identified as characteristics of leaders in an effective school.

In this age of ubiquitous high-stakes testing, expectations for academic and social behaviour and the clear communication of those expectations to the school community by the school leader are consistently identified as characteristics of leaders in effective schools. In *The Times Educational Supplement*, Darren Evans (2011) pointed out that headship is not just about "bells, budgets and budgets" because society is asking more of school leaders. The so-called "turnaround" schools are probably the toughest test for any school leaders and excellent research by Hitt and Meyers (2018) developed five domains that characterise effective school leadership: vision, organisational engagement, organisational advancement, the student experience and external environment. So, in a turnaround school effective leaders develop a shared sense of vision, they restructure the school to support learning, they build teacher capacity, the instructional programme is improved and external partners are engaged in the rebuilding process. In reality, effective school leaders need to deliver this whole package of renewal, over time.

OUR BELIEF 3

> A leadership disposition that values and encourages fairness, openness, honesty, loyalty and integrity in relationships will facilitate the creation of a learning and teaching culture that is purposeful and empowering and subsequently renewal ready.

Whilst a renewal orientation has leaders of change valuing working with others, both individually and in teams, they do not strive to be popular, are not overly concerned with the needs of others nor do they seek to minimise conflict. A school leader's focus on people is demonstrated by their ability to connect with others easily and frequently; hence, a *team style*, which is motivated by a preference for participation in team activities, is evident.

While in totally collaborative school environments there is no need for the school leader to exercise a controlling role. Such a collaborative organisational culture emphasises a web of relationships, and points to the important role of the leader in defining and stimulating effective teamwork among teachers. This supports the proposition that school leaders engaged in renewal are at the centre of the web of relationships in the school. This is not without its associated benefits as it does afford the opportunity to the school leader to identify possible catalysts for change among staff (see Chapter 15). There is a common understanding in team sports that is very applicable to the school environment: a team of champions will never perform better than a champion team.

The leadership disposition of the school leader along with the rate at which the desired change can be implemented in respect of a renewal agenda, is significantly influenced by the prevailing school culture. Overcoming and addressing the barriers presented by a prevailing school culture that is not change-willing or change-adept is a challenge that confronts all educational leaders. For many school leaders it is the point at which they proceed with renewal as a change paradigm or shy away from it. We are first to concede that leading change can be a most stressful situation for any school leader. The more complex the change the more stressful it can be, and school leaders need to demonstrate real courage, for the sake of the students. That is the moral imperative that guides all school renewal endeavours.

References

Burkhauser, S., Gates, S.M., Hamilton, L.S., Li, J.J., & Pierson, A. (2013). *Laying the foundation for successful school leadership*. RAND Corporation. https://www.rand.org/pubs/research_reports/RR419.html

Coleman, J.S., Campbell, E.Q., Hobson, C.J., McPartland, J., Mood, A.M., Weinfeld, F.D., & York, R.I. (1966). *Equality of educational opportunity*. Washington, DC: U.S. Government Printing Office.

Evans, D. (2011, 18 February). Headship isn't just about 'bells, budgets and buses'. *The Times Educational Supplement Cymru*.

Hitt, D.H., & Meyers, C.V. (2018). Beyond turnaround: A synthesis of relevant frameworks for leaders of sustained improvement in previously low-performing schools. *School Leadership & Management*, 38(1), 4–31. doi:10.1080/13632434.2017.1374943.

Marzano, R., Waters, T., & McNulty, B.A. (2005). *School Leadership that Works*. Alexandria, VA: ASCD.

3 School leader efficacy and change

(If you're not part of the solution ... Then you are a part of the problem)

Our initial conceptualisation of school *Pedagogic Leadership* has been strongly influenced by Bandura's (1977) notion of efficacy; which recognises that effective school leaders' behaviours are influenced by a belief in their own capacity to perform the roles and responsibilities associated with their positions. According to Bandura's definitions (1977, p. 3), self-efficacy is "… the set of beliefs a person has about their capabilities and more importantly the judgements they make about them to execute particular courses of action and to do specific things within their belief parameters".

OUR BELIEF 4

> School leader efficacy is an essential factor that underwrites successful and sustainable pedagogic change.

Bandura (1997) argued that, although locus of control was primarily concerned with casual beliefs about action-outcome contingencies or an individual's estimate that a given behaviour would lead to certain outcomes, personal efficacy was concerned with the conviction that one can successfully execute the behaviour required to produce the outcomes desired.

There is now extensive research showing consistent relationships between self-efficacy beliefs, task performance and predisposition towards change. The concept of self-efficacy is now widely used in general conversations, and Kendra Cherry (2019) listed four accepted characteristics of self-efficacy: view challenging problems as tasks to be mastered; develop a deeper interest in the activities in which they participate; form a stronger sense of commitment to their interests and activities; and recover quickly from setbacks and disappointments. We maintain that when the efficacy construct is applied to teachers' pedagogic practices, then it has significant implications for schools and professional learning activities, which is why schools need to develop teachers' professional beliefs and personal well-being.

The voluminous research on the possession of a high efficacy orientation by school leaders has shown that they are more effective educators than school leaders lacking this sense of self-efficacy. The disposition of efficacious leadership to change initiation and organisational improvement is recognised as a highly desirable leadership behavioural characteristic. Organisational research also shows consistent relationships between self-efficacy beliefs, task performance and predisposition toward change.

We believe that the constant companions of self-efficacy are courage and sensible risk-taking. School leaders think about the likely end-results of their behaviours and this influences the goals they set, the effort they commit to the task at hand, and their actual performance. Consequently, they have an orientation toward seeing themselves as the origin or master of their own destiny, in contrast to people who view themselves as pawns who are at the mercy of luck or fate. Such a concept sits with the notion of external and internal locus of control. Efficacious school leaders perceive themselves to be in control of their lives and, therefore, responsible for taking action if there is a desire for events to unfold in a certain direction or manner. In the school context such leaders adopt the role of being an initiator of desired action. They see themselves as the agents who must precipitate such action and a subsequent disposition toward proactive behaviours with a predisposition to action.

As we have demonstrated, school renewal activities require strong pedagogic leadership competency, traits not demonstrated by less efficacious leaders. School-based research has also supported the contention that in school climates where achievement is encouraged and supported, a positive sense of efficacy is more likely to exist. It follows that those with high leadership efficacy would have a greater tendency to engage in renewal and whole-school change activities than their less self-efficacious counterparts.

Pedagogic leaders in a positive, high-achieving environment believed that what they do has important consequences for student educational outcomes and that individual contribution made a difference in the overall learning and teaching enterprise. Conversely, low self-efficacy is seen as the root cause of avoidance behaviour, particularly in respect to decision-making activities. The implication that such a finding has for school renewal is significant as it implies that school leaders possessing key behaviour attributes with a disposition associated with change agency are more risk-willing and proactive in initiating and developing a school renewal orientation.

Individuals who have a strong belief in their capabilities think, feel and behave differently from those who have doubts about their capabilities. Those who doubt their capabilities will shy away from difficult tasks and problems as they have low aspirations, weak commitment to the goals they choose to pursue and are risk-averse in their orientation towards moving from the familiar to the unfamiliar. Our contention is that such a construct has major implications for school leadership engagement in school renewal actions, as school leaders will engage in quite distinct patterns of practice that are shaped by how they think about their role.

We believe that there is a significant difference between individuals' possession of knowledge and skills, and their being able to use them well under difficult or testing conditions. Particularly, this is the case with respect to leadership efficacy within a change scenario where cognitive, social, motivational as well as behavioural attributes of the school leader as a pedagogic leader must be organised and effectively orchestrated to serve numerous purposes.

A school leader's beliefs and values play key roles in motivating and creating a predisposition to action within a school. Individuals motivate themselves and through the process of forethought, acting in anticipation of a given outcome occurring. Therefore, the motivating potential of outcome expectancy as a result of initiating a change paradigm is partly governed by an individual's assessment of their capability to accomplish the desired outcome.

Unfortunately, values are rarely discussed, but are identified in literature on leadership to be the core to a leader's public image. Within a school context the school leader's leadership image carries with it symbolic meaning. This is evident with respect to the perception of the leader within a broader school community context. It is a task of the school leader to interpret and model the organisation's espoused values in a very public way. As a consequence, these values are seen to be manifest in the overt behaviour disposition of the leader within the cultural setting of an organisation. It is the school leader's role to articulate values for the school in a way that gains acceptance of them at both the whole organisation and/or individual teacher level.

A school leader reflecting about her personal sense of efficacy remarked:

> I have never doubted that what I wanted to achieve would make for better learning outcomes for the students at my school and therefore it would be better for the whole school community – I have often doubted my ability to get the job done and have the changes maintained.

The leader's values and behaviour disposition have the potential to put a school's renewal agenda and associated mission and vision on the critical path to success. The idea advanced at this juncture is that once a school staff begin to experience a change in school culture that results from the introduction of a renewal agenda, their individual and combined passion would be expected to emerge and be in itself self-sustaining and reinforcing.

The leader's personal value base is seen to be translated into their level of personal commitment to, and implementation of, change in the school. They know what changes they want to achieve, have a clear picture of the how, why and when it can be implemented, and have the necessary self-efficacy to realise it. A school leader's values, therefore, provide the necessary leverage for the school vision, and it is through their vision for renewal that improved outcome achievement can be obtained.

School leader comment:

> I achieved the learning and teaching approach I wanted by establishing a clear vision of the school that centred on student learning and not resisting from making the hard decisions in relation to the school's teaching and learning practices. By ensuring that school structures and

curriculum supported student centred pedagogic approaches. By not letting structures (school timetable, etc.) to dictate classroom pedagogy. I got into classes and taught alongside staff. By encouraging collaborative teaching and empowering those with sound student focused teaching to take a lead role in the school. By being approachable to parents and letting them see that I was really interested in their children.

Leadership of change and proactivity are also associated with the notion of change agency. Whenever successful change or reform occurs, it is usually possible to identify certain key individuals who were crucial for its initiation and implementation. These individuals may have stimulated the change, supported the change process or provided leadership at various stages in it. Their role is directly associated with a particular project or innovation and they had the capacity to cause, facilitate or enable change to occur in the organisation.

School leader and teacher pedagogic efficacy

In line with the Bandura (1977) definition, *Pedagogic Efficacy* is seen to be concerned with the conviction held by a teacher that they can implement successfully the pedagogic behaviour required to produce exemplary and desired learning outcomes. The converse also applies; poor pedagogic efficacy beliefs result in poor performance by the leader and also the teachers. Bandura (1997) argued that, although locus of control was primarily concerned with causal beliefs about action-outcome contingencies (or indeed, a person's estimate that certain behaviours would lead to certain outcomes), personal efficacy was concerned with the conviction that one successfully can execute the behaviour required in order to produce the outcomes desired. We argue that the same maxim applies to teaching and that a teacher's pedagogic efficacy is influenced by a belief in their capacity to effectively perform the roles and responsibilities associated with the teaching function.

In the United Kingdom, a four-year research project conducted by Day, Stobart, Kington, Gu, Smees and Mujtaba (2006) examined the factors that influence teachers' long-term effectiveness. Self-efficacy was a complex and key factor in determining the quality of teachers' professional lives:

> Teachers who are committed to their work have an enduring belief that they can make a difference to the learning lives and achievements of students (efficacy and agency) through who they are (their identity), what they (knowledge, strategies, skills) and how they teach (their beliefs, attitudes, personal and professional values embedded in and expressed through their behaviour in practice settings). Commitment is the expression over a career of a desire to be the best possible teacher and provide the best possible teaching for all students at all times through care and competence. Commitment occurs, then, in both real time and is an enduring aspiration (Day, et al., 2006, p. 10).

Pedagogic efficacy asserts that teachers' personal expectations about teaching exert powerful influences on their classroom behaviours and, as a consequence, on their willingness to initiate and engage in pedagogic change. The term self-efficacy or personal efficacy is used in the literature to refer to the set of beliefs people have about their capabilities and, and the judgements they make about their capabilities to execute particular courses of action. Pedagogic efficacy considers educators' beliefs within the parameters of the teaching function.

At a school level it is observed that teachers differ in their general pedagogic efficacy, and these differences have behavioural correlations in terms of classroom learning outcomes and practices. In particular classrooms where teachers have enhanced pedagogic efficacy are identified as having greater student engagement in learning tasks, evidence of a repertoire of teaching practices, a significant commitment to the education of the whole child, a change-adept and willing orientation, a valuing and fostering of relationships, team and coalition-building.

Some consistent relationships between pedagogic efficacy, teaching performance and proclivity towards change is observed. What a teacher thinks about the likely end-results of their behaviour has a powerful effect on the classroom goals and expectations they set, the effort they commit to the teaching task at hand and on their actual performance. This supports the contention that a teacher's perception of their teaching ability and pedagogic knowledge and skills (pedagogic efficacy) is more critical than the actual curriculum knowledge they possess.

Pedagogically efficacious teachers perceive themselves to be in control of the learning and teaching process and, therefore, responsible for taking action in their classrooms if there was a desire for events to unfold in a certain direction or manner. Such teachers adopt the role of being an initiator of informed learning and teaching action. They demonstrate skills in problem solving and information seeking. Pedagogically efficacious teachers are seen to possess a strong self-image, and consequently, are self-assured and confident about their teaching. They have confidence to engage in collaboration, are open to observation of their classroom practices and seek advice and information about teaching and learning from a wide variety of sources.

Teachers with high pedagogic efficacy mobilise more effort in pursuit of learning and teaching goals than those with low pedagogic efficacy. That is, those who believed in their ability to perform in expected areas are more likely to strive harder to succeed often persevering even in the presence of obstacles and negative outcomes. They perceived a failure as only a temporary setback, rather than a final result. Conversely, those with low pedagogic efficacy are more likely to adopt avoidance behaviours, particularly in respect to classroom practices and the taking on of new approaches and ideas.

Pedagogic efficacy arises from the gradual acquisition of complex teaching skills often gained through experience. Individuals appear to weigh, integrate and evaluate information about their capabilities. Accordingly, they regulate their choices and efforts.

In applying the construct of pedagogic efficacy to the teaching function the relationship between situational and organisational variables needs to be considered in any such assessment. This is because pedagogic efficacy has a situation context that may affect its generalisability, specifically that success in one situation impacts on an individual's beliefs that they can bring about a similar outcome in a different context. Taking cognisance of this cautionary remark the question becomes how a teacher's pedagogic efficacy orientation can be enhanced.

Teachers' pedagogic knowledge bases

A key component of teachers' pedagogic efficacy is the teachers' pedagogic knowledge bases. Examining teachers' pedagogic knowledge bases, Lee Shulman (2004, pp. 219–248) in the 1980s identified seven components of teachers' knowledge bases: content knowledge, pedagogic knowledge, pedagogic content knowledge, curricular knowledge, knowledge of learners, knowledge of the educational context and knowledge of educational goals. Rosie Turner-Bisset (2001), some fifteen years later, re-analysed Shulman's work and identified twelve knowledge bases for teaching (see Table 3.1) but Shulman's conceptual framework still retained a high degree of utility.

As pedagogic efficacy refers to teacher's judgements about their capabilities to execute particular courses of action within their classrooms, it is concerned not so much with the actual skills the teacher has, but with judgements about what that teacher can do with those skills. It refers to teachers' beliefs about their ability to influence educational learning

Table 3.1 The knowledge bases of teaching

The knowledge bases of teaching	
Bisset-Turner	**Shulman**
Content knowledge	Substantive subject knowledge
	Syntactic subject knowledge
Curricular knowledge	Beliefs about the subject
Pedagogic knowledge	Curriculum knowledge
	General pedagogic knowledge
Knowledge of learners	Knowledge/models of teaching
	Knowledge of learners- Cognitive
	Knowledge of learners- Empirical
	Knowledge of self
Knowledge of the educational context	Knowledge of the educational contexts
Knowledge of educational goals	Knowledge of educational ends
Pedagogic content knowledge	Pedagogic content Knowledge

outcomes. Teachers who have a strong belief in their capabilities think, feel and behave differently from those who have doubts about their teaching capabilities, whereas teachers who doubt their capabilities shy away from experimentation and rich learning tasks and opportunities.

It is erroneous to believe that pedagogic efficacy is developed merely through adding more technical knowledge and skill as it is strengthened through practice and through the conditions and consequences that accompany the practice of the craft to be learned. But the practice must be accompanied by informative feedback about teaching performance. Therefore, formative and summative feedback needs to be constructive, and teachers must learn that they are the cause of their performance. That way feedback will have a positive effect on their perception of competence. School leaders modelling appropriate pedagogic practice can convey rich information about how the teaching task should be actioned.

Student learning and teachers' efficacy

Students' learning and teachers' commitment, resilience and efficacy are a part of an exquisite equation that influences teachers' professional lives. The *Variations in Teachers' Work, Lives and Effectiveness* research empirically revealed the factors that influenced teachers' ability to withstand the daily grind of teaching. Teachers' efficacy is significantly affected by commitment and effectiveness, and Day et al. (2006) found:

> It was not only in teachers' minds that commitment was perceived to be closely associated with perceived effectiveness – we found, also, there was a statistically significant association between commitment and effectiveness defined by pupil attainment. (p. 221)

Student attainment was a factor that strengthened teachers' efficacy, effectiveness and commitment. However, the other side of the equation is that teachers' professional life phase also affected students' learning:

> Pupils of those teachers in each professional life phase who were on an upward trajectory and sustaining their commitment were more likely to attain results at or above the level expected, regardless of school context (70% -cohort 1; 65% - cohort 2). Pupils of teachers in each professional life phase who were on a downward trajectory and not sustaining their commitment were more likely to attain results below the level expected, regardless of school context (27% - cohort 1; 31% - cohort 2). (Day et al., 2006, p. 257)

Students' achievements are not only the big picture numbers but the thousands of small achievements that early childhood teachers see daily: Jacob writing the number three and Emma recognising three sight words are milestones in each child's achievements and they are no less important in strengthening a teachers' efficacy, effectiveness, commitment and resilience than having a class member win a national prize for high achievement. Knowing the students really well allows teachers to rejoice in the micro-level achievements, which is far more difficult for teachers in secondary schools who teach up to 120 students each week. The depth of student contact must be a contributing factor to the higher attrition rate for secondary school teachers.

A primary school school leader stated that he:

> Talked all the time about Learning and Teaching, I visited all classrooms, I took all the "time out" to support staff in relation to student discipline, I facilitated the new accountability process with all teaching staff. This was very helpful as I was able to ask the hard question and comment with demonstrable knowledge re the answers.

Current theory associated with the efficacy construct asserts that an individual's self-efficacy expectations exert a powerful influence on subsequent behaviours and, as a consequence, on their willingness to initiate change. The term self – or personal – efficacy refers to the set of beliefs a person has about their capabilities and, more importantly, the judgements they make about their capabilities, to execute particular courses of action and to do specific things. When applied to the leadership domain in a school context, the theory that school leaders' perceptions of their abilities to bring about positive organisational changes are an important factor in an individual's willingness to engage in school renewal.

Building teacher capacity for achieving effective learning outcomes might necessitate administrators looking at ways to enhance pedagogic efficacy of staff by getting them to think about their teaching in new and challenging ways. Teaching practices had been long dominated by tradition, mythology, personal beliefs and ideology; and then John Hattie's (2003) meta-analyses burst into classrooms and gave teachers evidence-based guidance. Suddenly *effect-size* became a part of teachers' informed conversations as the list of teaching strategies were examined. As a result, we saw an improved commitment to educating the whole child, with an improved repertoire of teaching practices.

Charting a path for school cultural change calls for a clearly defined image of the outcomes that will be achieved articulated by the school leader as a pedagogic leader. A vision is a statement which provides: a mental image of a possible and desirable future state of the organisation, a view of a realistic, credible, attractive future for the organisation. As such it needs to be a realistic, credible, and an attractive future proposition for the organisation that is so compelling that staff will readily ascribe to it.

Working with teacher self-efficacy instruments

Many of us were brought up in the presence of the much-repeated aphorism: "Nothing succeeds like success", and parents used this wise saying as an incentive and a guide in the life planning for their children. However, this guide to action was in constant use by every thinking person, and then in 1977 Albert Bandura developed the variant theory of *self-efficacy*, in which individuals who understood their personal strengths then further developed their abilities to succeed. Interestingly, Mihaly Csikszentmihalyi (1997), in his work on the concept of *Flow*, described what he called an autotelic (self- goal-setting) personality that appeared to be a manifestation of self-efficacy. Csikszentmihalyi said, "Applied to personality, autotelic denotes an individual who generally does things for their own sake, rather than in order to achieve some later external goal" (p. 117).

In teaching and school leadership self-efficacy is extremely important because it influences risk-taking, professional learning, professional judgements, courage, change agendas, negotiations, convincing staff about the efficacy of planned improvement programmes, and all of the things that we do every day. A school leader who does not have sufficient self-efficacy to be able to effect change simply reverts back to being a school manager, who is forced to wallow in the status quo.

Megan Tschannen-Moran and Anita Woolfolk Hoy (2001, p. 783) observed that, "Teacher efficacy has proved to be powerfully related to many meaningful educational outcomes such as teachers' persistence, enthusiasm, commitment and instructional behaviour, as well as student outcomes such as achievement, motivation, and self-efficacy beliefs." The link between teacher self-efficacy and pedagogic mastery was further acknowledged by Tschannen-Moran and Woolfolk Hoy (2007, p. 954) when they confirmed Bandura's prediction that mastery experiences made the greatest contribution to teachers' senses of self-efficacy.

The teacher self-efficacy test (24 items), developed by Tschannen-Moran and Woolfolk Hoy (n.d.), was titled "Teacher Beliefs – TSES" and it closely examined three factors that influence teachers' self-efficacy:

- Efficacy for management
- Efficacy for instructional leadership
- Efficacy for moral leadership

In our use of this instrument we found that it was very difficult to differentiate teachers against these three factors but the individual item responses were far more useful.

Teacher efficacy and change

The task of creating environments conducive to learning rests heavily on the talents and self – efficacy of the school leader and teachers. Ongoing school-based research has confirmed this concept where self-efficacy is defined as one's belief in one's ability to succeed in specific situations or accomplish a task. We have argued that one's sense of self-efficacy can play a major role in how an individual approaches goals, tasks and challenges.

There is clear evidence that indicates that a classroom's atmosphere is largely determined by a teacher's beliefs in their own pedagogic efficacy. Teachers who have a high sense of pedagogic efficacy devote more classroom time to academic learning, provide students who have difficulty learning with the help they need to succeed and praise them for their accomplishments. In contrast, teachers who have a low sense of instructional efficacy spend more time on non-academic pastimes, and they are quick to give up on students if they do not get first-time results and criticise them for their failures. Therefore, it has been observed that teachers who believe strongly in their instructional efficacy create mastery experiences for students in their classrooms. On the contrary those with self-doubt create classroom environments that are likely to undermine a student's sense of efficacy and overall cognitive development.

Teachers who believe strongly in their instructional efficacy support development of student's intrinsic interests and academic self-directedness, whereas teachers who have a low sense of efficacy shy away from difficult tasks, which they perceive as personal threats. Those teachers who have a low sense of instructional efficacy favour a custodial orientation that relies heavily on extrinsic inducements and negative sanctions to get students to engage with their learning. They have low aspirations and with commitment to goals they choose to pursue. When faced with difficult tasks, they dwell on their personal deficiencies, on the obstacles they will encounter at all kinds of adverse outcomes. They slacken their efforts and give up quickly in the face of these difficulties. They fall easy victim to stress and depression.

A strong sense of efficacy enhances personal accomplishment in many ways. Teachers with high efficacy approach difficult tasks as challenges to be mastered, rather than as threats to be avoided. Such an efficacious outlook fosters interest and a deeper engagement in activities. They set themselves challenging goals and maintain strong commitment to them. They maintain a task diagnostic focus that guides effective performance. They heighten and sustain their efforts in the face of failure. They perceive failure as resulting from insufficient effort or deficient knowledge and skills which are acquirable. They quickly recover after failures or setbacks such as efficacious outlook produces personal accomplishments reduces stress and lowers vulnerability to depression.

Putting it all together: Collective efficacy

In schools it is relatively easy to identify school staff members who demonstrate self-efficacy in a variety of ways, and it is these people (gardeners, cleaners, education assistants, teachers and administrators) who, often unconsciously, help create public opinion of the school's effectiveness. Efficacious staff members are worth their weight in gold to every school leader.

However, having a number of self-efficacious staff members is good for a school, but it is the next step of developing a collective efficacy, and making a great efficacious team that turbo-charges school renewal.

Schools are complex social organisations, and the challenge for school leaders is the development of collective efficacy and the move toward an efficacious school status. The research on this specific topic is now just over two decades old and we can see how the researchers addressed this issue. In 1998 (p. 241) Megan Tschannen-Moran, Anita Woolfolk Hoy, and Wayne Hoy examined Collective Efficacy as a part of their notes on Directions for Future Research, and they posed a series of questions that still face school leaders every day as they develop their school renewal processes.

Collective teacher efficacy is defined as the "… perceptions of teachers in a school that the efforts of the faculty as a whole will have a positive effect on students" (Goddard, Hoy, & Woolfolk Hoy, 2000, p. 480). The research questions in this field of study ask if, and how, personal self-efficacy can be transferred to an aggregation of collective efficacy. Furthermore, self-efficacy may obstruct collective efficacy when the goals are not shared strongly, which is the basis for school renewal.

Collective efficacy is a term that is widely used across a variety of situations in relation to human endeavour. "Collective efficacy is a social construct that partially explains how demographic characteristics of neighbourhoods, such as concentrated disadvantage, ethnic heterogeneity, and concentrated immigration, lead to higher rates of neighbourhood crime" (Lackey & Tomsett, 2018, p. 148). Likewise, the concept of team and teamwork are now impacting on the way we think about school operations, and they give support for better school leadership.

It is fortunate that educational research benefits from the spin-off of research into collective efficacy in other organisational structures such as team building in sport and business enterprises. For example, in a team situation Katz-Navon and Erez (2005, p. 439) noted that the change from self-efficacy to a collective efficacy may occur in two stages:

> … first, individuals shift their reference from the individual to the group level when they evaluate team efficacy. Second, the agreement among all team members elevates the construct itself to the group level. Thus, collective-efficacy reflects the shared beliefs of the group members in their group's capabilities to mobilize the motivation, cognitive resources, and courses of action needed to produce given levels of attainments on a specific task. What happens in sporting teams also occurs in school teams, as collective efforts are initiated to address whole-school goals.

If we look at sporting team captains (chosen for their role in collective efficacy) and the school leaders of renewing schools, parallels are obvious. The research by Huang, Huang and Chang (2019, p. 825) shows that goal orientation is important in team performance and leaders play a critical role. The goal orientation can be seen in school leaders' leadership styles where the

LGO (learning goal-oriented leader) believes in improvement, and the acquisition of new skills. This leader behaviourally models the actions and standards expected, with an aggressive approach to task completion. In contrast, the performance goal oriented (PGO) leader may instil:

> ... feelings of helplessness, a tendency to experience negative emotions in the face of obstacles, a habit of seeking to avoid or withdraw from achievement, based situations and a lack of effort when it comes to completing tasks. Such team leaders are likely to have a negative reaction to challenging tasks and related environments, and to create a passive climate for team members. Through their interactions in the course of team processes, team leaders may potentially instil a common attitude of avoidance in team members, which is characteristic of low team efficacy. (p. 828)

We have all seen these situations in many schools and the goal orientation-efficacy relationship is still being investigated.

Concluding comments on chapter

Our treatment of school leader self-efficacy considerations as a precursor to successful school leadership behaviours aligns significantly with more recent organisational studies in the area of entrepreneurship. While the research in this field is limited at this stage early data confirms that entrepreneurial actions by a leader are significantly impacted by their personal self-efficacy. Titled Entrepreneurial Self-Efficacy, this discourse has explored the link between entrepreneurial leadership action and personal attributes, inclusive of a person's self-efficacy, as an antecedent to determining a leaders disposition to initiating significant change (J. McGee, M. Peterson, S. Mueller, & J. Sequeira, 2009). Studies across the business sector have indeed shown that there is a positive correlation between the concept of Entrepreneurial Self-Efficacy and the likelihood of a person being change-willing and risk-averse.

We maintain that Entrepreneurial Self-Efficacy can be seen as a multi-dimensional construct that further supports the leadership and management of schools' dichotomy that we have proposed.

It is acknowledged in educational literature that being actively involved in a process as complex as pedagogic renewal can be both daunting and at times isolating for teachers as well as a school's leadership. Engagement in teaching and cultural change requires certain behaviours and personal attributes from the individual, including a strong sense of self-efficacy.

What was interesting from our own observations is that those teachers who openly engage in discussions about learning and teaching are able to identify colleagues with a similar disposition and engagement. It is these colleagues with whom they are comfortable in developing a critical friendship relationship. We found the path to school renewal exciting, and the milestone results were fulfilling to us and our staff.

References

Bandura, A. (1977). *Social learning theory.* Englewood Cliffs, NJ: Prentice-Hall.

Cherry, K. (2019). *The everything psychology book: Explore the human psyche and understand why we do the things we do.* Holbrook, MA: Adams Media Corporation.

Csikszentmihalyi, M. (1997). *Creativity: Flow and the psychology of discovery and invention.* New York: HarperPerennial.

Day, C., Stobart, G., Sammons, P., Kington, A., Gu, Q., Smees, R., & Mujtaba, T. (2006). *Variations in teachers' work, lives and effectiveness* [Research Report RR743]. London: Department for Education and Skills. www.dfes.gov.uk/research/data/uploadfiles/RR743.pdf

Goddard, R.D., Hoy, W.K., & Woolfolk Hoy, A. (2000, Summer). Collective teacher efficacy: Its meaning, measure, and impact on student achievement. *American Educational Research Journal*, 37(2), 479–507.

Hattie, J. (2003, October). *Teachers make a difference: What is the research evidence?* Melbourne, Australia: Australian Council for Educational Research.

Huang, C-Y., Huang, J-C., & Chang, Y. (2019). Team orientation composition, team efficacy, and team performance: The separate roles of team leader and members. *Journal of Management & Organization*, 25(6), 825–843.

Katz-Navon, T.Y., & Erez, M. (2005, August). When collective and self-efficacy affect team performance: The role of task interdependence. *Small Group Research*, 36(4), 437–465.

Lackey, J.H., & Tomsett, C.J. (2018). A model of rural delinquency: Collective efficacy in rural schools. *Journal of Rural Mental Health*, 42(3), 148–160.

McGee, J.E., Peterson, M., Mueller, S.L., and Sequeira, J.M. (2009, July). Entrepreneurial self-efficacy: Refining the measure. *Entrepreneurship Theory and Practice*, 34(3), 966–988.

Shulman, L.S. (2004). *The wisdom of practice: Essays on teaching, learning and learning to teach.* San Francisco: Jossey-Bass.

Tschannen-Moran, M., & Hoy, A.W. (2001). Teacher efficacy: Capturing an elusive construct. *Teaching and Teacher Education*, 17(7) 783–805.

Tschannen-Moran, M., & Hoy, A.W. (2007). The differential antecedents of self-efficacy beliefs of novice and experienced teachers. *Teaching and Teacher Education*, 23(6), 944–956.

Tschannen-Moran, M., Hoy, A.W., & Hoy, W.K. (1998, Summer). Teacher efficacy: Its meaning and measure. *Review of Educational Research*, 68(2), 202–248.

Turner-Bisset, R. (2001). *Expert teaching: Knowledge and pedagogy to lead the profession.* London: David Fulton Publishers.

4 Moral leadership guiding school change and vision setting

(If you always do what you have always done, you will always get what you have always got)

A vision, although describing a desirable future, has its importance in the present by guiding actions and decisions that will create that future. School leaders have key roles in formulating the agreed vision, and implementing it, while being publicly acknowledged as the primary *go-to* person. Thus, a vision may be seen to refer to the shared values and aspirations agreed to by the members of an organisation, and it guides their present actions and decisions in order to create a desirable future. This is nicely summed up by Bennis and Nanus (1985, p. 89) who observed that "leaders articulate and define what has previously remained implicit or unsaid; then they invent images, metaphors, and models that provide a focus for new attention. By so doing, they consolidate or challenge prevailing wisdom".

OUR BELIEF 5

> Re-culturing a school requires a clearly defined and well communicated vision of an agreed future, which generates commitment, not compliance.

The notion of a *vision* has been defined in many ways: as an internal compass for an organisation (Conley, Dunlop, & Goldman, 1992); a force or dream guiding the development of a school (Chance, 1991), or more simply, it is a statement that describes an ideal future state. In a school, a vision refers to the stated priorities, preferences and directions of school initiatives and activities and, therefore, it is an important and integral part of the school's planning.

In schools, a shared vision is an important statement about an agreed sense of future direction. While the statement has a guiding importance, it is the shared visioning process that gives the statement validity in the community's eyes. The visioning process is an exercise in leading and listening for school leaders. Consequently, the school leader must be a superb listener, particularly when advocating new or different images of the emerging reality. Effective school leader leadership is marked by a core philosophy (values) and a vision of how the organisation wishes to make its mark.

A major challenge in leaders' efforts at articulating a vision is their pedagogic leadership credibility, particularly in getting stakeholders to believe in the change agenda that is being articulated. The reputation and relationship that the school leaders have with staff and within the wider community are deemed important considerations, particularly in terms of their perceived integrity and trustworthiness, and the consistency between the words and deeds of the communicator of the vision.

School renewal and change are more likely to occur when the school's leader, community and the teachers are connected to each other by a commitment to common ideals. In this respect we fully support Fullan's (2001) assertion that leadership based on moral purpose coupled with change agency, with a focus on shared goals and a sense of common purpose, is the key to continuously renewing a school's pedagogy and culture. Thus, our hypothesis is that change and renewal cannot survive unless moral purpose is strongly linked to change agency. School leaders who see themselves as leaders of renewal also perceived themselves as active agents of change and moral purpose.

Highly effective school leaders have positive, detailed and compelling visions of the future. The vision they articulate provides a sense of purpose and direction for the school. It is important to note that the school-based visioning process:

> ... is that it is not about being judged by outsiders, or trying to meet criteria that have been set by other people. Instead, it is a learning journey where teachers, students and friends of the school work together to take stock of what has already been achieved – in terms of those intangible, values-related 'achievements' often missed by national exams and inspections – and what is still needed. (PERL, 2014, p. 5)

It is this vision that provided a sense of direction and purpose for stakeholders in the organisation.

In the language of school and organisational development, the terms *vision, mission* and *purpose* are of critical importance because they represent public statements about present and the future. *Mission* and *purpose* are often used interchangeably in educational literature. A school's purpose statement typically makes statements about the school cultural environment, optimising students' learning, facilitating students' movement to the next stage of learning, and establishing the foundations for good citizenship and a better society. The school's purpose statement is a practical document that guides parents and staff about what is, or what ought to be, happening in the school. In contrast, the vision is a statement of an optimal future. Both the vision and mission are heavily influenced by the school's statement of values. In terms of whole-school direction, the vision and purpose are seen as key strategies in the school's organised response to a set of perceived needs. The vision and purpose can be seen as important parts of a change process, but they can also be seen as strategies promoting conservatism when the stakeholders view the current vision and purpose statements as iconic. The interaction between the school's vision and the school's leadership is of critical importance to the influence of the vision.

The mission and vision as the starting point for change

It is not enough to simply acknowledge that the mission and the vision are the starting point for change. Missions and visions are different in every school and organisation because they respond to each specific community's needs and aspirations. To be the starting point of change, the vision must do three things:

- paint an attractive and engaging picture of the future (it must capture a following);
- reinforce an ethical connectedness with the community's aspirations, and,
- must be significantly different to the present situation (not changing is not an option).

The Moordijt Nyungar Indigenous school's vision is a good example of a vision that has been used to inspire that school's community:

> **Nyungar – old people dreaming**
>
> The moon was high and full in a cloudless night sky, lighting the land between the two creeks. Around the remains of a large fire the old people sat talking and worrying about the past, the future and their children.
>
> The oldest man leaned forward, took a handful of the warm white ash from the edge of the fire and threw it into the air.
>
> As the group watched the mist of ash in the moonlit air they saw the future- clean, bright, well dressed Nyungar kids leading in the Wadjela* world. Champion sportsmen and women.
>
> Champion musicians and actors.
>
> Champion business people, doctors, lawyers and teachers.
>
> Nyungar people supporting each other and making our culture strong.
>
> This is the Dreaming of the old people.
>
> We can all make it happen. (MacNeill, 2006).
>
> *Nyungar – Indigenous Language Group. Western Australia; Wadjela -White man (Nyungar term).

Educators examining vision and purpose statements need to look at the vision and mission statements to determine their capacity to drive change. The quality of the vision and mission need to be examined, not simply accepted unquestioningly, for without the capacity to inspire, the vision is lacking. Also, the point being made by Frick and Frick (2010, p. 118) is that we have a commitment to distributed leadership in schools, but more important for successful, visionary change is the *ethic of connectedness* with the school's community base.

When Martin Luther King intoned the words, "I have a dream", he was articulating a vision statement, which has motivated generations of people across the world. Visions can exist at a personal level, group level, school or organisation level, state and national levels. In management, the vision has become an important part of the planning process. The link with corporate planning can be seen in Wriston's statement: "Look, for me a long-range plan is a dream with a deadline" (Bennis & Townsend, 1995, p. 48). It is this dream quality that is the essence of vision. Senge (1995) made the point that the concept of a vision can be seen in most corporate plans but it is often one person's, or one group's, vision which requires *compliance, not commitment*. "A shared vision is a vision that many people are truly committed to, because it reflects their own personal visions" (Senge, 1995, p. 206). A shared vision is uplifting and creates an important synergy of the team members. And an important point is that personal visions and shared visions can exist side by side. Senge noted that "(I)f people don't have their own vision, all they can do is sign up for someone else's. The result is compliance, never commitment" (Senge, 1995, p. 211).

The real measure of the presence of a shared vision and a sense of mission can only be seen in the commitment and actions of teachers, administrators, parents and students. Although vision development should not be grounded in the current environment, attention needs to be given to these conditions before embarking on a visioning process. The vision and mission are important statements about the school's learning culture. Effective innovations are driven by whole-school understanding and beliefs and the *Innovation and Best Practice Project* showed that schools have to "… develop a shared understanding and set of beliefs about best practice for their student population and a preparedness to test strategies against alternative options" (Cuttance, Angus, Crowther, & Hill, 2001, p. xxv).

A relevant insight into the vision and purpose can be seen in Cavanagh and MacNeill (2002) who argued that there were six assumptions underwriting the visioning process in schools:

1 Sense-making underpins professional growth.
2 School culture affects improvement.
3 Reality should not deny idealism.
4 Success is more important than failure.
5 Teachers must be efficacious.
6 Experimentation is not risk-taking.

Firstly, it must be recognised that for teachers to grow professionally and be committed to the vision and purpose, they must make sense of those statements, preferably through involvement in their development. King and Newmann (2000) saw a link between the vision and sense of professional belonging:

> To be sure, high-quality instruction depends on the competence and attitudes of each individual teacher. But teachers' individual knowledge, skills, and dispositions must also be put to use in an organized, collective enterprise.

The vision for social resource development among staff members can be summarized as the development of a schoolwide professional community.

Secondly, it is almost a truism to state that school culture directly influences school improvement. For change to be embedded and result in improvement there has to be staff commitment to the change and there is a raft of cultural factors that facilitate that willingness to undertake change. Thirdly, there is a need to foster idealism. Reality must never be allowed to crush the flame of idealism that burns in most teachers. Regardless how bad the situation within the school is, it is rare not to find a teacher who wants to improve things for the students. Fourthly, success is more important than failure in that it enables schools to build on from successes, no matter how small. Fifthly, teachers have to be personally and professionally efficacious. The sense of efficaciousness enables teachers to undertake experimentation (the sixth assumption).

The purpose statement and pedagogy

The primary purpose of the vision and purpose statements are to provide the school with a sense of direction. In the development of a shared vision, which develops group ownership, it is the process of development that is important in developing a cadre of stakeholders who will advance the vision. At the end of the day, while the agreements, vision and purpose statements are important, they are only as important as the stakeholders want to make them. That is why getting the process of school renewal right is critical to its success. It is the process that has the capacity to form the cadre that will bring about change in the school community. The cadre of believers in the school's vision become the torch bearers for an achievable ideal.

The purpose statement is a statement about the school's corporate, educational goals and it is the measure against which the school's performance can be judged. Typically, a school's purpose statement will contain four statements that indicate the school's pedagogic intent:

- a statement about the learning environment;
- optimising the individual student's learning;
- facilitating transition to the next stage of learning (high school, tertiary study or work); and,
- producing good citizens (adapted from Sizer & Sizer, 1999).

In an organisational sense the purpose statement underwrites school development planning, accountability and performance management.

The purpose statement is a key part of a school's strategy to give a common purpose and sense of direction to stakeholders in the school community. As Elmore (2002, p. 20) reported, "Schools do not succeed in responding to external cues or pressures unless they have their own internal system for reaching agreement on good practice and making that agreement evident in organization and pedagogy". When schools have a strong commitment to their purpose statements, it serves as a strong internal accountability system. Elmore (2002, p. 20) has argued that internal accountability precedes external accountability and underwrites all school improvement plans.

There are five characteristics of effective purpose/mission statements that allow the evaluation of students' learning and then give direction to teachers' pedagogic responses.

- Are clear.
- Are specific. (What exactly are students supposed to learn?).
- Are measurable. (How do we know students have learned?).
- Provide for failure. (How do we respond when students don't learn?).
- Future-oriented.

While to mission/purpose statement has a whole-school application, its directions must be put into place in the classrooms. The translation of the vision and the mission into classroom practice is the measure of pedagogic leadership, because unless the mission/purpose positively influences students' learning, they serve little purpose.

A vision without leadership becomes an historical artefact of well-meaning intentions. The leadership that makes the vision become a working document can be drawn from any member, or combination of members in the school community. Starratt (1995, as cited in Lashway, 1997):

> ... emphasizes the importance of institutionalizing the vision. No matter how inspiring it sounds on paper, the dream will wither unless it takes concrete form in policies, programs and procedures. At some point, curriculum, staffing, evaluation, and budget must feel the imprint of the vision, or it will gradually lose credibility.

The mechanical application of an existing vision, for a school leader, may be seen more as a managerial act, rather than leadership. The visionary leader's task is to excite others in the translation of the vision into a working document. In this way the mission statement becomes a document that guides teachers' actions and the vision and mission are embedded in the schools' and teachers' accountability.

With an engaging and viable vision there is an expectation that the vision can be translated into action. Collins (2001, p. 42) in his multi-site study of great leaders found that "... great vision without great people is irrelevant". A corollary to this observation is that a great vision, without action, remains simply an interesting piece of writing. Collins's (2001, p. 13) bus metaphor shows clearly where the vision sits in creating a renewed school or organisation:

> We thought that good to great leaders would begin by setting a new vision and strategy. We found instead that they first got the right people

on the bus, the wrong people off the bus, and the right people in the right seats- and then they figured out where to drive it.

Collins had in fact argued for a shared vision, in which the stakeholders had a sense of ownership and which allowed the talents of the organisation to be utilised.

As the school leader of a large primary school indicated, his credibility as an educational leader in the school evolved:

> By establishing a clear vision of the school that centred on student learning and not resisting from making the hard decisions in relation to the school's learning and teaching practices. By getting into classes and teaching alongside staff. By being approachable to parents and letting them see that I was really interested in their children.

He achieved this by:

> Determining an agenda for change: we really are breaking new ground. You simply are in action research mode. You need time to catch your breath as you self-reflect while at the same time locating and empowering learning and teaching leaders.

It is important to realise that the vision is the starting point and constant navigational reference as the school charts its way forward, but as Collins (2001, p. 74) explained: "Yes, leadership is about vision. But leadership is equally about creating a climate where the truth is heard and brutal facts confronted."

Visions and purpose statements vary in their ability to win the engagement of the stakeholders, and they must be defendable. So, the quality of the vision and mission statements must be considered when assessing the ability of vision and mission statement to excite and win commitment. In schools, the pedagogy decides a whole range of decisions influencing students' learning, so the pedagogic intent of the vision and purpose statements are of key importance. Successful pedagogic leadership is dependent, in no small part, on the vision and mission statements being driven by a pedagogic intent.

Effective school leaders who engage in school renewal activities, have visions not only of a preferred outcome but, also, of the process of renewal through which that outcome was to be attained. However, we maintain that a school leader having a vision for the desired school change and then securing commitment to that vision is just the starting point in instituting effective renewal within a school community. To be effective the vision needs to be articulated in a way that enables it to be institutionalised so that it shaped the everyday activities in the school.

It stands to reason, therefore, that a school leader's self-efficacy expectations largely determined the amount of effort and degree of persistence exhibited and maintained in pursuit of the school's vision and implementation of change.

Research regarding change indicates that there were two ways in which leaders help to alter the status quo, especially in respect of a desired renewal paradigm shift; either by drawing attention to an issue and then setting forth a vision for it; or, alternatively, by heightening perceptions held by the school community by pointing out desired and mutually agreed upon outcomes.

School leaders, by the very nature of their position within the organisation, are required to function as the driving force behind the educational reforms that take place within the school system.

The development of a school vision should be an inclusive and reflective process in order to create a vision representative of everyone's values and goals. This implies that not only must the school leader exercise leadership in promoting a vision but the staff must also be cohesive enough to be willing to buy some shared set of goals. In this respect, therefore, the school leader as a leader becomes the steward of the school's vision.

Effective schools are identified as having credible, strong (i.e. having a sense of presence) and efficacious educators as their school leaders. In these schools the school leader is primarily viewed as an educator – a pedagogical leader –- who does not let school organisational and managerial tasks hinder or obstruct the schools learning and teaching focus. Such leaders employ effective change management behaviours that facilitate the school's attainment of its vision and goals, continually focusing on its pedagogical activity. There is an expectation by the school's leadership and staff that all students would be engaged in their learning, and as a consequence, students would be expected to engage well with their learning. Students are expected to achieve and demonstrate improvement in learning outcomes they achieve.

Such a scenario requires of the school leader a vision for the school, and through this, a responsibility to provide a sense of purpose and direction to the school's learning and teaching programmes.

School leaders must be confident in their pedagogical understandings and ability to accomplish successfully the visions implementation within the school. It stands to reason, therefore, that in order for a school to achieve a degree effectiveness and the desired improvement orientation, it is of vital importance that the school leader, as the pedagogical leader, be possessed of a strong sense of personal self-efficacy. These self-efficacy beliefs we know have behavioural correlates. In particular, these are identified as being associated with a tendency towards leading change, fostering relationships, team and coalition building and providing a sense of direction for the organisation.

OUR BELIEF 6

> School leaders' self-efficacy beliefs, in association with their personal behavioural dispositions, impact directly on school improvement, effectiveness and renewal endeavours.

The proposition we make here is that effectiveness within a school is linked to the personal qualities of the leader and depends on their personal assessment of their own capabilities and their beliefs about their leadership credibility. More effective leaders possess particular behavioural characteristics that make them more effective in defined situations, and this effectiveness can be attributed to their personal predisposition.

Renewing the culture of a school requires teachers to also develop new beliefs, attitudes and values about instructional processes that will lead to change in-classroom practice and improved educational outcomes by students. Consequently, renewal of a school's learning and teaching programme requires re-culturing to occur at the individual classroom level through the development of alternative beliefs and attitudes towards pedagogy and curriculum.

We see that a school leader's strong pedagogic focus in the school environment translates to increased student achievement and learning outcomes and improved effectiveness. School leaders committed to improving the education of students are thus often described as instructional leaders as they have an identified and credible understanding of the teaching and learning process. These leaders display a credible knowledge of pedagogy and become actively involved in the school's instructional programme and student learning. However, the exercise of curriculum and pedagogic leadership is often tempered by the demand for attention to non-instructional, management-oriented demands and issues arising within the school and from the educational system or authority.

Fullan (2001) expanded this theme through a discussion of what he termed a leader's sense of moral purpose. Moral purpose in this case refers to the desire to act with the intrinsic intention of making a positive difference in the lives of employees, customs and society as a whole. However, as Fullan (2001, p. 5) stresses repeatedly, moral purpose without an understanding of the change process "will lead to moral martyrdom".

That some leaders have specific personal characteristics (leadership attributes) that make them more skilled in the administrative processes was highlighted in research undertaken by Silcox (2003). A tenet of the author's research was the suggestion that effective leadership made some traits more important than others in different situations. This observation of the need for a match between the traits of the leader and the situation suggested that leadership was not an isolated phenomenon and drew attention to the situational context of leadership. Situational leadership concept research sought to identify situational variables that could be related to effective leadership. The path-goal theory that House and Mitchell (1974) proposed saw leadership behaviours as not being fixed; consequently, at different times a leader could be directive, supportive, achievement-oriented or participative. Hersey and Blanchard (1982) took this concept even further with the development of the situational leadership paradigm indicating that leadership practices and behaviours were influenced significantly by the maturity of subordinates within the organisation and its pre-existing culture. They maintained that the situation, inclusive of environmental factors helped determine the leader's disposition to action in a given scenario and supported the proposition that the situation or context plays a key role in deciding whether certain leadership approaches will be effective or not. What they argued indicated that the leadership behaviours a school leader may exhibit in one school situation may not be as effective in another context.

The implications of this thesis for a school leader working towards re-culturing a school through the implementation of a renewal agenda therefore becomes a significant consideration. The leadership approach the school leader employs will consequently need to be adaptive in order to accommodate the range in maturity and the level of pedagogic understanding of staff in the school. In Figure 4.1 below, we synthesise the situational leadership model to more appropriately align it with a school leader's efforts at leading school level change and or re-culturing, recognising that the school leader's leadership style will depend upon the school's current learning and teaching culture and, the competence and commitment of staff to the change

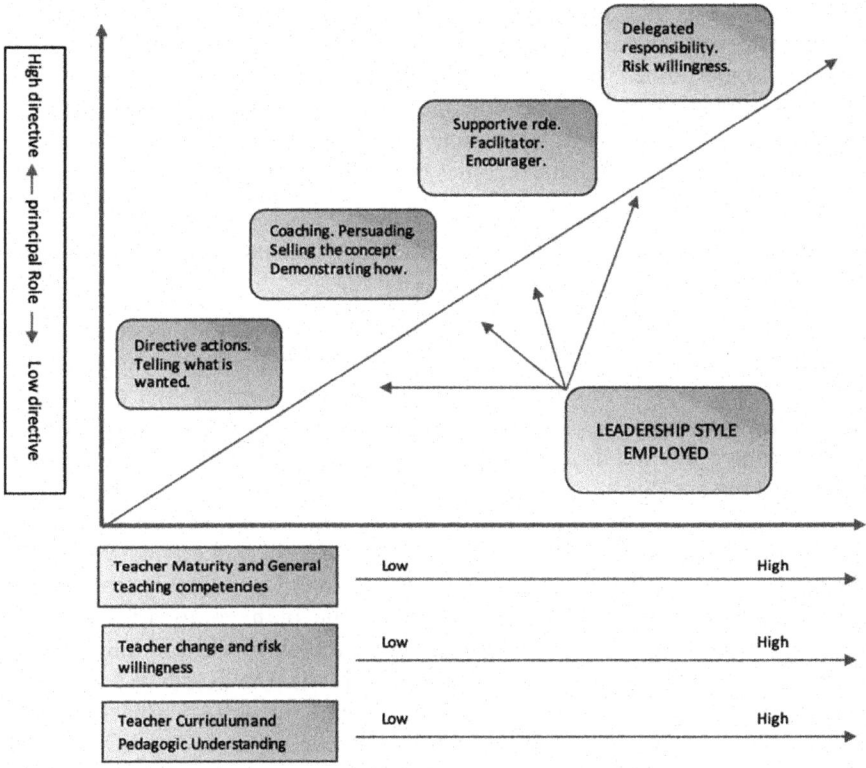

Figure 4.1 School leader leadership style accommodating staff behavioural dispositions.

agenda proposed. In each case the school leader would need to be conversant with the needs of his/her staff, then adjust the leadership style to that which most appropriately aligns with those needs; if necessary moving seamlessly from one type of leadership style to another.

We recognise that there may indeed be certain factors inclusive of staff and community disposition to either the proposed change agenda or relationships within a school that could impact on both the school leader's sense of self-efficacy and subsequent leadership behaviours exhibited.

There are many possible variables that influence a school leader's behavioural disposition, which in turn, are influenced by it. Not only specific internal school factors but also other influences external to the school could affect their predisposition to engage in initiating and implementing school change. For example, the relationship the school leader had with the District Director/superintendent, or collegial relations within the school, staff and community attitudes and beliefs about learning and teaching, social support networks and community involvement activities all are likely to affect the school leader's behavioural disposition and proactivity towards renewal. Some of the evidence reviewed points to the fact that a leader's personal beliefs in their capability to bring about the desired change agenda is not only related to their sense of self-efficacy developed through a learned process but that it is also somewhat situation specific. This assertion, underpinned by research, would tend to contradict system level initiatives of posting successful pedagogical leaders identified in one situation to schools where there are identified significant learning and teaching and cultural issues, while expecting similar outcomes to be obtained.

The impact of a school leader's personal motivation and flow on their change predisposition

Massive transformational change was visited upon school systems in the 1980s and 1990s as a response to perceptions about the lack of general economic competitiveness in the changing global economic environment. In Britain and Australia, this ideological push for change in government services became known as New Public Management; and in the United States, neoliberalism (Hursh, 2008).

As a consequence, across the Western world, the impact on school leadership has been evident with increased managerialist demands for greater efficiency and outcome attainment. Consequently, school leaders are increasingly required to undertake more of the managerial administrative type roles at the expense of their pedagogic leadership, while simultaneously teaching and learning practices have changed with the associated increased external demands of accountability through such agency as national testing regimes. The impact on school leadership as a consequence has been, as one school leader complained, "an increase in the amount of paperwork and 'administrivia' to the extent, now see myself as an office manager more than a pedagogical leader in the school".

In many jurisdictions, school leaders are being placed under increased accountability and scrutiny of their schools' operations. This has meant that a school leader's time for pedagogic and curricular issues in their school is significantly impacted upon, which then affects their ability to address the real issues and core business of education, specifically, improving student learning.

Flow theory has evolved from research into the motivation and resilience of modern school leaders in response to these external impacts. It was the Hungarian/American psychologist Csikszentmihalyi (1997) who developed the concept of flow to describe the psychological state experienced during and after optimal performance. Flow theory sits comfortably within the rich context of related theories including self-efficacy and peak performance.

In discussing the concept of flow, the moral dimension of the school leader's job is identified as most important. A real concern is that the motivation that influences school leaders' job satisfaction remains elusive within the current context of the role and the ambiguities associated with it, particularly in difficult often low-socio-economic schools. Flow experiences occur more often when the job is challenging and has clear achievable goals. School leaders are more likely to experience a sense of flow when they are actually immersed in activities that serve a greater purpose, such as helping students learn, and when they can see the results of their work through student outcome achievement.

We acknowledge that as a consequence of unrelenting change, increasing demands on the school leaders' time, more explicit accountability and enhanced community empowerment, the school leaders' tasks have become far more complex. This has resulted in a corresponding reduction in job satisfaction, which in itself has significant implications for recruiting the next generation of school leaders across some jurisdictions. In fact, as Topsfield (2012) reported, systems and schools are struggling to attract school leaders into the role given the potential for long working hours, lack of support and insufficient play and what are termed *helicopter parents*.

With acknowledged stress impacting on school leaders across the world as we see higher rates of school leader burnout and fatigue. Whittaker (1990) said of educational leadership in America:

> These principals are competent, hard-working professionals are experiencing frustration on the job and are having second thoughts about remaining in their roles as principals. Many frustrations are related to sheer role overload, unable to accomplish the many tasks and responsibilities assigned to the role of the principal. Other frustrations experienced by principals include site-based management and shared decision-making, declining resources, increased paperwork, and greater expectations from the public and central administration by higher student standards. (p. 60)

School leader leadership and flow

Flow is an interesting concept and one that not many have given much thought to in the past as it pertains to education and in particular, the teaching enterprise. As educators, do we ever lose our flow? According to MacNeill (2013) apparently not. It appears that flow merely ebbs and then rises again as new emotional, mental or social challenges and situations arise. Flow is momentum, and momentum is not only caught up partly in one's personal motivation for a particular task but is also deeper than that – it relates to how things get done, how one goes about tackling a task.

This is not to say that the strength of the flow is constant, de-motivating activities such as an ineffective bureaucracy or poor and ineffective line management, personal health or insecurity can impede the flow, but not stop it. When such events take place, boldness increases and one is more prone to engage in greater risk-taking and experimentation. When challenges are being met an individual's flow increases, often carrying all before them; increasing personal efficacy and confidence and as barriers disintegrate adding focus and force to my activity. Urgency often results in an increased flow, channelling the focus and actions to achieve a desired timeline and outcome.

Flow relates to an ability to adapt to circumstances, and underpins both the strategies and methods one applies as a teacher. The degree of flow is linked with the risk-willing disposition of a school's leadership and staff. It is about creativity, a working disposition that has one working to other than set ways and traditional conventions and consequently has an air of unpredictability about it. An educator's flow is ongoing, and helps identify the momentum and self-efficacy to tackle any task or action encountered. One's flow is retarded at times by blockages that are strewn in the path which directly retard momentum and impact subsequently on motivation, but it is always there: builds up and eventually helps break through the barriers. So, at times the flow may be disrupted but it is never stopped.

Mental flow is increased when a situation calls for new ways of thinking, looking outside the envelope for solutions. Such events are uplifting and liberating for an individual. New knowledge and finding ways to apply it increase our flow and desire to seek out more knowledge. However, this can also be depressing when one comes to the realisation that there is so much more to learn, so little time and a workforce that is not abreast of the knowledge that it takes time for them to catch up with of thinking currency. When one avenue of mental flow is disrupted it emerges with new thinking in a different area or sphere. The flow is merely channelled elsewhere, not stopped.

Emotional flow, how one reacts with others and to events is more erratic than mental flow. Emotional flow is disrupted in having to deal with situations that tend to evolve from the more irrational side of human interaction and thought. Dealing with selfishness, personal agendas that having nothing to do with the organisations greater good and self-promotion affect an individual's emotional flow, particularly when these events interrupt the momentum of the whole school. Constantly dealing with the naysayers disrupts emotional flow and at times motivation. The best reaction is usually to seek a counterbalance and not to let such irrational thinkers get in the way.

The importance of moral leadership in school vision setting

Today schools and teachers are rarely out of the headlines as schools have replaced churches as society's moral educator because they are increasingly being looked to for social leadership and responsibility; this includes moral leadership. If children do not have consistent, local, role models of moral responsibility, then schools are increasingly asked to address this issue.

Many schools today have purpose statements that are typically an expression that translates the shared vision of a school into attainable goals. The shared vision therefore is a shared covenant that bonds together leader and follower in a moral commitment.

In playing their part in the moral and educative development of students, schools are contributing to the maintenance of social cohesion by morally and technologically socialising people. Consequently, at the school level, written statements of the school's moral obligation to students and society, usually underwrite a schools' vision and purpose. The purpose statements of schools typically comprise of four moral intents or obligations:

- The school will optimise students' learning.
- The school will facilitate students' transition to the next stage of learning (high school or work).
- The school will create a happy and productive learning environment.
- The school will ensure that students have the necessary skills and understanding to contribute to a democratic society.

While teachers make individual judgements about aspects of students' learning, there is a universal requirement, often unstated yet implied, that students will also receive a moral education, within a moral educational context. Teachers, therefore, have come to understand that learning itself is intrinsically a moral activity, which involves them by necessity in attending to the moral character of what the community has called upon them to do, thus redefining the learning and teaching function not in technical terms but moral terms.

Moral purpose and shared leadership

Have you ever watched a movie like *Stand and Deliver*, or *Goodbye Mr Chips*, or *To Sir with Love*, or *Lean on Me*? They are often inspired by true life drama and stories of passionate and committed teachers. Usually they are based in schools located in low socio-economic areas, involve cultural diversity, more often than not inter-racial and idealistic middle-class teachers who are faced with the challenge of teaching a multiracial collection of students whose lives, aspirations and world views are often confused and lacking direction.

Teachers who genuinely respect their students and want to understand them, realise that they can make a difference in their lives. While such depictions carry the additional weight of being based on real-life examples, perhaps enhanced somewhat in the telling of the story, they are nevertheless films that often resonate with the viewer. These "hero school leader or teacher" movies portray individuals who bring to their work a real sense of responsibility for their charges, a committed presence to their students' needs and interests and a refusal to be anything less than authentic. These virtues capture much of what is perceived to be the best characteristics in the *ideal* teacher model.

In each of these films however, we see schools portrayed as a constant struggle against the hopelessness of colleagues, and the inflexibility of the bureaucracy within which they work. The hero teacher is depicted as a lone figure who stands for high ideals in the midst of apathy or overt opposition. The schools, as depicted in these films, lack either a strong sense of moral purpose, or a culture of collaboration. Unfortunately, quite often the "heroic" school leader or teacher has as much to worry about in the staffroom as he/she does in the classroom.

However, a major problem in education has been this myth of the hero school leader or teacher and a belief that the power-of-one is a singular measure of good leadership. In reality, the long-term prospects of the mythical, singular, martyr principle is similar to the fate of man in Hobbes's *Leviathan* ... solitary, poor, nasty, brutish and short; which is why distributed leadership is so important in schools (more about this topic later). We argue that school leaders are currently seen as being overburdened, overworked and often overwhelmed by the many tasks they must complete. Therefore, the era of promoting the singular hero leader has finished as organisational theory has now acknowledged the need for collective leadership and collective efficacy, which in essence represents a staff's shared belief in its capabilities to organise and execute the course of action required to produce given student levels of attainment.

Michael Fullan (2001) reminded us that more good things are likely to happen in schools where there is a sense of collaboration around a shared moral purpose. Much has already been said and written about shared leadership with its many labels and many forms, but less attention has been paid to what shared moral purpose might look like in practice, and to the connection between this and shared leadership.

What is a shared moral purpose?

Whether labelled as "shared whole school vision and goals" (Cuttance et al., 2001) or as "overarching values" or, as in the work of MacBeath and Mortimore (2001) as just plain "moral purpose", a shared moral purpose has been consistently identified in the literature as one of the fundamental necessities for bringing about the kind of change and improvement which will deliver desirable student learning in schools into the future.

A shared moral purpose is a compelling idea or aspirational purpose. A shared belief is that as a team people can achieve far more for their end users together than they can alone.

An alternative perspective is provided by Moos (1999) who writes that: "While most people agree that democratic schools and democratic leadership are good ... They do not agree on what it means" (p. 65). It may be that an ill-founded sense that beliefs are shared could be as damaging as open disagreement. There is a need for this shared sense of purpose to be grounded likewise in a shared commitment to *explicit* values (Andrews & Lewis, 2004). In other words, it is not sufficient to have a broad aspiration, there also needs to be clarity and detail in the way the purpose is understood by stakeholders, and in particular about the values which underpin it. There is a demonstrated link in research that shows that the kinds of decisions we make as individuals are influenced by the norms at work in the groups in which we operate and by the issues at stake. These norms operate in conjunction with our beliefs and values to create attitudes and dispositions to act (Duignan & Bezzina, 2004). Shared norms are really a manifestation of what we are here calling shared moral purpose.

The challenge is to find a way for this moral purpose to surface and then to make it part of the discourse of the school so that it can be embedded in its pedagogic practice.

Shared leadership

In a study of leadership, Duignan (2003) advocates the need for an important shift in the meaning, perspective and scope of leadership in schools, in order to build organisational cultures that promote, nurture and support shared leadership. His is one voice among the many in the chorus which argues that, for reasons which range from survival, to efficacy, through to principle, the practice of investing leadership solely in individuals is no longer sustainable.

A range of reasons has been put forward for the pursuit of shared leadership. Shared leadership actually works in practice; it builds commitment among those involved; and it is intrinsically ethical as a practice. In practice, shared leadership has been shown to enhance student outcomes. However, Elmore (2002) cautions that collaborative work by teachers will not, alone, lead to changed teacher practices and improved learning outcomes, as there must also be a clear organisational focus on large-scale change and whole-school improvement – a shared moral purpose, if you will.

With respect to school improvement and change, there is an extensive body of research, which confirms that strong collegial relationships, mutual trust, support and a focus on enquiry are crucial for effective improvement.

Shared or as we prefer, distributed leadership also promotes a sense of belonging among participants, a sense of being valued members of the school community and a deep commitment to collective action for whole-school success. Such a commitment to collective action is in itself an expression of moral purpose. Shared leadership is intrinsically ethical. We pick up this theme in greater detail in Chapter 7. However, when responding to paradoxical problems, a shared moral purpose developed in dialogue with colleagues provides a firm foundation for decision-making.

Moral leadership and authentic learning

It seems to us that what these big-screen teaching heroes had in common was a preparedness to ask the most fundamental of questions: "What must I do if I am to make a genuine difference to the lives of my students?"

Like them, we need to connect the learners' search for meaning and purpose in their lives to a variety of personal experiences in the academic curriculum. We need to enable learners to continuously transform their understanding of themselves and their worlds and to use this to face the challenges and possibilities of their lives and their future. This type of learning is authentic, and it is truly transformative.

The open challenge to educators, therefore, is to infuse academic learning with a dimension of personal meaning, and thereby in doing so enrich the whole learning process. Learning which is not authentic to the needs of the students' life world is not only *inappropriate* but *unethical*, and goes to the very heart of what we do as educators. The pedagogic leader's role is to act courageously. If we take our work as educators seriously, and seek to be ethical in its practice, we must also be constantly in search of ways to make learning authentic.

What does authentic learning look like? Among other things, it promotes:

- Development of personal meaning.
- Awareness of the connection between the learner and the subject.
- Respect for the integrity of what is being studied.
- Appreciation of implications for the trajectory of the learner's life.
- Application of a rich understanding of the subject/object of study in practice; and ultimately
- Transformation into a more fully human individual (Duignan & Bezzina, 2004).

This type of learning is not just about taking new knowledge and skills for oneself but is more about giving of one's unique humanity to others and to the community. It is deeply relational. Authentic learning is itself a fundamentally moral activity because it engages students in a deeper understanding of the nature and purpose of their lives and in determining how they can best contribute to the greater good of the community and society. In the everyday busy-ness of schools, it may be easy to forget, but all of us engaged in the privileged work of teaching are engaged in a profoundly ethical activity.

Naming authentic learning as the goal of our work assumes values and ethics which often go un-named and undiscussed. The challenge for educational leaders is to find ways to make these explicit – to give them expression and to promote ownership. This is not always easy.

Moral purpose and shared leadership – a potent brew indeed!

References

Andrews, D., & Lewis, M. (2004). Building sustainable futures: Emerging understandings of the significant contribution of the professional learning community. *Improving Schools*, 7(3), 129–150.

Bennis, W. & Nanus, B. (1985). *Leaders: The strategies for taking charge*. New York: Harper & Row.

Bennis, W. & Townsend, R. (1995). *Reinventing leadership*. London: Piatkus Publications.

Cavanagh, R., & MacNeill, N. (2002). School visioning: Developing a culture for shared creativity. *The Practising Administrator*, 24(3), 15–18.

Chance, E. W. (1991). *Restructuring, the principal, and an educational vision: Key to success*. ERIC Document Reproduction Service No. ED340 103.

Collins, J. (2001). *Good to great: Why some companies make the leap ... and others don't*. London: Random House Business Books.

Conley, D. T., Dunlop, D. M., & Goldman, P. (1992). *The 'vision thing' and school restructuring*. Eugene, OR: Oregon School Study Council, The University of Oregon.

Csikszentmihalyi, M. (1997). *Creativity: Flow and the psychology of discovery and invention*. New York: HarperPerennial.

Cuttance, P., Angus, M., Crowther, F., & Hill, P. (2001). *School innovation: Pathway to the knowledge society*, (pp. xiii–xxix). Canberra: DETYA.

Duignan, P. (2003, September). *Formation of capable, influential and authentic leaders for times of uncertainty*. Paper given at the Australian Primary Principals' Association National Conference, Adelaide. www.educationalleaders.govt.nz/Culture/Attitudes-values-and-ethics/Formation-of-capable-influential-and-authentic-leaders-for-times-of-uncertainty

Duignan, P., & Bezzina, M. (2004). *Leadership and Learning: Influencing what really matters*. Paper presented at the Teacher Education Council Conference, Strathfield, ACU National.

Elmore, R.F. (2002). *Bridging the gap between standards and achievement: The imperative for professional development in education*. Washington, DC: The Albert Shanker Institute. www.shankerinstitute.org/Downloads/Bridging_Gap.pdf

Frick, J.E., & Frick, W.C. (2010). An ethic of connectedness: Enacting moral school leadership through people and programs. *Education, Citizenship and Social justice*, 5(2), 117–130.

Fullan, M. (2001). *Leading in a culture of change*. San Francisco: Jossey-Bass.

Hersey, P., & Blanchard, K. (1982). *Management of organizational behavior: Utilizing human resources*. Englewood Cliff, NJ: Prentice-Hall.

Hobbes, T. (1968). *Leviathan*. Ringwood, Australia: Penguin Books.

House, R.J., & Mitchell, T.R. (1974). Path goal theory of leadership. *Journal of Contemporary Business*, 3, 81–97.

Hursh, D. (2008). *High stakes testing and the decline of teaching and learning: The real crisis in education.* Lanhamm MD: Rowman & Littlefield.

King, M.B., & Newmann, F.M. (2000). Will teacher learning advance school goals? *Phi Delta Kappan,* 81(8), 576–580.

Lashway, L. (1997). Creating a learning organization. *ERIC Digest,* Number 121. Eugene OR. ERIC Clearinghouse on Educational Management. ED420897.

MacBeath, J., & Mortimore, P. (2001). *Improving school effectiveness.* Buckingham, UK: Open University Press.

MacNeill, C.N. (2013). *An examination of Csikszentmihalyi's concept of flow in Western Australian school leaders' work and learning* (Unpublished doctoral dissertation). Curtin University, Bentley, Western Australia.

Moos, L. (1999). New dilemmas in school leadership. *Leading & Managing,* 5(1), 41–59.

PERL (2014). Growing a shared vision: A toolkit for schools. Partnership for Education and Research about Responsible Living. https://iefworld.org/fl/PERL_toolkit3.pdf

Senge, P.M. (1995). *The fifth discipline: The art and practice of the learning organization.* New York: Doubleday.

Silcox, S.B. (2003). *An investigation of the roles of school principals in leading school renewal in a Western Australian school district* (Unpublished doctoral dissertation). Curtin University, Western Australia.

Sizer, T.R., & Sizer, N.F. (1999) *The students are watching: Schools and the moral contract.* Boston, MA: Beacon Press.

Topsfield, J. (2012, 9 July). Schools hit by principal shortage. *The Age* (Melbourne). www.theage.com.au/victoria/schools-hit-by-principal-shortage-20120708-21pmv.html

Whittaker, C. (1990, September). *Accountability in the Public Sector: A brief and personal overview of the Australian perspective.* Paper presented to the Nation Think Tank on Library and Information Statistics, Kings Ambassador Hotel, Perth.

5 System reforms as catalysts for school renewal

Change in schools can be initiated as a result of external inputs (community, system or district) or from internal initiatives based on addressing local needs. In this chapter we examine how school staff can handle the external demands, which are often mandatory in public schools. The challenge for schools is to ensure that the external requirements are thought through and local strategies put into place to ensure that the students benefit from the act of compliance, which could be beneficial anyway. There are specific challenges posed for pedagogic school leaders when systems or districts decide to impose change on schools.

Examining the characteristics of school leadership descriptions from around the world, one can be forgiven for believing that there is a sense of conformity and sameness to them. The moulds that press out thousands of models of schooling may have slight variations and imperfections, but in essence there is an underlying common template of schooling. This sameness ensures that teachers and school leaders are easily recognisable in the schooling models and the stereotypical representations in the literature and television, and as a consequence, they have generally not been kind. However, circumstances have changed and nowhere is this change more evident than in the world of modern school leadership where a more independent version of leadership is promoted.

A typical description of school leadership as presented in the literature to this point in time involved a colourful, clichéd example of what had been expected of school leaders in the past, where their schools remained under more centralist, bureaucratic control. However, as indicated, the world of school leadership has undergone a significant transformational change, particularly in the public-school sector with the development of Charter Schools and other variants of this model. This approach to micro-level management of the school leader's role was seen as no longer reflecting the required leadership role that was necessary to implement the new, dynamic paradigm of schooling. However, occasionally breakthroughs can occur when system level reforms provide a sufficient impetus for school leaders to embark on a renewal agenda. Such a scenario is presented to school leadership when a more centralised governing body, state government, district or department, is forced to reduce its controls from a more micro-management perspective to a more macro approach. A loosening of the reins of control with tighter accountability.

In more recent history, examples of such reform type changes (top-down) have tended to relate to human resource management, financial controls or accountability measures. For example, with system delegation of human resource functions to schools, school leaders then have greater ownership of the staff selection processes and therefore are able to select staff that more appropriately meet the school's learning and teaching ethos and requirements. This also had the added benefit of enabling curriculum and re-culturation processes to be more achievable.

Not all schools are the same and this needs to be more widely recognised, as it is at the school level where the unique demands of the local community can be best accommodated. Members of a school staff and community need to be given the opportunity, as well as the authority to make decisions necessary to improve teaching and learning, although school communities vary in how much authority they need. We maintain that the school community is best placed to set directions for their school to ensure every young person has the greatest opportunity to be successful in education and in life.

The vision for schools that has evolved in the United States, United Kingdom, Australia, New Zealand and Canada is to give greater responsibility for student outcome achievement to school leaders and communities while simultaneously recognising that this needs to occur within a framework where policy and budget is determined for implementation locally.

The problems associated with a centralised system of governance with respect to schools have long been recognised. We have previously referred to this scenario as the leadership versus management dichotomy!

OUR BELIEF 7

> The enabling of schools to be empowered with the authority to make decisions that reflect the needs and aspirations of the individual school and the local community will enhance community perceptions about the value of learning and teaching.

For schools to be able to respond quickly to situational demands, they must be provided with the choice to make all the necessary decisions themselves. That is, they should be as autonomous as possible. It has therefore been critical that centrally held powers affecting the ability of a school to respond quickly to market forces be devolved to the schools.

The system reform: Moving towards greater local empowerment

The empowering of school communities to establish appropriate and relevant directions for their schools based on the educational, social, emotional and physical needs of their students can be seen in most Western educational jurisdictions. Of this change model, Amanda Keddie (2016, p. 714) observed that:

Commitment to school autonomy is set against a political backdrop of moral panic about the dire state of public schooling in contexts like the USA, the UK and Australia (Apple, 2010; 2013). This moral panic has provided a warrant for increasing schools' public accountability to external measures of school effectiveness (e.g. the publication of comparative school performance data on standardised tests) in an effort to drive up standards. The notions of competition and choice are key here.

School leaders, teachers and staff want to work with parents, local businesses, community groups, local government and the wider community to improve learning outcomes for school students. This aim will be better fostered, we argue, if the unnecessary red tape that currently inhibits school leaders from being innovative is removed.

Teachers have indicated that central system education policies and reforms are not reviewed often enough to take into account the changing circumstances and conditions within their particular classroom, school and community.

CASE STUDY 4

Independent public schools and a new model of school leadership

The Western Australian model of Independent Public Schools (IPS) was developed by the authors while working with the shadow Minister for Education, and presented to government as a concept in 2008. We saw the concept as a way to encourage schools to accept greater ownership in their decision-making, and further as a means to arrest the decline of the client-base of public schooling evident in the state. At this time, the state's Education Department was highly centralised, bureaucratised and strongly hierarchical.

The programme that eventuated from these discussions was titled *Empowering School Communities* and was based on the precept of growing greater school community ownership of their local schools through important delegations for decisions to school leaders and local school boards. It acknowledged that such a model would foster the principal and the school board members having a closer relationship because they would need to have a more intimate knowledge of the contextual issues that influence their particular school's operations.

The Independent School model we proposed and that was subsequently accepted as an important electoral plank of the incoming government required school leaders to have a different mix of knowledge, skills and values from those needed in the previous more management-oriented models of school administration. In reality, the bureaucratic model of school leadership that the previous model encouraged was situated in the field of *management* rather than *leadership* because the levels of decision-making were always about low-level compliance and accountability under the oversight of directors or superintendents.

> The new model proposed facilitated:
>
> a Firstly, the school leader being seen as the true educational leader in the school.
> b Secondly, the school leader having a degree of separation from the educational hierarchy that more aptly describes the bureaucratic model of school administration at the time.
> c Thirdly, the potential dissonance between the school and system's interests no longer would exist. The education system/department would be relegated to becoming a support and resource structure for the school boards. Finance and outcomes would, therefore, become the main drivers of conversation in the relationship the school had with the system/department.
> d Fourthly, the school leader would be able to develop a relationship with the school board that was different to that which they had previously with directors and superintendents, and more akin to that of the role of CEO of a company to his/her board.
>
> The process entailed schools applying for the new delegations. The initiative was warmly accepted by schools with over 75% of the state's public schools applying for inclusion in the programme.

Advantages of a devolved system of education

The major advantage of a devolved system of education is that a school is able to individually tailor its decisions to achieve the best outcome for its students and teachers. Those at the coalface – teachers, parents, administrators and students – are ideally placed to make the vital decisions that produce a quality educational environment, as opposed to a centralised system of decision-making, whereby policy is determined by bureaucrats who are removed from the day-to-day operations of a school. Devolution of such decision-making to schools also allows those that are equipped to manage available resources to be given the opportunity to do so. This places them in a position to tailor these resources to the most appropriate areas, doing away with the onerous and unnecessary accountability procedures that often exist under a more centralised structure.

For example, a heuristic example of performance management that evolves from such an approach can be seen in the template used by New Zealand Schools' Trustees' Association (NZSTA, 2015) which outlines the purpose of the performance management agreement as providing:

- A clear understanding of the board's expectations for the principal.
- Measurement of principal's contribution to the school's strategic objectives.

- An indicator of learning and development targets for the principal.
- A measure of the principal's achievements in the professional standards.
- A formal process to provide determination of principal career allowances.
(The framework for the annual performance review NZSTA, 2015)

A devolved system of education instils a sense of belief and ownership when schools are making decisions based on the best outcomes for their school community. It also allows for a more targeted and appropriate recruitment of teachers, and the ability to retain teachers who feel involved and linked to their school.

This approach is particularly significant when addressing behaviour management issues. Schools with greater autonomy can negotiate and implement an effective behaviour management programme that reflects the values of the local school and community. The school will not be constrained by a bureaucracy that is out of touch with the specific issues within a school community.

CASE STUDY 5

Newspaper report on school principal reactions to new level of autonomy

HEADLINE: Independence brings flexibility in lots of flexible ways

A new era for education opens this year with the first 34 Independent Public Schools setting the trend for greater autonomy and flexibility to meet the needs of their local communities, two school principals share their approach to the flexibilities that the new policy provided.

For one school it allowed the principal to allocate resources where they were needed most. An elementary school principal indicated:

"We applied to become an Independent Public School because we needed more flexibility in how we operated so we could continue – and indeed expand – the opportunities we provide our students and their families. The flexibilities meant we could ensure that we had the right staff, the right staffing model and the right programs to contribute to the development of the community in ways that extended beyond school learning."

After being selected as a participant in the program a secondary college principal remarked that he immediately went out to stakeholder groups, teachers, parents and community to seek their views and aspirations for the college with the new delegations in place, as it was clear that the school needed to develop a more independent way of thinking in terms of stated priorities.

"Over the past few years the principal had fostered and promoted experimentation and broad thinking, and encouraged innovative practices – all essential ingredients for successful teaching and learning programs. Now an opportunity was provided to have a more significant dialogue with stakeholders on the development of the vision, ethos, values and beliefs that underpin our learning and teaching endeavour."

> Using the flexibilities that were now provided the school was able to develop further its two greatest strengths – a more highly qualified staff and greater community ownership of the decision-making processes – to set us apart. "Our priorities and desired outcomes are specific, measurable, achievable and realistic in their scope." he said. (*School Matters*, February, 2011)

While an efficient and effective school organisation provides access for staff to access the skills and knowledge necessary for improvement and change, an empowered environment goes so much further. It encourages schools and its leadership in particular, to use the more autonomous decision-making provision that comes with greater independence along with, available resources and organisational support to engage more effectively, and appropriately in meeting local community desires and expectations.

We have long argued that greater school-based autonomy facilitates school re-culturation and curriculum change endeavours. It enables and encourages schools to focus their attention, resources and expertise on addressing the community's expectations and in meeting the school's learning and teaching priorities. Enhanced autonomy removes many layers of bureaucracy, improves the schools focus on client needs and facilitates teacher responsiveness to them.

OUR BELIEF 8

> That one template of schooling does fit all school situations, because there is never one right design or one structure that will suit every school in a variety of situations.

It is interesting to note that the *one size fits all* way of doing business is sometimes referred to as Procrusteanism. Procrustes was a mythical Greek robber who killed his victims by fitting them to an iron bed. He stretched short victims and amputated the legs of tall ones, thus ensuring a perfect fit! Merriam-Webster (2019) notes that a "procrustean bed" is a scheme or pattern into which someone or something is forcibly fitted.

The autonomy that comes with greater independence from systemic management, even at a graduated level, enables schools to achieve a certain degree of freedom from compliance aspects in exchange for demonstrable greater effectiveness in terms of student performance. Centralised structures and accountability processes have generally grown piecemeal over time in response to issues that were urgent at the time, more often than not evolving from a situational political imperative. Autonomy for schools meant staff selection with greater control over budgets, and the dynamic changes from a focus on compliance to a focus on school and student performance.

It is acknowledged that it is highly unlikely that central or district education systems will ever surrender total control over compliance, unless schools are able to demonstrate enhanced student outcomes performance. This becomes a dilemma as schools are better able to achieve greater student achievement when they are provided with greater autonomy to respond to student needs.

What is required now is a mind-shift in the practice of most central, hierarchical oriented authorities and bureaucracies in terms of the gap in rhetoric about devolution and autonomy and the movement towards increased control and compliance processes. This of course highlights the tension between central planning with its system policy development and compliance requirements, and a schools' ability and overall flexibility to develop a local response to student learning needs. Both have the aim of improved student outcome performance. However, it is argued that giving schools more autonomy is a greater enabler.

Building classroom relationships

So, what have we identified as the best practices for improving student/teacher relationships? Furthermore, how do students' differences in ability, learning preferences, culture, age and gender affect their motivation and behaviour? How do teachers' personalities and experience influence their management styles? How are schools assessing the effectiveness of behaviour management strategies? How are experienced teachers coaching beginning and substitute teachers? How can teachers manage classrooms with a human touch?

OUR BELIEF 9

> The professional relationships that teachers establish with their students form the bases of an inclusive pedagogy.

We maintain that:

- Accountability and individuation are the imperatives of modern education and they influence the daily learning and teaching at classroom level.
- Secondly, there is a danger that social-emotional learning (SEL) will be ignored as schools push for better rankings on standardised testing programmes.
- Appropriate, inclusive pedagogy must be employed if what happens in classrooms is to model the directive statements of the school purpose statements.

The external factors influencing classroom culture

The twin imperatives *accountability* and *individuation* are shaping what happens in classrooms across the Western World. Accountability, linked to the difficulty in attracting tax dollars to education from an ageing taxation base, coupled with an increasingly litigious and sceptical society increasingly influences teachers' pedagogic practices. As a result, there has been a change in the focus of a teacher's actions and the development of a narrower curriculum based on identified standards for accountability. Secondly, at the individual student level, teachers are becoming more accountable for students' progress. The inexorable path to individuation is strewn with potential pitfalls for individual teachers and schools. While growing societal and moral pressures require teachers to adopt individually appropriate pedagogy that facilitates inclusion, it must be acknowledged that there are limits to what teachers can do.

Pedagogy: A better way to go

While many writers use *instruction* as a synonym for *teaching* or *pedagogy*, instruction, in reality, is a limiting, clinical term that relates to one part of the teaching and learning cycle. Instruction does not encompass the formative or summative assessment that effective teachers do as a matter of course. Instruction does not consider the influence of the teacher's body language or discourse that helps create a learning environment that promotes academic risk-taking. Instruction does not describe the influence of the class culture on students' understanding of democratic decision-making. As Van Manen (1993, p. 9) warned, "(I)t is possible to learn all of the techniques of instruction but remain pedagogically unfit as a teacher."

While *pedagogy* is a contested concept, it covers a wider range of aspects of the teaching act than instruction. Pedagogy is derived from *paidagogos*

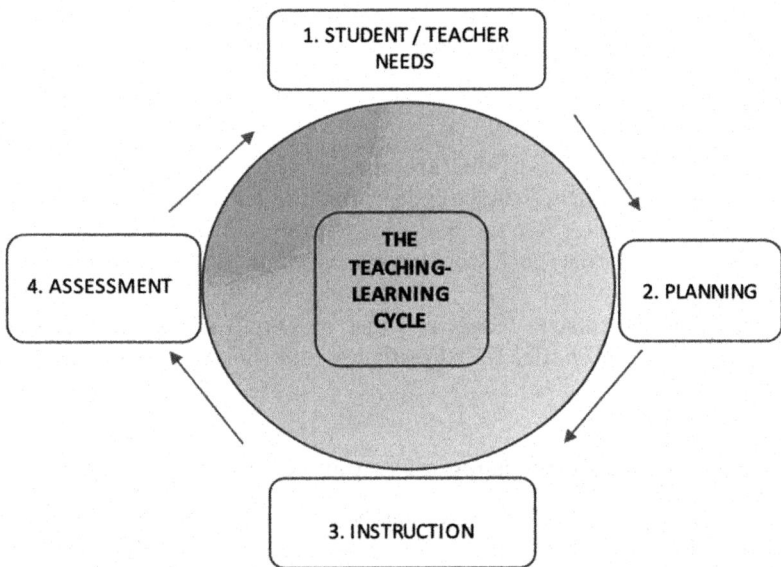

Figure 5.1 A typical teaching and learning cycle.

(Greek) meaning, the teacher of children, the intentional use of the term *pedagogy*, instead of *instruction* or *teaching*, in modern times, can be conceptual, geographical and/or ideological. The term *pedagogy*, while relatively uncommon in a decade ago, is currently being used more frequently in publications and teachers' discourse. This Van Manen (1993, p. 11) attributed to an upsurge of North American interest in Western European philosophy and educational theory. There appear to be three, inter-related clusters of meaning of pedagogy in the literature:

- Pedagogy as a synonym for teaching but not instruction (Mortimore, 1999; Newmann et al., 1996);
- Pedagogy as a political tool for the enculturation students and others (Freire, 1977; Smyth, 1988); and
- Pedagogy as student-centred learning and teaching, and specifically excluding didactic teaching (Hamilton & McWilliam, 2001).

We have defined pedagogy as learning-oriented, purposeful human interactions that acknowledge the social, personal and political influences in the learning content and context, which results in informed learning.

Pedagogy must take into account the "Why?" "How?" and "When?" of learning, not just the "What?" Pedagogy is based on dialogue, not monologue, and the learners are essential participants in the discussion. Evans (1999, p. 11) made the point that school leaders who are not guided by pedagogic choice "... resort to a thoroughly bureaucratized way of relating to teachers" and as a result teaching becomes an occupation defined by expectations.

Supporting teachers

It is extremely difficult to change teachers' preferred teaching methods (Stigler & Hiebert, 1999). In an effort to describe a pedagogy of inclusion, based on student-centred approaches, the authors developed a 'Pedagogic Profile' that described successful informed practice in cooperative learning teams. (An example of such a profile is provided in the appendix.) As a part of the teachers' performance management discussions with the school leadership they were asked to plot their levels of performance on the profile matrix and then identify potential areas for further development. It was noted that the teachers' self-analysis of pedagogic development was empowering for both new and experienced teachers alike as they reported that the Pedagogic Profile gave them a sense of direction in their teaching.

Secondly, experience has shown that teachers learn best from each other, so scenarios can be orchestrated by the school's leadership that encourages teacher collaboration and school peer support networks. By way of example, through the effective use of double classroom spaces and timetable adjustments it is possible to ensure that teachers teaching the same year levels have common preparation times each week.

The creation of a culture of inclusion, based on caring, professional relationships, is as important for newly appointed graduate teachers and experienced teachers, as it is for students and their parents. The pedagogy that a school promotes is the key in establishing and maintaining a culture of inclusion and further, it defines the interpersonal relationships between stakeholders. It is claimed that a mix of explicit teaching and cooperative learning in teams is a successful practice that engages students in their learning. However, in education there is not one correct way of doing things and as a pedagogic leader the school leader is in a good position to encourage peer interaction among teachers; facilitating visits to other classrooms and promoting collaborative teaching endeavours. Finally, a comment that needs to be made here is that the teachers should not be allowed to rest on their pedagogic laurels; the learning and teaching practices suiting one group of students will rarely suit the next group and getting the relationships right is the fundamental key ingredient to engaging students in learning.

As jurisdiction's move away from a centralist conformity based on the economic rationalist influences of the bureaucracy and New Public Management (NPM)/Neoliberalism there is a need to enact the changes spawned as *school systems* metamorphose into *systems of schools*.

The fundamental purpose of a pedagogic leader in a school is to encourage professional and personal growth: growth in both teaching and support staff enhancing their professional capabilities, growth in the students in their academic, social, physical and emotional well-being and outcome attainment and growth in the wider community in their ability to enhance the life chances of their children.

We recognise that school leader pedagogic leadership is a personal journey that is underpinned by a commitment to care for (and about) others in the school community. Such a leadership ethos will therefore, require the use of inclusive processes to engage stakeholders in a learning journey that is future focused, acknowledging that the individuals who comprise the wider school community will in turn provide the context for the leadership journey and will be an important consideration in determining the nature and outcomes of that journey.

School leadership must be focused on the capacity to build and sustain positive relationships, and the inclination to do so in ways that affirm the integrity and credibility of the leader. For a school leader to be seen as pedagogically effective and to be seen as credible opportunities to apply their expert knowledge, skills and abilities to solve existing and emerging learning and teaching problems. Engaging in a school renewal process is one such avenue.

We acknowledge that although participative processes will always underpin any school renewal actions, there will be occasions when tough decisions will need to be made in the interests of the school as a whole. However, by building relationships that create trust through care and acceptance leadership integrity will always emerge and be seen as quality most admired and acknowledged by stakeholders involved in the process.

School leaders must be seen as both administratively competent and pedagogic experts, modelling supportive and inclusive behaviours that will be seen by the school community as compelling evidence that the school is committed to its learning and teaching endeavours and in turn will lead to successful learning outcomes for students. A pedagogic school leader who builds relationships underpinned by integrity can construct a renewed and sustainable culture in their school.

The failure to recognise that business models give us a better understanding of what is happening in some education change models

Educators often look askance at parallels drawn between education and the perceived tawdry profit-driven world of business and industry. While American writers have been keen to label the new directions in education as *neoliberalism*, they have failed to develop the name-calling links with what they see in Main Street every day.

The fast food industry, an industry that impacts on everyone's lives, is a prime example of business franchising in action, and this is an efficient way to get market impacts while leaving the day-to-day administration to local franchisees. The arm's-length control is affected by comprehensive franchising agreements that set out:

- product being offered;
- quality standards of the products;
- promotion of the brand;
- support from the franchise owner;
- the franchisee takes the financial risk;
- payments for named services are closely defined; and
- a fine-grained set of standards for which the franchisee is held accountable are included in the franchise agreement.

The Franchising Model has many variations, but the commonalities we believe are easily interchanged with the independent/ charter model schools.

In the move towards the franchising model of schooling, it is often forgotten that a different type of leadership is required to that of the school leader-managerial type of leadership that are safely ensconced in many unchanging school systems.

The illusion of autonomy

What is poorly understood in the development of the so-called independent and autonomous schools is that like in any puppet theatre, the puppeteer still pulls the strings, and the illusory concept of Punch's autonomy is an end of a continuum that is never reached in system change or puppetry. While philosophers realised that humans can be truly free in a state of nature, the

Table 5.1 Comparisons between Franchising Model and Independent/Charter type schools

	Franchising Model	Charter Schools (not stand alone)
Brand	Brand driven	Brand driven
Start-up costs	KFC $1.4 m; Dominos $250,000 (Donohoo, 2019)	Start-up costs: buildings, school-type equipment, staffing.
Accountability	Accountable to Franchise owner for contractual requirements	Accountable to the Charter founders
Profitability	Profit-driven	Profit-driven
Business share	Trade on name	Trade on name
Standards of products	Advertised	Advertised
Standards service	Publicised, complaints processes	Publicised. Complaints not expected
Advertising	Franchiser-driven	Franchiser and franchisee responsibility.
Decision-making	Franchiser-strategic; franchisee Local decisions	Franchiser-strategic; franchisee Local decisions
Leadership type	Highly active, entrepreneurial	Highly active, entrepreneurial

moment they enter into a *social contract* to live in society, those freedoms are compromised. In education, the same situation holds, and autonomy within an educational contract cannot happen.

However, the rhetoric of autonomy, grunion-like, has spawned thousands of variations on this theme. School leaders and school communities must accept that true autonomy will never happen, but there are fantastic possibilities for school renewal and school improvement when working within the defined constraints for the betterment of students' educational opportunities. System and district changes can always be seen as an opportunity to improve teaching and learning.

References

Donohoo, J. (2019). Strengthening collective efficacy – How educators' beliefs impact student learning. https://gazette.education.govt.nz/notices/1H9qTp-jenni-donohoo-strengthening-collective-efficacy-how-educators-beliefs-impact-student-learning/

Education Department of Western Australia (2011). *School matters*. Government printers.

Evans, R. (1999). *The pedagogic principal*. Edmonton, Alberta: Qual Institute Press.

Freire, P. (1977). *Pedagogy of the oppressed* (M.B. Ramos, Trans.). Harmondsworth, UK: Penguin Press.

Hamilton, D., & McWilliam, E. (2001). *Ex-centric voices that frame research on teaching*. In V. Richardson (Ed.), *Handbook of research on teaching* (pp. 17–43) (9th edition). Washington DC: American Educational Research Association.

Keddie, A. (2016). School autonomy as "the way of the future": Issues of equity, public purpose and moral leadership. *Educational Management, Administration & Leadership*, 44(5) 713–727.

Mortimore, P. (Ed.) (1999). *Understanding pedagogy and its impact on learning*. London: Paul Chapman Publishing.

Newmann, F.M., et al. (1996). *Authentic achievement: Restructuring schools for intellectual quality*. San Francisco: Jossey-Bass.

NZSTA (2015). Performance management templates. www.nzsta.org.nz/board-as-employers/principals-performance-management/templates/

Smyth, W.J. (1988). *A "critical pedagogy" of teacher evaluation*. Geelong, Australia: Deakin University.

Stigler, J.W., & Hiebert, J. (1999). *The teaching gap*. New York: The Free Press.

Van Manen, M. (1993). *The tact of teaching: The pedagogical meaning of thoughtfulness*. London, Ontario: The Althouse Press.

6 Situational factors and their impact on school leadership and change

> A person, who no matter how desperate the situation, gives others hope, is a true leader.
>
> Daisaku Ikeda

When applying the construct of efficacy and school renewal to the school leadership domain, the relationship between situational, personal and organisational variables needs to be considered in any assessment. This is because self-efficacy, by definition, is situation specific.

The divergence and convergence between personal dispositions and the context in which leadership is exercised causes the school leader to behave in certain ways. This situational view of school leader leadership has been previously been represented diagrammatically in Figure 2.2.

The belief we will present here is that the combined influences of the prevailing school culture (including stakeholder dispositions) and school leader behaviours and attributes, influence whether or not the leader adopts an approach that will lead to initiating a renewal agenda, or alternatively, makes a determined effort to stay within the status quo and maintain the existing school learning and teaching culture.

OUR BELIEF 10

> A measure of good leadership is the accommodation of the multitude of situational factors that impact significantly on school leadership strategies and decision-making.

Whole-of-school cultural change is always difficult to initiate and achieve when existing behaviour and dispositions are based on deep-seated beliefs and assumptions about learning and teaching that may have been shaped over prolonged periods of time. The transformation of school culture essential for the renewal of schools requires highly efficacious school leaders with their efficacy deriving from moral and ethical beliefs they hold about education and schooling. These school leader beliefs are of significant importance when a school leader is confronted with situational specific barriers to the changes that are proposed.

Barriers to change

Many well-intentioned reform agendas have been frustrated or negated by a conservative staff reaction. In schools the main problem, in respect to change, is not the absence of innovation, but the presence of too many disconnected, episodic, piecemeal, ideologically driven projects. Having staff on side with the change process is seen as both desirable and essential in implementing whole-of-school renewal activities. Therefore, besides coming to terms with this juxtaposition of the present and future view of the school there are certain issues that a school leader would need to consider before embarking on the initiation and implementation of a renewal agenda. These issues in large part relate initially to a staff willingness to engage in the necessary self-reflection that is an essential part of the school renewal process and, further, to participate in collaborative educational debate at the school level on what the possible futures could in fact look like.

For example, a school leader commented that:

> I realised early that the assumptions that the renewal of our approach to learning and teaching would result in improved student outcomes would require a great leap of faith on the part of staff and to a lesser degree the parents. Now some years down the track there is no turning back and staff resistance is confined to only one or two malcontents.

There are also contextual issues relating to either school or system human resource practices and further, possible student cohort issues that may need to be factored into situational context considerations. Later, we will discuss, in some depth, two such issues that a school leader may encounter.

While the attitude and disposition of teaching staff is clearly identified as a possible significant impediment to initiating change agendas in schools there are others, both internal and external to the school that also need to be considered. Therefore, it is appropriate to first mention some situational barriers, specifically those associated with negative staff attitudes, union resistance to changes, parent interest or the lack thereof, and the impact of externally imposed system policies, resources and requirements on a school. After discussing some of these albeit superficially, we will then undertake a more in-depth examination of two very significant potential barriers; a toxic school teaching and leadership culture and sycophantic human resource practices and the impact that they have on staff cohesiveness and morale.

Staff resistance

Often the greatest resistance to renewal tends to come from experienced teachers who are suspicious of change, and or who may have had negative experiences with change efforts in the past. Staff resistance to change can be in the form of the more passive mindset of teachers in the way they think about their work, to a more active, oppositional and almost confrontational resistance which primarily revolve around entrenched staff attitudes and behaviours. Factions on the staff, the disenfranchisement of some through previous change processes can, it is acknowledged, create a very change resistant culture among staff.

Interestingly, Silcox (2003) identified that the greatest resistance to renewal tended to come from experienced teachers who were suspicious of the changes proposed, or who may have had negative experiences with change efforts in the past. These teacher-related barriers to change were seen to emanate from either a general lack of understanding of curriculum implementation and or the pedagogical mind-shift required by them to implement the changes at the classroom level.

School leader comment:

> The lack of teacher knowledge about learning and teaching was a major barrier that I encountered. Previously teachers had not reflected about and discussed their work with their peers.

Developing strategies to overcome staff resistance is an important consideration for school leaders in promoting a renewal agenda in their school. However, resistance to proposed change scenarios can be addressed by school leaders by initially adopting behaviours that enable them to articulate a clear sense of direction to staff and community where and when required, and then be achieved by using either directive behaviours of informing (telling) those involved what the change would look like, or by selling the renewal agenda as a better way of achieving desired outcomes to the staff and community alike.

School leader comment:

> I was prepared to live with a certain degree of staff discomfort and possible conflict in the initial phase of introducing change that would impact on the way things were traditionally done in the school and was willing to engage them (staff) in a direct way because I was confident that they would derive benefit and enjoyment from the experiences offered in renewing the schools learning and teaching program.

Once the desired culture of trust develops, staff participation increases and resistance, as a result, tends to reduce.

Staff union resistance

Many school leaders interviewed in the research undertaken by Silcox (2003) identified the various staff unions as being a significant impediment to their attempts at initiating a school renewal and change agenda. In fact, they argued that the staff unions tended to often adopt a significant anti-change orientation. For example, as one school leader interviewed remarked:

Some teachers were very Union oriented and very much opposed to change. If at any time they felt threatened by the renewal agenda, they would seek solace in the arms of their union representatives.

In a similar vein another school leader indicated that:

Some staff used the Union to try to block the proposed pedagogic and curriculum changes that other schools were already putting into place; portfolios, literacy net, learning journeys, student outcomes.

As a consequence of the threat of union resistance, many school leaders indicated a degree of reluctance, or were tentative, in their efforts to engage and/or to involve union representatives in their respective change programmes. As one school leader remarked: "I involved the union only after we had been a long way down the renewal process so that any efforts at retarding the progress of the change agenda would be harder to initiate because they always defended the status quo."

Consequently, leadership of school renewal requires not only the school leader possessing but also exercising well-developed behaviours in the communication and interpersonal area to facilitate negotiating through potential union resistance.

Parents

It is important for school leaders to engage parents early in the implementation phase of the school renewal process as the value of getting parents on side is recognised. Experience would indicate that quite often parents can be significant drivers behind school renewal efforts and if engaged in the process appropriately can be effective as partners in the changes proposed for the school.

This willingness by parents to engage may have a direct relationship with the socio-economic status of the school or at least, in part, be influenced by it. In respect to the school socio-economic profile data there is evidence of a strong relationship between parent involvement and interest in the school renewal agenda and the socio-economic environmental context in which the school is located. The schools located in low socio-economic areas retain strong parent support, even though they may not have been well equipped to help resource appropriate renewal actions.

However, there can also be very evident divisions within the parent body between long-time residents (perhaps those with a similar church connection) and parents new to the community. Significant conservatism among either group can often impede a school leader's attempts at initiating whole-of-school change.

School leader comment:

A group of traditional parents was very influential with the past school leader in determining changes within the school. They became obstructive and divisive when they did not agree with decisions made or changes planned, bullying tactics applied to other parents and towards me. They had a strong commitment to maintaining status quo and openly argued an anti-change disposition.

Community apathy, the other end-point on the continuum of parent involvement, is also identified as a significant issue and barrier to change. However, by establishing a clear vision for the school that focuses on student learning, not avoiding making the hard decisions in relation to the school's learning and teaching practice; getting into classes and teaching alongside staff, being approachable to parents and letting them see that the schools interests are centred on their children's learning and, by ensuring that renewal changes initiated in the school all have their roots in curriculum and pedagogical thinking and informed successful teaching and learning practice are but some of the fundamental behaviours successful pedagogic leaders have employed.

System level barriers

Several barriers associated with system level policies, resource allocations made to the school and curriculum imperatives while significant, are not seen to be insurmountable barriers. System level human resource practices, department dispositions to centralisation with respect to some decision-making processes and inappropriate timelines associated with the introduction of curriculum reforms are commonly identified potential barriers.

However, the greatest impediment to renewal from a system perspective is the human resources dimension. In particular issues relating to industrial constraints, enterprise bargain requirements, restrictions on local selection of staff, transfer policies, lack of flexibility allowed in school timetabling operations and the provision of non-teaching time for staff to undertake duties other than teaching can all impact on a school leader's renewal attempts.

School leader comment:

> I think that Departmental staffing attitudes are appalling. I would like someone to point out a successful large organisation who runs its staffing in such an inward-looking way.

And another school leader comment:

> Where do I start? Human resource practices. Even though the school has the benefit of local merit selection it is still very difficult to move staff on who are not contributing to the vision of the school, or to dismiss poor performing staff.

Nevertheless, while the identified staff, union, parent and system constraints may exist, they are not insurmountable barriers with the more effective school leaders able to work around the barriers as they present, inclusive of seeking fellow school leaders' advice in tackling issues.

At this point we raise two specific issues relating to changes aimed at re-culturing a school to which we believe school leaders will need to pay closer attention. These relate to the existence of a toxic culture among school staff and or its leadership and sycophantic human resource practices.

Piggy in the middle (keep away).

The ubiquitous children's game, *Piggy in the Middle (Canada)*, or *Keep Away (America)* is a ball game where two players throw a ball to each other while making certain that the third player (in the middle) does not catch it. The metaphoric intent of this game can be transferred into business and adult decision-making when one key person (Piggy) is caught between two conflicting parties.

There are three basic types of conflict (Shonk, 2020): task conflict, relationship conflict, and values conflict and in schools every member of the school community may experience one, or a combination of these conflicts regularly. But often school leaders can become the Piggy in the Middle when conflict develops between external governance and parents. For example, In the United States, Standard 3 of the Professional Standards for Educational Leaders (National Policy Board for Educational Administration, 2015) states: "Ensure that each student has equitable access to effective teachers, learning opportunities, academic and social support, and other resources necessary for success." This particular standard can be found in every liberal democracy, and school leaders are caught between the daily dilemma of equity and equality issues. The equality measure is easier for school leaders, but a problem arises when the principle of equity requires a differentiated distribution of resources and time to some students. The equity issue often escalates beyond the school site and school leaders have to explain their juggling acts to a variety of involved parties.

Toxic management: A culture devouring its future!

When examining school and organisational performativity, the elephant in the room must be the linking of the word "toxic" with "leadership". While examples of *toxic culture* are quite commonly quoted in educational literature, we argue that *toxic leadership* cannot exist because of a definitional incompatibility, and so, when the term "toxic leadership" is uttered the speaker is seen as having a limited understanding of the contemporary meaning of *leadership*.

Leadership has long been differentiated from management. While leadership is about creativity, the ethical intent of doing good, and pushing extant boundaries; management is confined to following rules and making sure that the organisation operates efficiently by maintaining the status quo.

"Transformational" leadership. like management, is also transactional in nature. *Ipso facto*, transformational leadership is always a consequence of a transactional equation that occurs when we change x, and then there will be perceived benefits for y and z. Even charismatic leadership is undoubtedly transactional.

Toxic management

The topic of toxic management has been largely neglected in the literature and can be categorised as either intentional or unintentional in form.

Unintentional toxic management occurs when weak managers are appointed to schools or organisations.

Organisational accountability has been somewhat diluted in recent times with education systems moving away from direct supervision of schools by superintendents. Until the advent of New Public Management (NPM) school superintendents had been selected because they were identified as expert school leaders, and their experiences were such that they could support and mentor developing school leaders while also passing judgements on their performance. However, in many cases the untidy mix of the coaching and umpiring roles proved to be not conducive to facilitating school leaders' professional growth. New Public Management changed that equation almost overnight, and struggling school leaders were left floundering, because to ask for help publicly perhaps signalled a personal weakness that they thought was often better concealed. The same scenario held for weak superintendents or Directors, who in avoiding the hard to make judgements that would potentially generate conflict, never actively addressed cases of toxicity in school management.

Intentional toxic management can be best demonstrated using as a reference an extract from the movie "A Few Good Men" which portrays a tough, military culture of violence and blind obedience. Marine Colonel Jessup (Jack Nicholson) represents the epitome of toxic management. Colonel Jessup is questioned about ordering a Code Red (disciplinary violence), which resulted in the punitive death of a marine.

LTJAG: (Tom Cruise): Did you order the Code Red?
COLONEL JESSUP: I did my job.
LTJAG: Did you order the Code Red?
COLONEL JESSUP: You're God damn right I did!

This mythology of toughness continues to haunt modern, androcentric, military leadership. For example, Aubrey (2012) in addressing the issue of toxicity in organisations rightly claimed that culture was the key factor for toxicity:

> When focusing on toxic leadership, many researchers emphasize the symptoms of toxicity (individual characteristics, traits) and not the

disease (culture, climate, outcomes). Although characteristics and traits may be helpful in identifying toxic leaders, they fall short of a holistic view by failing to identify or discuss how an organization's culture may contribute to toxicity in its leaders. Culture is a key strategic factor in predicting behaviours and outcomes (p. 1).

There is always a dynamic interaction between key individuals and their situational and cultural contexts. However, the culture factor is fragile, and if placed on Maslow's *Hierarchy of Needs* it often comes a poor second to survival. Tracking back through examples of toxic management it is noted that they are often mired by conflicting views of causation; often because there is rarely a single attributable cause.

OUR BELIEF 11

> A toxic school culture, if not excised by the school leader, will derail any attempts to initiate school pedagogic or cultural change.

Toxic school culture

The concept of toxic school culture was initially popularised by Deal and Peterson in their ground-breaking book, *Shaping School Culture* (1999). Most experienced teachers have experienced, or at least have an awareness of the concept of a toxic school culture. Of significant concern is the direct toll that this toxicity has on the overall well-being of an organisation, particularly in respect to unsupported school leaders. **Such a culture is divisive, excluding, and often it is based on very hierarchical views of schooling.**

Deal and Peterson maintained that the reasons for toxicity in a school's culture can be varied, however, resistance to change among the incumbent staff and a general lack of understanding and unwillingness to accept changes proposed for the school's learning and teaching programme tend to underpin such a disposition (pp. 118–119).

Research by Silcox (2003) described in some depth observations of such toxic school cultures. Such schools he maintained were characterised by distrust and fear. Parents were kept at a distance from the school and consequently their children's learning. Teachers were very private and afraid of "being exposed" in the performance of their teaching role. Students were treated with little respect – even to the extent of being openly disliked and discussed in disparaging terms in staffroom conversations. Students' learning was a low priority in staff discussions, with the curriculum often being dumbed down. The school change culture was best described as resistant and reluctant even openly hostile, slow on uptake of system imperatives, with a lack of teacher knowledge and currency. Teamwork could best be described as dysfunctional and unprofessional due to lack of teacher and/or school leadership. In such a school culture he argued there is a tendency for cliques to have formed with long-term staff undermining the endeavours and ideas of those newly appointed to the school.

As one school leader remarked:

> The school's learning and teaching culture I inherited was reminiscent of the 1950s. I had no choice but to initiate and implement a renewal program across the school, pedagogically focused and driven using curriculum provision and student engagement as the desired outcomes. Curriculum and pedagogy issues drove my decision-making agenda in the school.

As another school leader remarked:

> Primarily the barriers I encountered revolved around entrenched staff attitudes and behaviours towards learning and teaching. Factions on the staff, the disenfranchisement of many in previous decision-making processes had created a very change resistant culture among staff.

A school with a toxic culture can be readily identified using these key indicators:

- Talk in the staffroom is more about problems than solutions with teachers seeing students as the problem rather than as their valued clients.
- There is little recognition of staff achievements with staff preferring instead to share stories and historical perspectives on the organisation that are often negative, discouraging and demoralising.
- The school is not seen as a place of successful informed practice and innovation. Staff often express a belief that they are doing the best they can and consequently they do not pursue new ideas, approaches or professional development opportunities.
- There is a tendency to complain, criticise and distrust any new ideas, approaches or suggestions for improvement that are made.
- Staff do not have a feeling of pride about their teaching or the school the school has few ceremonies or traditions that celebrate what is good and hopeful about their place of work.
- There is a reluctance among staff to operate as a team often with the evolution of negative subcultures or cliques that are hostile and critical of change. Staff rarely share ideas, materials or solutions to classroom problems that are raised.

Toxic, reluctant managers and toxic, self-promoting managers

In a similar vein toxic school management is readily identifiable and, in many cases, can be linked to the rise of a similar culture in a school. Toxic management is seen to present in two ways: First in the general inability of the leaders to manage, and therefore they foster the elements for toxicity in the schools learning and teaching approaches; and second in terms of leaders' personal leadership styles and characteristics and the way that they interact with staff.

The school leaders' lack of an innate efficacy, and affinity for and understanding of the basic requirements of the leadership or management role are crucial elements underpinning the development of a toxic school learning and teaching environment. This is usually evidenced initially through their general inability to articulate a clear sense of direction to staff and community for change where and when required. It is recognised that school leaders need to be prepared to live with a certain degree of staff discomfort and possible conflict in the initial phase of introducing change, particularly that which would impact on the way things are traditionally done in the school. Such a disposition requires the leader and manager to have the confidence to engage staff in a direct way so that they will derive benefit and enjoyment from the experiences offered in improving the schools learning and teaching programme.

In the change process, before collective action and dialogue can take place, certain relationships need to be built among teachers and stakeholders within the school context, particularly in overcoming identified *balkanisation* and an individualist orientation commonly identified among staff. However, it is recognised that the elements of a participative and collaborative teaching culture do not occur through simple decree by well-intentioned leadership, or as a result of teachers' mutual respect. Such collaborative approaches require the direct involvement and intervention of a school's leadership as an agent of change. If the school leadership lack the essential efficacy to undertake such a process, then the opportunity offered becomes conducive to the development of a toxic school culture, as described previously. The perspective presented here (Table 6.1) is that leadership of a school requires the exercise of well-developed behaviours in the communication and interpersonal area to facilitate negotiating through resistance encountered to reach the High-High standard.

Pelletier (2010) recognised that school leaders identified as having a toxic management disposition exhibited consistent identifiable behaviours and approaches to their management of staff and of school learning and teaching

Table 6.1 Understanding moral intent and staff efficacy in organisations

High Staff Efficacy Low	Low-High Solved by initiating a leadership change.	High-High A high-performing school. Excellent morale among staff, students and community.
	Low-Low A toxic school culture and/or toxic school management.	High-Low Solved by investigating different staff options.
	Low Moral Intent High	

improvement endeavours. Significant among these behaviours included aspects relating to:

- Their demeaning, marginalising of staff who were offering an alternative perspective to their personal agenda. This was often achieved by attacking individuals' self-esteem and by stifling and dissent.
- Their tendency to want to blame others or bend the rules unethically to suit their particular purpose, at the same time showing a lack of personal integrity.
- Their propensity to adopt a very volatile, coercive and emotionally charged response to staff questioning of their actions, often resorting to abusive attacks on the individual/s concerned.
- Both in an overt and covert way their marginalising of staff through either socially excluding, ostracising practices or by disenfranchising them from the decision-making processes in the school and therefore encouraging disengagement.
- Their promotion of sycophants (and consequently, a culture of sycophantocracy and a general inequality in the way they allocated resources and rewards among staff).
- Their threatening of a staff member's job security.
- Their ongoing self-promotion.

Toxicity in organisational operations poison relationships, and organisational efficiency. Such an orientation is often counter intuitive to the aims of the organisation which are then driven to excise the large cancerous parts involved. Governmental organisations generally take a more cautious approach to the problem and often resort to removing key individuals in an attempt to turn the non-performing sections around. The real danger of this cautious approach is that high-performing leaders are often fed to the toxic low-level cliques that still control basic organisational operations. In these situations, underlying beliefs in the efficacy of democratic processes need to be put aside until the new leaders have developed a critical support mass. Real leaders cannot afford to turn their backs on any forms of toxicity.

However, there is hope for a leader intent on addressing a toxic culture in a school. The steps that the authors recommend that school leaders take are:

1. Confront the negativity head on.
2. Shield and support positive cultural elements and staff.
3. Focus energy on the recruitment, selection and retention of effective, positive staff.
4. Rabidly celebrate the positive and the possible.
5. Consciously and directly focus on eradicating the negative and rebuilding around positive norms and beliefs.
6. Develop new stories of success, renewal and accomplishment.
7. Help those who might succeed in a new district make the move to a new school.

Toxic culture survey

The authors designed this questionnaire for school leaders to measure the influence of a toxic culture on their school's operations. Every question needs to be answered.

1.1 Some staff view students as problems rather than as their valued clients. YES/ NO
1.2 Some staff view parents as problems, who have too much influence in the school. YES/ NO
1.3 Some staff believe that District Office supports complaining parents. YES/ NO
2.1 Some staff are sometimes part of negative subcultures that are hostile critical of change. YES/ NO
2.2 Some staff look up to staff leaders who knock education and the system. YES/ NO
2.3 Some staff leaders believe that the current school system is hostile to teachers. YES/ NO
3.1 Some staff believe they are doing the best they can and won't search out new ideas. YES/ NO
3.2 Some staff believe that there is nothing wrong with how they have always taught and see the changes in curriculum and pedagogy as pointless. YES/ NO
3.3 Some staff refuse to attend after-hours professional development. YES/ NO
4.1 Some staff frequently put the point that the past is better than the present and the future YES/ NO
4.2 There are sections in the staff room where you know the conversations will generally be negative. YES/ NO
4.3 Some staff believe that the changes being implemented at present will not last and we will go back to the old way of teaching. YES/ NO
5.1 Some staff actively discourage new or younger staff member from taking on leadership roles in the school. YES/ NO
5.2 Some staff will always openly criticise new ideas and programmes. YES/ NO
5.3 Some staff are reluctant to take roles on committees for fear of criticism from the negaholics on staff. YES/ NO
6.1 There is not a culture of welcoming and sharing new ideas in this school. YES/ NO
6.2 Staff generally do not adopt a team approach to teaching and learning in this school. YES/ NO
6.3 Talk in the staffroom is more about problems than educational solutions. YES/ NO
7.1 The staff do not encourage recognition of staff achievements in the teaching and learning programme. YES/ NO

7.2 Staff promote this school as a place of good learning and educational innovation. YES/ NO

7.3 Staff have a feeling of pride about the teaching and learning programme offered in this school. YES/ NO

8.1 All staff are happy at school. YES/ NO

8.2 There is a lot of laughter in the staffroom. YES/ NO

8.3 The staff willingly operate as a team. YES/ NO

Marking scale for each section

1 Yes = Low on the toxic culture scale; 2 Yes = medium level toxic culture; 3 Yes = high level toxic culture.

Toxic cultures dimensions:	*SCORES (Yes scores)*
1. View students as the problem rather than as their valued clients.	
2. Are sometimes part of negative subcultures that are hostile and critical of change.	
3. Believe they are doing the best they can and don't search out new ideas.	
4. Frequently share stories and historical perspectives on the school that are often negative, discouraging and demoralising.	
5. Complain, criticise and distrust any new ideas, approaches or suggestions for improvement raised by planning committees.	
6. Rarely share ideas, materials or solutions to classroom problems.	
7. Have few ceremonies or school traditions that celebrate what is good and hopeful about their place of work.	
8. (Added to Peterson's list). Are not happy and motivated and do not operate as a successful team in the school.	

A culture of sycophantocracy is a barrier to change initiatives

We know a sycophant as being a person who acts obsequiously towards someone important in order to gain some form of advantage. In its broadest sense it is taken to refer to someone practising obedient flattery. It can also refer to someone who practises "insincere flattery". Sycophants, it can be argued, have had a ubiquitous presence within most if not all organisations.

Typically, a sycophant imitates leaders' opinions, and often seeming to share their opinions enthusiastically. Sometimes this is taken to absurd lengths with sycophants honing their compliments to impress. Accordingly, the weaker the leadership target, the easier it is to ingratiate and impress. It is also noted that sycophantic behaviours tend to manifest and become most noticeable in hierarchical organisational situations (Perlman, 2018).

Leadership studies have been characterised by the application of political and psychological theories to the more recently developed schools of thought such as educational leadership, bureaucracy and organisational development. Interestingly, the concept of sycophantocracy has existed as long as humans have lived in social co-existence, but now in an era of resurgent, raw narcissism it becomes more identifiable in government and administration contexts.

OUR BELIEF 12

Weak school leaders tend to create and foster a more sycophantic staff culture.

Students of administration and governance were all exposed to the development of The Westminster Model of government, with its associated independent public service. At the bureaucratic-personnel level, however, the conflict between patronage and merit was an ongoing problem. In 1854 the Northcote–Trevelyan reforms of the Civil Service attempted redress this problem of patronage and its associated sycophantocracy. While they hoped that the Civil Service attracted the ablest and most ambitious youths, it was often not the case: "The character of the young men admitted to the public service depends chiefly upon the discretion with which the heads of departments. and others who are entrusted with the distribution of patronage, exercise that privilege" (1854, p. 6). While patronage is a two-edged sword, it is the patronage that is diverted into personal benefits that causes systemic problems.

Leaders' Achilles' heels

Leaders' roles are complex, often stressful and there is fear of failure. It is this leadership vulnerability, workload and task complexity that forces leaders to trust others to get the job done. With trust comes two-way dialogue that impacts on the personalities of all parties. However, weak, vulnerable leaders need constant propping-up and this is the hunting ground for the sycophantocracy with artful flattery.

Examining flattery, Fogg and Nass (1997) found that gaming software writers played on the users' susceptibility to flattery to keep them engaged. In studying the effects of flattery on targets (the receivers of the flattery) the authors found that:

- targets tend to believe that flatters speak the truth;
- flattery creates a positive effect in the target;
- targets like those who flatter them; and
- targets judge the performance of flatters more favourably.

And, the payoff for the flatterer/sycophant is that "Not only does the target rate the flatterer's work performance more favourably, but the target also perceives the flatterer to be more intelligent" (p. 553).

Sycophantocracy in school systems

In a punchy statement about the sycophantocracy in schools, Trotter (2011) explained the development of the sycophantocracy:

> (When) ... new superintendents come to town come apparently thinking that they are "playas for life" [*sic*] — as if landing their big new jobs entitle them to more women (or more men, depending on the gender or orientation), more financial and ridiculous perks that they assume, and the inalienable right to promote only kiss-ups and sycophants.

And the author then goes on to explain that merit and integrity are seen as dangerous to weak leaders who prefer to be surrounded by a sycophantocracy than a meritocracy:

> If a person maintains integrity and honour, this seems to be a liability to (weak leaders). I have told many educators that one of the reasons that their particular assistant principal or principal or superintendent doesn't like them is because either (1) they pose a threat to them because they are popular with the students (and the students' parents) or because (2) they have integrity, and this just scares the crap out of the dishonest administrators.

Common among the issues experienced in organisations that are identified as having a sycophantic culture is the overall toxicity that it creates among staff. This toxicity can become manifest in a variety of staff behaviours including the development of a silo mentality among faculty members with a corresponding impact on their communication and interpersonal interactions. A sycophantic culture can be described as divisive, excluding and grounded in a very limited world view.

School leader comment:

> Barriers that I encountered upon appointment to the school and to changes in general were many. Primarily they revolved around entrenched staff attitudes and behaviours. A sycophantic faction on the staff appointed by the previous principal and the disenfranchisement of many others through previous decision-making processes had created a very change resistant culture among staff that I had to contend with.

A perspective of such a sycophantic culture that aligns with the more extreme toxic learning and teaching culture is one where a school staff/community has an attitude to change that is best described as resistant and reluctant. Such school cultures tend to be generally slow on the uptake of system and change imperatives often due to lack of knowledge and pedagogic currency among its leadership. Teamwork in such cases could best be described as dysfunctional.

The reasons for school leaders adopting a sycophantic approach to staff selection and promotion and is seen to evolve from a leader's personal insecurity, conservatism and a general lack of both trust and willingness to accept alternative dispositions on policy and implementation matters.

School leader comment:

> When I was first appointed to the school the teaching was didactic, threatening for students. The parents and the teachers were at war. None of the teachers liked me or my two new deputies and one teacher refused to speak to me. The out-going acting school leaders had carried out questionable selection process and appointed several his friends to key positions in the school.

Issues relating to power and control come into play in a **sycophantocracy** as leaders prone to making staff selections based on the promotion of personal favourites (sycophants) do so as they believe they can trust such appointees to reinforce their own position and personal self-image.

Developing a field guide for identifying the sycophantocracy

The literature clearly shows variations of the operations of the sycophantocracy in a variety of organisations. In establishing this first field guide the authors recognise three types of sycophantic behaviours, which adjudge behaviours against two sets of variables: overt-covert behavioural displays, and overt-covert rewards and payments. The three models sitting on this continuum of sycophantocracy are:

1   Aggressive public displays and pay-offs.
2   A hybrid model that mixes Type 1, and Type 3.
3   Subtle, covert, opportunistic sycophantic behaviours often with unobserved rewards.

Type 1. Overt sycophantic behaviours that result in public rewards and favouritism. Nepotism is a great example of Type 1 sycophantocracy. Parker and Parker (2017) tell the story a bishop who found when he was ushered in to meet with the Duke de Vendome that the Duke conducted his meetings while sitting on a portable lavatory. When the Duke rose and wiped himself the Bishop was offended so, for the next meeting the bishop sent the cleric Giulio Alberoni who was known for his inoffensive nature. Alberoni was treated in the same manner as the bishop but he shouted, "O culo d'angelo" (roughly translated, "Oh, ass of an angel!"), and he "ran to kiss" the duke's behind. His long career within the church and among European courts was assured".

Type 2. In this model some sycophants are publicly identifiable, and others are not. A classic example are *les claquers* who accept free tickets to ballet or opera, and they are expected to actively acknowledge performances by clapping and shouting "bravo".

Les Claquers: (from the French to clap or slap), are audience members at ballet or opera, who were rewarded to applaud plays or speeches, and this formalises the more overtly commercialised, transactional aspects of the sycophantocracy. While the "claquers" at the Bolshoi Theatre in Moscow are rewarded with valuable passes to ballets to motivate audiences, they also claim to have an educative role in explaining to an audience what is good in a performance:

> "The audience does not trust itself; it trusts someone else," said the ballet critic Vadim Gayevsky, who fell in with the claquers as a boy in the 1940s. "If it hears someone applauding very aggressively and intensively, they think that something extraordinary is going on which they did not grasp, and they feel generally that they should not look like fools, that they should join in, so that nobody sees they missed it." (Barry, 2013)

The claquers can also be present at political rallies and in meeting stacking exercises. Claquers receive a transactional reward for the defined services that they offer individuals or organisations. However, sycophants offer subtle, non-negotiated actions often in the hope of some future reward.

Type 3. Subtle, opportunistic flattery. Type 3 sycophants are often learning their craft, and they use incidental flattery to try and gain some advantage. Fogg and Nass (1997) showed that even computer software gaming users were extremely vulnerable to computer generated flattery, which says something about human foibles.

What to do

An ability that leaders must develop is a *sycophant early warning system*, because as Attila the Hun warned: "A king with chieftains who always agree with him reaps the counsel of mediocrity" (Roberts, 1987, p. 101). Mediocrity is a pestilence that damages the operations and public perceptions of a leader's performance. Apart from the problem of lack of excellent advice from the sycophantocracy, an added burden is that the quality of leaders is judged by those they surround themselves with.

A rule of thumb that has guided astute leaders is to recruit staff who complement the leaders' profile and cover potential weaknesses. For strong leaders, the best advisers are those who are loyal, not afraid to give powerful advice, and have the best interests of the organisation at heart. And, in the case of school leaders we need to start identifying those qualities in teachers whom we recruit as graduates.

School leader comment:

> My administrative staff, the deputy principals were kindred spirits in terms of the desire to change the existing school culture. I consulted with them in an ongoing professional way. The proved to be great supporters of the renewal initiative in the school.

The leadership hierarchy common to most if not all organisations provides an ideal breeding ground for the sycophant. In more recent times given the ever-expanding human, physical and financial portfolios and legal frameworks that leaders must deal with on a day-to-day basis it is not surprising therefore to see a very real or perceived corresponding rise of a more overt sycophantocracy. Managing this perception, real or not, becomes a challenge for the leader. A challenge that is more ably met by a leader who has a confidence in their own skill set and organisational knowledge and who operates with an underlying integrity in dealing with subordinates. The basic premise that is offered here is that weak leadership promotes an environment in which a sycophantocracy can flourish.

General comment on chapter

Before collective action and dialogue can take place in respect to initiating a renewal agenda in a school, it is clearly evident that certain relationships needed to be built among teachers and stakeholders within the school context, particularly in overcoming any identified balkanisation and or individualist orientation among staff. The renewing of a school with an emphasis on the development of a collaborative culture among teachers can positively alter the staff dynamic. However, we would be remiss in not recognising that the elements of a participative and collaborative teaching culture do not occur through simple decree by well-intentioned leadership, or as a result of teachers' mutual respect. A collaborative approach requires the direct involvement and intervention of the school leader as an agent of change. Renewing a school's learning and teaching culture and ethos is a leadership concern. The bigger the change, the more it must be well led.

While the disposition of some teaching staff may be seen as barriers to the implementation of renewal in a school, the use of identified key staff as catalysts in the implementation of the change agenda is a very successful strategy that can be employed (see Chapter 16). These significant staff are those identified as being either fully engaged and/or willing to engage in the desired pedagogical and curriculum reform at the classroom level. Through such staff, school leaders can lever a greater risk-willing mentality and disposition to change across the whole school by highlighting and promoting their teaching practices.

School leader comment:

> Once I had a critical mass of staff behind me and the changes proposed, the barriers I had previously encountered fell away.

School leader comment:

> As the school was able to utilize its merit selection processes to introduce a critical mass of staff who exhibited the pedagogical approaches and

curriculum understanding needed to bring about change. I guess I used a divide and conquer approach.

Renewal as a form of changes has its roots in curriculum and pedagogical thinking, and informed successful teaching and learning practice. To this end, a school leader's beliefs about learning and teaching must be driven by an understanding that students (and teachers) learn best by constructing their own realities and therefore cannot progress in didactic situations. From this belief about maximising deep learning, we believe that the learning situation, not necessarily classrooms, should maximise active learning in authentic situations.

References

Aubrey, D.W. (2012). *The effect of toxic leadership.* Carlisle, PA: United States Army War College. https://apps.dtic.mil/dtic/tr/fulltext/u2/a560645.pdf

Barry, E. (2013, 14 August). Designated cheering spectators thrive at the Bolshoi Theatre. *The New York Times.* https://www.nytimes.com/2013/08/18/arts/dance/designated-cheering-spectators-thrive-at-the-bolshoi-theater.html

Deal, T.E., & Peterson, K.D. (1999). *The principal's role in shaping school culture.* Washington, DC: U.S. Department of Education.

Fogg, B.J., & Nass, C. (1997). Silicon sycophants: The effects of computers that flatter. *International Journal of Human-Computer Studies,* 46, 551–561.

National Policy Board for Education Administration (2015). *Professional standards for educational leaders.* Reston, VA: author.

Northcote and Trevelyan (1854). *Report on the organisation of the permanent civil service.* London: House of Commons. www.self.gutenberg.org/articles/eng/northcote-trevelyan_report

Parker, D., & Parker, M. (2017). The 10 biggest sycophants from literature and history. *Electric Literature.* https://electricliterature.com/bootlickers-ingratiators-and-lapdogs-10-sycophants-from-literature-and-history-d1a1c16c3640

Perlman, M. (2018). Sycophants, yes-men, and forelock-tuggers. *Columbia Journalism Review.* https://www.cjr.org/language_corner/sycophants.php

Pelletier, K.L. (2010). Leader toxicity: An empirical investigation of toxic behavior and rhetoric. *Leadership,* 6(4), 373–389.

Roberts, W. (1987). *Leadership secrets of Attila the Hun.* Rohnert Park, CA: Warner Books.

Shonk, K. (2020). *3 Types of conflict and how to address them.* Daily Blog. Program on Negotiation. Harvard Law School.

Silcox, S.B. (2003). An investigation of the roles of school principals in leading school renewal in a Western Australian school district (Unpublished doctoral dissertation). Curtin University, Western Australia.

Trotter, J.R.A. (2011, 10 June). Georgia teachers speak out: Another great playoff game. My Heat lost. Robert's Mav's won. But, we watched meritocracy in action. Too bad that public school systems don't operate on meritocracy but on sychophantocracy … (sic). https://georgiateachersspeakout.com/2011/06/10/another-great-playoff-game-my-heat-lost-roberts-mavs-won-but-we-watched-meritocracy-in-action-too-bad-that-public-school-systems-dont-operate-on-meritocracy-but-on-sychophantocracy-in-o/

7 Pedagogic leadership
A view of what real school leaders do

(The attributes of school leaders as pedagogic leaders)

As educational leaders, we acknowledge that education per se is in a state of constant flux, but a constant priority is the establishment of pedagogic relationship-based classroom cultures. The holism of the relationship between the teacher and student is under threat as teachers' pedagogic practices are becoming more impacted by teacher specialisation, system and school-imposed targets and standards; and a variety of implications from the inexorable drives towards individuation and external accountability testing. As a consequence, the act of teaching is being reduced to that of *instruction* (a mechanical process) as test-driven curriculum and instruction impact on our classrooms today.

OUR BELIEF 13

> School change to be effective and sustainable requires demonstrated pedagogic leadership from the school leader.

We contend that by teachers and school leaders making appropriate pedagogic choices, the managerialist and clinical tendencies dictating the current directions of education identified can be reversed, thereby re-asserting the importance of relationships between the learners and the facilitators of that learning. The Nutbrown Report (2012) in the UK, when discussing pedagogy in early childhood settings supported this inspirational and inclusive view: "Ultimately, all early years practitioners should aspire to be leaders, of practice if not of settings, and all practitioners should be capable of demonstrating some pedagogical leadership regardless of qualification level" (p. 55).

Towards an understanding of pedagogic leadership

The term *pedagogy*, while relatively uncommon a decade ago, is currently being used more frequently in publications and teachers' discourse. In western, Anglophonic counties, pedagogy represents a fresh start, and an alternative view of the broadest aspects of teaching and learning. This, Van Manen (1993, p. 11) attributed to an upsurge of North American interest in

Western European philosophy and educational theory. As previously noted by Van Manen (1993, p. 9), "It is possible to learn all of the techniques of instruction but remain pedagogically unfit as a teacher."

There are five pedagogic lenses in the literature:

1 Epistemological

- Pedagogy as the transmission of knowledge (Lingard et al., 2003).

2 Socio-Ideological

- Pedagogy as a political tool for the enculturation students (Freire, 1977; Morton & Zavarzadeh, 1991; Smyth, 1988; Van Manen, 1999);
- Pedagogy – ideological practices of constructing subjectivities necessary for reproducing existing social organisations (Morton & Zavarzadeh, 1991).

3 Pedagogy as a participative ideology, seeking co-construction of learning through active involvement, dialogue and shared knowledge. It seeks to empower and release personal agency and is concerned with building relationships with parents, professionals and the wider community (Murray & Clark, 2013). Social

- Pedagogy as a relationship that produces knowledge (Van Manen, 1999);
- Pedagogy as social practice (Daniels, 2001).

4 The pedagogic act (The mechanical aspects of *how* knowledge is transmitted).

- Pedagogy as an inclusive view of all aspects teaching but not simply instruction (Mortimore, 1999; Newmann et al., 1996; Zierer, 2011; Nutbrown, 2012);
- Any conscious activity designed by one person to bring about learning in another (Ireson, Mortimore, & Hallam, 1999).
- Recognises structural and performative aspects of pedagogic act (Danielewicz, 2001).

5 Pedagogy separated from didactics

- Pedagogy, in the European usage, related to culture and children's learning, while didactics relates to the subjects to be taught (Alexander, 2004, p. 10; Hamilton & McWilliam, 2001).

Taking these aspects into consideration our working definition of *pedagogy* that summarises a conceptual framework that accommodates all views of pedagogy is:

> Pedagogy is a planned action, designed by human agency, that acknowledges the socio-political, moral context of the learning act, and which

directly facilitates the acquisition of new knowledge, beliefs or skills for the learner.

The key points associated with this working definition of pedagogy are that:

- Pedagogy is a result of planned human agency, which includes computer assisted learning, and environmental design (Perez, Fain, & Slater, 2004).
- Pedagogy is an action that allows, or causes, the learner to acquire new knowledge, skills or beliefs.

Pedagogic leadership takes a broader view of the learning and teaching acts than *instructional leadership*, as it takes into account the "Why?" "How?" and "When?" of learning, and not just the "What is taught?" typical of instructional/curriculum leadership. Pedagogic leadership is based on dialogue and engagement with learners as essential participants in the discussions about learning. Evans (1999, p. 11) made the point that school leaders who are not guided by pedagogic choice "… resort to a thoroughly bureaucratized way of relating to teachers" and as a result teaching becomes an occupation defined by expectations not dialogue.

Pedagogy and curriculum

Education in the last century, and teaching specifically, was dominated by curriculum and as a result of its close association with mandated reforms, the term *curriculum leadership* in schools has become an oxymoron as *curriculum management* seems more fitting. As Fink and Stoll (2005, pp. 17–18) observed:

> These reform policies have certain common features. Important decisions about students' learning, such as what they are to learn, when they are to learn, and how they are to demonstrate their learning have been removed from local settings and assumed by bureaucrats in distant offices. Conversely, resources have been devolved directly to schools to make local "site based" decisions, usually accompanied by a reduction in support.

A second problem with curriculum is that the underlying philosophies that underpin it are never declared. The consumers of education get more information about the butter they put on their toast in the mornings, than about the philosophical underpinnings of the curriculum that influences students' life options.

Thirdly, the advocacy of curriculum alone cannot match the rich human nature of pedagogy. *Pedagogy* is a more appropriate approach to learning and teaching because it emphasises the professional primacy of the human stakeholders involved. The connotations of the concept of pedagogy are indicative of active and reflective learning and professional, consultative decision-making at the school and classroom level. Pedagogy represents a more global, humanistic way of looking at the teaching act and interactions, while curriculum is still tainted by being, more often than not, the domain of experts in Education District and Central Offices. Pedagogic leadership is a better, more democratic and inclusive description of leadership in the teaching and learning context than *instructional or curriculum leadership*.

School leader comment:

> I visit classrooms almost every day and believe I have a good relationship with the kids. I communicate my expectations to students, staff and parents on a daily basis. I can see what is happening in classes and I reckon if the teacher-student relationships are right, then the classroom climate is right, and the school climate and culture will be right too. I indicate to teachers the importance of building relationships with their students. I stand by the school gate and chat to parents. I know from the warmth of people's smiles that the school is heading in the right direction. My office door is always open to anyone.

Pedagogic obsolescence: School leaders as the endangered species in education

We maintain that the micro-changes that have affected school leaders' roles in the last 30 years were too small to raise concern, but cumulatively these ratchet-like micro-changes have embedded changes that are becoming almost impossible to reverse. As a result of these bracket creep reforms, and associated role expectations, school leaders are in danger of becoming the endangered species of education.

The Public Management Movement and its implications for school leadership

The introduction of the ideology of New Public Management changed expectations of school leaders. New Public Management (NPM) was part of the managerialist reforms that accompanied the introduction of the so-called economic rationalist approach to government (Pusey, 1992), that heavily and irreversibly influenced government policies in the 1980s and 1990s. As a result of this ideological change, government services and administration were redesigned and this impacted on schools, especially publicly funded public schools.

> Hood (as cited in Moos, 1999, p. 44) noted that the changes in British schools included: active, visible management; set goals and targets; resources linked to performance and results; a move towards smaller units of operation; decentralised budgets; competition; a business-oriented management style; and an emphasis on doing more for less. Table 7.1 sets out the themes and components of NPM in the public service in England (Dunleavy, Margetts, Bastow, & Tinkler, 2006, p. 471). The components that are identifiable in education are italicised.

Table 7.1 Themes and components of The Public Management policy push

Themes	Components
Disaggregation	Purchaser-provider separation; Agencification; Decoupling policy systems; Growth of quasi-government agencies; Separation out of micro-local agencies; Chunking up privatized industries; *Corporatization and strong single organisation management; De-professionalization; Competition by comparison; Improved performance measurement; League tables of agency performance.*
Competition	Quasi-markets; *Voucher schemes*; Outsourcing; Compulsory market testing; Intra-government contracting; *Public/private sectoral polarization*; Product market liberalization; Deregulation; Consumer-tagged financing; *User control.*
Incentivization	Respecifying property rights; Light touch regulation; Capital market involvement in projects; Privatizing asset ownership; Anti-rent-seeking measures; De-privileging professions; *Performance-related pay*; PFI (private finance initiative); *Public-private partnerships*; Unified rate of return and discounting; Development of charging technologies; Valuing public sector equity; Mandatory efficiency dividends.

As a result of school leaders' increased administrative and budgetary powers in the New Public Management model, Berg (as cited in Moos, 1999, p. 51) reported that in England, head teachers would not play a role in teachers' curriculum decisions or methods of teaching.

The pressures of New Public Management reform on school leaders' perceptions of their roles was profound. By necessity, school leaders became more preoccupied with issues of accountability and were drawn away from the practicalities of teaching and learning in classrooms. School leaders' time is finite, and they constantly have to juggle a range of conflicting demands, and as Cotton (2003, p. 3) observed,

> Three-quarters of all school leaders say that the job has become too complex, and nearly half report feeling under great stress several days a week or more ... While most school leaders report having a great deal of control in hiring teachers and making decisions about teachers' schedules, fewer than half have great control over removing teachers or over curriculum and instruction.

Indeed, the MetLife (2012, p. 3) examination of school leadership ranked financial issues as one of the greatest challenge for school leaders, which supported the belief that managerialist pressures impact heavily on school leaders in the contemporary environment. With a set of sanctions in place most school leaders will ensure that the accountability aspects of the role are attended to, even at the risk of ignoring the key purpose of schooling, students' learning.

The danger to the school leadership, as we know it, is that school leaders are being forced out of teaching and learning into an oversight of all school operations, which has the potential to pedagogically deskill and marginalise them.

Pedagogic leadership and Public Management policy

Pedagogic leadership focuses on changing the school's culture by engaging in and leading teachers' learning, and therefore it is broader than the instructional leadership. Pedagogic leadership takes the broad view of teaching and learning that acknowledges the relational basis of learning and accepts that the culture and context of classroom influence students' learning.

As we have indicated pedagogy is a planned action, designed by human agency that acknowledges the social, political, religious and moral context of the learning act, which directly results in the acquisition of new knowledge, beliefs or skills for the learner. Consequently, pedagogic leadership can be regarded as a mutually transformative, learning relationship that improves teachers and school leaders' repertoires of pedagogic practices within a culture of school improvement, which in turn results in improved student learning. This perspective of leadership subscribes to a collegial model of teacher and school leaders' pedagogic learning, and anything less than a statement of mutual transformative learning misrepresents the nature of pedagogic learning in schools.

Fullan (1993) describes the belief that a school leader should be focused on fostering the development of children as their underpinning moral purpose and that such and orientation concerns the enculturation of the young as well as the provision of access to knowledge. Those school leaders committed to improving the education of students can often be described as pedagogic leaders as a consequence of their overt displaying of a credible knowledge of pedagogy and their active involvement in the school's instructional programme and subsequent student learning. However, it is also recognised that the exercise of curriculum and instructional leadership can often be tempered by the demand for attention to non-instructional, management-oriented demands and the day-to-day issues arising within the school and from the educational system. Leadership of the renewal of a school's learning and teaching activity, particularly with performativity in mind implies a different perspective for school leaders, teachers and learners.

OUR BELIEF 14

> The leadership attributes associated with initiating and leading sustainable school change and those anticipated to be required in generating school renewal, require differentiation, particularly in terms of the school leaders' roles and their understanding of pedagogy and curriculum implementation.

Proactive leaders facilitate organisational learning and view their leadership role in the specific sense of a learning organisation.

This neatly leads us once again into a further exploration of school renewal as a specific form of educational change. An anagram of "renewal" is "we learn" and this attitude underpins a school's pedagogical renewal. It is about nurturing the spiritual, affective and intellectual connections in the lives of educators working together to understand and improve their practice. Hargreaves (1991, p. 14) refers to the processes involved as one of, "re-culturing the school community".

School leader comment:

> I am a curriculum and pedagogical leader. Curriculum and pedagogy issues drove my decision-making agenda in the school. Priorities for school renewal fell out from this process. For every change the question was asked – how will this decision or change improve the quality of learning and teaching in the school?

This disposition was supported by comments of another school leader who maintained that:

> The pedagogy had to be made more real. We simply had to get teachers talking about pedagogical approaches in integrated settings. As well as which outcomes were being taught in a particular integrated task it was also critical as to what outcomes were not being taught.

Transforming schools, whether directed towards school reform or school renewal, concepts explored in some depths previously, is inextricably linked to the exercise of school leadership. The difference between effective leadership of renewal as compared to leadership of other processes of change (including educational reform) is a consequence of differing expectations of the end result of exercising leadership, and differing levels of commitment to attaining these ends. The expectations of specific outcomes associated with renewal are shaped by intrinsic philosophical beliefs about the future of education and society. In contrast, the outcome expectations associated with restructuring and reform are influenced by external demands for educational change, short-term goals or the promise of extrinsic rewards.

In the United States, Resnick and Glennan (2002, p. 162) noted that school leaders have had a diminishing influence on teachers' pedagogic practices:

> Meanwhile, district administrators, from principals to central office staff, spend relatively little time in classrooms and even less time analysing instruction with teachers. They may arrange time for teachers' meetings and professional development, but they rarely provide intellectual leadership for growth in teaching skill.

This view was supported by Downey, Steffy, English, Frase, and Poston (2004, p. 99) who studied the amount of time school leaders spent in classrooms:

> We know from research that most principals spend from 10 to 80 percent of their time in and around the office area. An additional 23 to 40 percent is spent in hallways and on the playground. About 11 percent is spent off campus, and only about 2.5 to 10 percent is spent in classrooms.

The tension between competing roles had much earlier been identified by Murphy and Hallinger (1992) who asserted it that it was impossible for one person to give adequate attention to the multiplicity of roles inherent in the school leadership. They suggested the need for empowering others to assume and exercise leadership roles. In addition, they had suggested that leadership be viewed in terms of what it enables others to do rather than prescribing what others should do.

School leadership of teacher learning is also diminished when school leaders do not have pedagogic credibility – the capacity to meaningfully engage teachers in dialogue about teaching and learning. Fink and Resnick (2001) posit that school leaders become removed from the instructional leadership when their knowledge and skills are outdated:

> Principals' time is filled by the many demands of administrative functions. Like most people, they also tend to gravitate toward doing what they know how to do. Unsure of what to look for or how to intervene when they visit classrooms, principals tend to visit rarely, perhaps only to make formal evaluations. With their knowledge of teaching growing dated they delegate questions of instruction and professional development to others.

This situation can be further exacerbated when teachers have a greater sense of empowerment through increased professional confidence and less reliance on guidance from the school leader,

The growing differences between teacher and school leaders' pedagogic knowledge bases are at the core of the issue. Shulman (2004, pp. 219–248) identified seven components of teachers' knowledge bases: content knowledge, pedagogic knowledge, pedagogic content knowledge, curricular knowledge, knowledge of learners, knowledge of the educational context and knowledge of educational goals. In England Turner-Bisset (2001), some fifteen years later, re-analysed Shulman's work and identified twelve knowledge bases for teaching (see Table 3.1) by breaking down pedagogic knowledge into its component parts.

School leader comment:

> I worked hard to focus on kids learning and used research to back up what I was saying. I made sure I was readily available to parents who wished to see me - this apparently was a huge change. I was also honest if I stuffed up, and admitted to my mistakes - I figured out very quickly that transparency in decision-making was the key and that playing games with

parents was futile. I also worked to take parents ideas on board in documentation such as the school plan. I find that my credibility has improved significantly. I worked hard to take the high moral ground - the P&C president also noticed that was my approach and commented on it.

He indicated that he:

> Led by example by modelling "change" strategies in classrooms, supporting teachers, praising and celebrating their efforts, presenting PD according to teacher needs and providing support for implementation. By demonstrating that I knew what I was talking about.

High schools are a special case in point, where a school leader who has not had training or experience in the range of specific subject content areas taught is limited to comments about students' motivation, students' behaviour; and the teachers' motivation and ability to maintain the students' interest. Using Shulman's model as a basis, school leaders should be able to comment on five of the seven components of pedagogic knowledge with a high degree of validity. In all levels of schooling, the school leaders' engagement in pedagogic support is made more difficult by lack of possession of in-depth knowledge about the curriculum in particular discipline areas. For example, Goddard (2003) noted the disdain of a high school physics teacher after the school leader with a background in English described his lessons as boring. The degree of subject specialisation in schools effectively excludes other subject specialist from making more than general comments about other teachers' lessons. The nub of this matter lies in differentiation between teachers' pedagogic knowledge bases.

Role discontinuity: Killing school leaders softly

In most countries all school leaders start as teachers at the commencement of their careers. A teacher's promotion to the school leadership is always joyfully celebrated because of the increased salary, responsibility, power and the perception of having greater control over the day's programme. Most of the newly appointed school leaders are promoted because they are very good teachers, and in the small rural country schools, with a staff of newly graduated teachers, they still teach and give helpful advice to their teaching staff. A typical career trajectory has a middle-aged, non-teaching school leader ensconced in a city or large regional centre school, with an equally middle-aged, experienced teaching staff. The day-to-day rigours of teaching have been replaced with sole responsibility for the school's finances, school operations, staff performance and oversight of community relations. The nature of sole responsibility in schools means that the buck stops with the school leader, and in a complex organisation like a school, the school leader is spread thinly across a range of key areas.

Loder and Spillane (2005) refer to the move between teacher and administrators' roles as *role discontinuity*. It is argued that the skills and knowledge of a teacher have little relevance to the skills and knowledge required of a school leader. For example, it is highly problematic that the school leader has learnt financial management on the job, without proper instruction or accreditation. Typically, the teacher will progress from being responsible for a cost centre to overseeing a whole budget on achieving school leader status. The effects of role discontinuity are exacerbated because of the lack of formal qualification and training for the components of the new role. Role discontinuity leaves school leaders stranded between to role of teaching (for which they were trained) and the role of school leader that they have learnt by observation and situated learning.

The way forward: The school leader as a significant and credible "other" in the work of teachers

Examination of the complexity of the school leader's role canvasses the proposition that the current approach to resolving this complexity is resulting in an imbalance that threatens to make the school leaders' leadership of pedagogy obsolete. Pedagogy is the core business of schools and while school leaders are becoming untrained office managers and book-keepers, the main game is passing them by. School leader are becoming caught in a time warp between the changing world of teachers and the professional lives of managers, for which they were never prepared. As a result of the role discontinuity, school leaders' pedagogic credibility suffers, and they are marginalised from teaching and learning.

If the future is to destroy the school leadership (as we know it) and replace it with committees of specialists then the plan is on track. In fact, this future is already with us now in many educational and school jurisdictions. Rhoda Halperin (2006, p. 180) described the board of new charter school in the United States separating the role of academic deans (pedagogic leaders) from the management team so that the academic deans:

> ... could be in the classrooms, spend time supporting teachers, and meet with the various instructional teams at primary, middle-school, and high-school levels. In return, the deans would be expected to respect the members of the management team, and coordination would occur weekly, with deans taking relatively passive roles.

We argue that Halperin's model of the future need not occur if school leaders refuse to be seduced by the current view of school leaders' roles and stay involved in the real purpose of schools, learning and teaching. Within the leadership role school leaders need to ensure that other people, who are better trained to look after the money, assets and property, take those responsibilities and educators stay in control of schools. Learning and teaching must remain the main game in town, and school leaders need to be major players in that or face professional extinction.

Staff resilience and work practices

A school that works effectively and efficiently must have a stable cohort of resilient staff at the interface, specifically the classroom, where the teaching is being done. Resilience in staff is developed through both empowerment at the ground level where staff have some degree of involvement in decisions that affect their teaching and having a sense of ownership where a teacher is able to either individually or collectively solve problems that matter to them, particularly those which have an impact on their classroom activity and subsequent student engagement.

In a similar way that it is important for the management structures of an organisation to not get in the way or retard desired work practices. Within an educational context the primacy of quality learning and teaching needs to be supported by appropriate leadership and school structures that empower teachers as facilitators of student learning and which do not impede practices.

A concern raised by Fullan (1992) is that micro-management approaches to supervision by a school's leadership can stifle teacher willingness to become more professionally engaged in a culture that is providing empowerment and devolved decision-making. In many respects the micro-management processes mirror some of the controlling and restrictive practices of many system approaches in respect to the school leadership. That same sense of frustration that is felt when school leaders are micro-managed is felt by teachers as well, particularly so when school practices and decision-making is seen as disenfranchising.

The problem is complicated by the paradox that while teachers and their associated pedagogy are the targets of school change (whether renewal or reform) they are also its implementers.

OUR BELIEF 15

Where empowerment is fostered, teamwork and collaboration thrive.

A key aspect of the process of engaging staff in reflective practice and pedagogical change is creating a culture that is purposeful and which encourages fellowship, and *communities of practice* through which teachers are empowered by an increased access to school decision-making. A transformational leadership style encourages an ethos of engagement among teachers. Such a style is underpinned by a leadership disposition that values and encourages the fairness, openness, honesty, loyalty and integrity in relationships across the school.

References

Alexander, R. (2004, March). Still no pedagogy? Principle, pragmatism, and compliance in primary education. *Cambridge Journal of Education*, 34(1), 7–33.

Cotton, K. (2003). *Principals and student achievement: What the research says*. Alexandria, VA: Association for Supervision and Curriculum Development.

Danielewicz, J. (2001). *Teaching selves: Identity, pedagogy, and teacher education.* Albany, NY: State University of New York.

Daniels, H. (2001). *Vygotsky and pedagogy.* London: Routledge Falmer.

Downey, C.J., Steffy, B.E., English, F.W., Frase L.E., & Poston, W.K. (2004). *The three-minute classroom walk-through: Changing school supervisory practice one teacher at time.* Thousand Oaks, CA: Corwin.

Dunleavy, P., Margetts, H., Bastow, S., & Tinkler, J. (2006, July). New Public Management is dead: Long live digital-era governance. *Journal of Public Administration Research and Theory,* 16(3), 467–494.

Evans, R. (1999). *The pedagogic principal.* Edmonton, Alberta: Qual Institute Press.

Fink, E., & Resnick, L.B. (2001, April). Developing principals as instructional leaders. *Phi Delta Kappan,* 82(8), 598–606.

Fink, D., & Stoll, L. (2005). Educational change: Easier said than done. In A. Hargreaves (Ed.), *Extending educational change.* Dordrecht, Netherlands: Springer.

Freire, P. (1977). *Pedagogy of the oppressed* (M.B. Ramos, Trans.). Harmondsworth, UK: Penguin Press.

Fullan, M. (1992). Visions that blind. *Educational Leadership,* 49(5), 19–20.

Fullan, M. (1993). *Change forces probing the depths of educational reform.* London: The Falmer PressGoddard, T. (2003). Leadership in the (post)modern era. In N. Bennett & L. Anderson (Eds.), *Rethinking educational leadership* (pp. 11–26). London: Sage.

Halperin, R.H. (2006). *Whose school is it? Women, children, memory and practice in the city.* Austin, TX: University of Texas Press.

Hamilton, D., & McWilliam, E. (2001). *Ex-centric voices that frame research on teaching.* In V. Richardson (Ed.), *Handbook of research on teaching* (pp. 17–43) (9th edition). Washington DC: American Educational Research Association.

Hargreaves, A. (1991). Contrived collegiality: The micropolitics of teacher collaboration. In J. Blasé (Ed.), *The politics of life in schools: Power, conflict and cooperation.* Newbury Park, CA: Sage.

Ireson, J., Mortimore, P., & Hallam, S. (1999). The common strands of pedagogy and their implications. In P. Mortimore (Ed.), *Understanding pedagogy and its impact on learning* (pp. 212–232). London: Paul Chapman.

Lingard, B., Hayes, D., Mills, M., & Christie, P. (2003). *Leading learning.* Maidenhead, UK: Open University Press.

Loder, T., & Spillane, J. (2005, August). Is a principal still a teacher? US women administrators' accounts of role conflict and role discontinuity. *School Leadership and Management,* 25(3), 263–279.

MetLife (2012). The MetLife survey of the American teacher: Challenges for school leadership. https://www.metlife.com/content/dam/microsites/about/corporate-profile/MetLife-Teacher-Survey-2012.pdf

Moos, L. (1999). New dilemmas in school leadership. *Leading & Managing,* 5(1), 41–59.

Mortimore, P. (Ed.) (1999). *Understanding pedagogy and its impact on learning.* London: Paul Chapman Publishing.

Morton, D., & Zavarzadeh, M. (1991). *Theory/Pedagogy/Politics: Texts for change.* Urbana, IL: University of Illinois Press.

Murphy, J., & Hallinger, P. (1992). The principalship in an era of transformation. *Journal of Educational Administration,* 30(3), 77–89.

Murray, J., & Clark, R.M. (2013). Reframing leadership as a participative pedagogy: The working theories of early years professionals, *Early Years*, 33(3), 289–301. doi:10.1080/09575146.2013.781135
Newmann, F.M., et al. (1996). *Authentic achievement: Restructuring schools for intellectual quality*. San Francisco: Jossey-Bass
Nutbrown, C. (2012). *Foundations for quality: Review of early education and childcare qualifications: Final Report*. Department for Education Publication. www.education.gov.uk
Perez D.M.C., Fain, S.M., & Slater, J.J. (2004). *Pedagogy of place: Seeing space as cultural education*. New York: Peter Lange
Pusey, M. (1992). *Economic rationalism in Canberra*. Cambridge: Cambridge University Press
Resnick, L.B., & Glennan, T.K. (2002). Leadership for learning: A theory for action. In A.M. Hightower, M.S. Knapp, J.A. Marsh & M.W. McLaughlin (Eds.), *School districts and instructional renewal* (pp. 160–172). New York: Teachers College Press.
Shulman, L.S. (2004). *The wisdom of practice: Essays on teaching, learning and learning to teach*. San Francisco: Jossey-Bass.
Smyth, W.J. (1988). *A "critical pedagogy" of teacher evaluation*. Geelong: Deakin University.
Turner-Bisset, R. (2001). *Expert teaching: Knowledge and pedagogy to lead the profession*. London: David Fulton Publishers.
Van Manen, M. (1993). *The tact of teaching: The pedagogical meaning of thoughtfulness*. London, Ontario: The Althouse Press.
Van Manen, M. (1999). The language of pedagogy and the primacy of student experience. In J. Loughran (Ed.), *Researching teaching: Methodologies and practices for understanding pedagogy* (pp. 13–27). London: Falmer Press.
Zierer, K. (2011, Spring). Pedagogical eclecticism. *The Journal of Educational Thought*, 45(1), 3–19.

8 The pedagogic wars
A challenge for school leaders

> Plans are nothing: planning is everything.
>
> Napoleon Bonaparte

Change in education can often be characterised by narrow, unsubstantiated, ideologically driven assertions that hopefully will result in some improvement. More often than not, discussion about change descends into false dichotomies championed by passionate, single-minded advocates who rarely acknowledged that there could be some good in the articulated opposing views. The *reading wars* are a good example of this. In America, as a result of imposed accountability, the "pedagogic war" between student-centred and teacher-centred pedagogy has now emerged from the shadows. Further complicating the issue, driven by strident calls for increased efficiency and accountability, high-stakes testing is heavily impacting on teachers' pedagogic decisions in the United States, the United Kingdom and Australia.

> **CASE STUDY 6**
>
> ***In a case study used by the Fogarty EDvance Program (2017)***
>
> (University of Western Australia)
>
> A case is made of the turnaround of a poorly performing school by the school leader who delineated eleven principles for the successful pedagogic change:
>
> - We must have strong beliefs that what we are doing is right.
> - Research and school-based trials are critical to the successful implementation of change initiatives.
> - Strong leaders across the teams are crucial to the success of any school.
> - Everyone has to embrace the change.
> - Having clear and high standards are central to successful outcomes.
> - Effective teaching increases when teachers learn from each other.
> - Development and measurement of student learning is critical.

- A positive school culture and supportive parents helps teachers perform in a trusted environment.
- There are two criteria for school-based change: improve the students' learning and, if possible, make the teachers' job easier.
- Understand that barriers exist, but know that everything is surmountable.
- Staff can never rest easy – We're constantly making sure we do better all the time.

Pedagogy as outlined previously in Chapter 7, is a broad concept that encompasses all aspects of teaching and learning. For example, in this book we are using a working definition of pedagogy:

Pedagogy is a planned action, designed by human agency that acknowledges the socio-political, moral context of the learning act, and which directly facilitates the acquisition of new knowledge, beliefs or skills for the learner.

In this context, the creation of classroom environments, and teachers' planning become pedagogic statements. Where are the desks and chairs placed? In fact, are there any desks and chairs? How is the learning experience communicated? What is the teacher's role? In this sense, pedagogy is broader and more inclusive than the narrower, term *instruction*.

The starting point for any examination of pedagogy is the teachers' beliefs of how students learn. Spillane (2002) examined the theories of change of district officials and teachers and then developed a pedagogic typology based on three epistemological learning theories: behaviourism, the cognitive view and the situated, socio-historical view (Spillane, 2002, p. 380). Brady, an Australian academic, developed five models of teaching (Brady, 1985, p. 10) that fit on a teacher-centred, pupil-centred continuum. The five models of teaching he identified are: Exposition, Behavioural, Cognitive developmental, Interaction and Transaction. Brady's model is now regarded as dated, and Cuban's (2009) triptych, representing student-centred, hybrid and teacher-centred pedagogies presents a modern, more simplified model of pedagogic change in our schools.

The current, ubiquitous swing towards a more teacher-centred pedagogy, as a result of high-stakes testing, is demonstrating a dangerous *Pedagogic Procrusteanism*, where the dominant teacher-centred pedagogy is applied to all students. It is also noted that accompanying high-stakes testing are new levels of school accountability. Cuban (2009) reported that a first-year teacher in the United States put the changes as: "The test is the total goal. We spend time every day doing rote exercises … The children sit and get drilled over and over" (p. 20).

In fact, little has changed since Dickens (1854) penned this description of teaching in *Hard Times*.

> Thomas Gradgrind now presented Thomas Gradgrind to the little pitchers before him, who were to be filled so full of facts. Indeed, as he eagerly sparkled at them from the cellarage before mentioned, he seemed a kind of cannon loaded to the muzzle with facts, and prepared to blow them clean out of the regions of childhood at one discharge. He seemed a galvanizing apparatus, too, charged with a grim mechanical substitute for the tender young imaginations that were to be stormed away. (p. 17)

As schools try to reverse poor test results, the push for targeted learning is associated with more teacher-centred pedagogies, such as direct instruction.

Student-centred pedagogy is the child of neo-progressivist trends in society. Jurisdictions across the world started to explore the use of open-area classrooms to facilitate a shift towards constructivist learning and student-centred pedagogy in the 1970s. This progressive change met its fate as American society swung back to a more conservative stance at the end of the Vietnam War era, as Larry Cuban (2004) reported:

> The national crisis gave rise to a perception, amplified by the media, that academic standards had slipped, that the desegregation movement had failed, and that urban schools were becoming violent places. This time the call was not for open education but for a return to the basics, again mirroring general social trends—namely, the conservative backlash against the cultural and political changes of the 1960s and early 1970s (p. 71).

However, student-centred pedagogies are considered the norm in kindergarten and pre-primary, pre-compulsory classes where, traditionally, the socialisation of young children is seen as the major purpose for this type of education. Student-centred pedagogy has impacted on many classrooms and constructivist, group and inquiry-centred practices are a part of most teachers' teaching skills.

Cuban's middle ground is the hybrid models of pedagogy. It helps understanding when the student-centred and teacher-centred positions are considered the end points of a continuum, and the hybrid models gravitate to either end according to the pedagogic *trend de jour* imposed by governments, school boards and systems. In examining the learning and teaching endeavour employed in classrooms it generally appears that the student-centred pedagogy, which dominates kindergarten classes, is proportionately used less, as students' progress through school. Teacher-centred content driven pedagogy becomes more the norm in the Year 8 to 12 secondary classes with students being prepared for tertiary institutions and post-secondary employment options. The movement within hybrid pedagogic models often reflects the responses of schools and systems to the publication of national test results. If the results are less than expected, a government or system initiated knee-jerk reaction will move the hybrid model toward more teacher-centred pedagogies.

The "pedagogic wars": Deskilling teachers

A major change that had taken place in the last twenty years is that teachers are required to develop and practise a broad range of pedagogies to engage all students successfully in their learning, because student engagement is no longer optional. Secondly, the new accountability has resulted in poor performing jurisdictions spraying the blame on poor students, unfocused curriculum and poor teaching to explain system failures. It is argued that these changes influence the pedagogic choices that teachers are forced to make in their respective classroom approaches.

A major challenge that is faced in schools, in times of high-stakes testing, is the drive to reduce curriculum and pedagogic offerings, particularly to the students who test poorly. Punishing the already disadvantaged students with repetitive iterations of basic education (as defined by the test) has serious implications for retention and breaking the poverty and achievement cycles. Cuban (2009, p. 57) noted that within the last decade a reading expert concluded that "... overall direct instruction worked best with students, particularly low-income minority children".

Using a full repertoire of teaching strategies: Tiger Woods's golf bag

How are the contents of Tiger Woods's golf bag seen as being important to education one may ask? Tiger Woods is a champion golfer, and like all of many golfers of his calibre learned to play golf using perhaps five clubs. Gradually he built on the competence that he had developed with those clubs until he could master the full range of clubs. On a good day, Tiger, like all professionals, will have perhaps as many as fourteen clubs in his golf bag, and these will vary depending on the environmental factors at the particular course being played.

In pre-service school-based experience, prospective teachers are introduced to the pedagogic equivalent of about the five clubs, which were enough to get the novice around the course without much style. Over time, with lots of birthday presents, and with the increase in skills, the novice golfers not only add to their golf club collection but they become consciously skilled in knowing when to use the clubs they have available. Unlike the golfers, teachers do not go into the pro golf shop and purchase the new club and then spend hours practising on the driving range. For teachers, the selection of new pedagogic strategies is not as simple as for the golfer picking up a new club, because there are no pro-teaching one-stop shops selling all of the pedagogies that beginning teachers would ever need. New pedagogic strategies are often forced into teachers' practices as the latest teaching fashion seeps into their classrooms, with little or no explanation or guidance in how to use this new strategy beyond a *follow the recipe* instruction.

As with golf, many teaching neophytes quit after a short time, having never progressed beyond the basic range of skills. However, the context of teaching is changing and education in schools is moving from the well-known course on which teachers have practised for the last ten years or more to a more focused teaching role. Consequently, teachers now need to re-examine their pedagogic club selection and learn and to practise a new set of pedagogic skills, while understanding that it is possible to play the course using those first five clubs, they can get much better results and provide students with much better opportunities by perhaps using a different range of clubs. It appears that the student-centred approach that many of the newer teachers have grown up with, will not survive intact with the next push into the new basics of the twenty-first century. Perhaps then it is now time for teachers and school leaders to revisit a specialised pedagogic pro shop!

In identifying the full range of pedagogic strategies available to teachers it is important to remember that one-size, or method will not fit every educational situation, and this is the mistake that ideologically and poorly trained educators make. For example, teacher cannot apply explicit direct instruction or collaborative learning, totally, to every situation, in every classroom, every day. However, understanding *when* to use certain pedagogic strategies is just as critical as the *which* ones to use.

A contention that we propose in this book is that students need teachers who can use a variety of pedagogic strategies that best fit the classroom situations. A round of golf is similar to teaching a lesson sequence, and a professional golfer might get away with using just one club (say, a putter) for a whole round, but the results would not be as good as having the option to use more appropriate clubs.

Audit of teachers' pedagogic skills

As school leaders soon come to realise teachers have been heavily exposed to collaborative learning processes (based on constructivist learning theory) during their pre-service training. In some instances, the pedagogic skills of teacher directed learning were frowned upon with pedagogic approaches more oriented towards teachers becoming the *guides on the side*. The downside of this purist approach was that teachers felt that they were failing the most vulnerable, disadvantaged students, and various state and national testing results amplified this fact. Basically, it was believed that the middle-class kids who had caddied for parents around the private golf courses dotting the greener, more affluent suburbs already had grasped the basics of playing golf, but for kids who had never seen a golf stick what was required was a more explicit teaching approach. Schooling is no different, and it is recognised that an appropriate level of instruction is needed to get students to a desired level of competence, and quickly at that. There is a need to find a way to give students access to the golf course in the first instance, with the right resources and practices so that they are then able to play the game.

Consequently, a pedagogically oriented school leader needs to pay particular attention to teacher practices, and further, become immersed in their professional development. This may incorporate a number of approaches including establishing a culture underpinned by a performance management process that is an accepted and valued process, staff coaching, peer observation and mentoring.

Performance management is a conversation with a purpose

We see performance management as a conversation with a purpose that requires first of all that the school leader establishes an atmosphere of trust, mutual respect, open communication and commitment to the process. Performance management provides a means of assessing the needs of staff for personal and professional development and of responding to accountability demands of the organisation. At all times the primary objective of performance management is about improving the staff potential. Therefore, performance management is seen as a planned review of performance and potential, aiming sympathetically, at personal and professional fulfilment within a framework of staff development.

As a school leadership-initiated activity, performance management needs to be viewed by those involved as a positive initiative, grounded in agreement, performance and the potential of an individual within the school context. To be effective the practice needs to be a positive one in which staff are personally invested, as it offers them the opportunity to develop professionally and personally to desirable, mutually agreed upon levels of teaching performance.

Unfortunately, in the past many performance management activities employed in schools have been hit-and-miss activities, paper-driven and done as a response to centrally determined policy imperatives. We maintain that an effective performance management process will have school leaders continually engaged in informal performance discussions with their staff about pedagogic practices, and that any more formal performance management schemes seen as a supplement to and not a substitute for this process. Experience would indicate that it is in the nature of the individual to want to discuss their performance.

So why is there often some resistance encountered to performance management processes? Historically performance management has often been poorly done. Departmental and system requirements have tended to make the task so complicated that many school leaders are reluctant to devote both time and effort to having the requisite conversations. Furthermore, an often-cited reason for school leaders to avoid performance discussions with staff or their general sense of discomfort with the process may also relate to their own credibility and ability to confidently discuss pedagogy and articulate expectations about teaching and learning with individual staff. They do so because they fear the feedback that is usually evoked by any evaluation procedure; doing it systematically opens not only their methodology but also the results of these discussions to criticism and attack.

The ingredients of a successful performance management process distilled from experience would overlap the school leader's role as a pedagogic leader in the school:

- Creating a school culture where the introduction of performance management processes is seen as developmental and supportive aimed at improving teachers' professional skills.
- Ensuring that the introduction of performance management agenda is perceived by staff to be transparent, participative, non-threatening and negotiable.
- Allocating adequate resources in terms of time and support.
- Following up discussions with identified professional training needs for individuals. Without this, confidence in the activity will evaporate very quickly.

OUR BELIEF 16

> Student learning will be enhanced when performance management conversations between the school leader and the teacher collegially address effectiveness, performance and improving students' learning.

Performance management to be meaningful needs to lead somewhere. Ideally an agreed upon schema of action is developed where firstly, the individual's strengths are utilised to a greater degree and secondly where a development plan, mutually agreed upon by the staff member is implemented.

Without an effective performance management system in place it is difficult to coordinate the professional development demands of its employees, let alone determine their point of professional need. Only when the needs of the individuals within the organisation are established, with planned professional development outcomes, will the system be able to truly bring about opportunities for staff and organisation improvement to occur.

The important thing to remember about all performance management systems is that they operate in the area of subjective human judgement and not scientific measurement. In the education arena performance management is one aspect of management in which we are still serving an apprenticeship.

Coaching

Coaching and mentoring are seen as two different, but complementary processes that are employed successfully by effective school leaders. Where mentoring usually involves a teacher selecting a peer to offer advice and career guidance, a coach is a person who through their interactions brings about school and teaching and learning outcome improvement. Knight (2015) emphasises that coaching focuses on research-based instructional strategies that can have a powerful impact in improving an individual's practice and is seen to incorporate a range of skills inclusive of skills listening, observing, modelling and collaborating.

Coaching therefore sits side-by-side with the school leadership role, and is built upon a foundation of frank and open communication between a school's leader and staff member. As such it involves focused, facilitated dialogue between a school leader and the teacher about future developments and agreed teaching and learning pedagogy and outcomes.

We recognise that coaching cannot take place unless there is a culture of willingness and openness on behalf of the teacher to accept the learning opportunities provided through the appointment of a coach. Since a coaching programme must be tailored to meet the needs of an individual or group of individuals some form of needs assessment, usually in the form of performance management discussions will precede actual coaching activities.

To be effective the relationship between the individual and the coach must be mutually cooperative and open. This relationship will need to build upon:

- mutual commitment, with the leader as coach and the teacher/s involved committed to the same thing;
- mutual trust, with both parties sincere in making a commitment to the process and also possessing the competence to meet that stated commitment;
- mutual respect, with both parties believing that the other is authentic, credible and sincere in their intentions;
- mutual freedom to express a point of view; an ability to speak freely, openly and with due respect for sensitivities involved.

It is essential that a feedback loop be created to enable self-correction and progress towards expectations that have been articulated for the process with both parties engaged in observation, reflection and action.

Mentoring and/or peer observation

Our preferred definition of mentoring is: *Assistance given by a school leader or teacher peer to another in making significant transitions in knowledge, work or thinking*. While a mentor is usually a more senior or experienced educator than the teacher being mentored, we recognise that in many cases in a school scenario it is a role undertaken by a credible peer. Mentoring encourages people to pass on their knowledge to others.

The mentor role is employed to facilitate one or more of the following school related outcomes:

- helping an individual teacher to improve classroom performance;
- assisting with an individual's career development;
- promoting the sharing of pedagogic and curriculum knowledge; and as
- a peer counsellor.

A significant role of the mentor is to help members of staff gain insights into themselves with an emphasis on their teaching quality (their strengths and weaknesses, in particular, how other staff see them), or classroom processes (how things operate in the classroom and best ways to get things done).

As such mentoring programmes follow a cyclical process involving the individual staff member and their mentor initially recognising the development need, addressing the development of that need (thereby increasing the capacity of the individual) in turn leading to individual empowerment and insight with the further identification of development needs.

Mentoring works best when it is learner-driven. As such it is expected that some relationships will take quite different paths when driven by different urgencies and situational contexts. It is acknowledged that it is ultimately a staff member's decision as to whether a mentoring relationship is wanted and acceptable.

OUR BELIEF 17

> A school leader who is engaged in school renewal must possess excellent communication and people skills, and actively be prepared to coach and mentor staff.

Pedagogic profile and performance management

As school leaders we have all experienced changes in education in our careers, but the biggest challenge facing schools, the profession and each of us individually, is broadening teachers' pedagogic repertoires beyond didactic instruction and engaging students in learning.

It is a rarity for school communities to define the pedagogic strategies that it values and expects to see in classrooms. We examined a number of school contexts, analysed the pedagogic and curricular changes that were being proposed at that time, and then examined available educational research and practice literature. Within a context of understandings related to the broad influences affecting modern education and with a recognition that teachers' pedagogic strengths within the school may need school leader leadership intervention, it became clear to us that a programme of pedagogic re-skilling may be needed in some instances to more orient them towards more appropriate teaching and learning strategies.

We developed the Pedagogic Profile (copy in Appendix 1) using current research and writing. The Pedagogic Profile has proved to be a useful tool for auditing current teaching practices and has been used successfully in many schools already. However, the real utility of the Pedagogic Profile is in the actual process of creating personalised descriptions of what the school community values in its teachers' practices. The upshot of a successful profiling process is a pedagogically improved and renewed school culture.

Rationale behind the Pedagogic Profile

The Pedagogic Profile was first created using the Principles of Learning, Teaching and Assessment of the Curriculum Framework (Curriculum Council, 1998), and the characteristics of authentic pedagogy (Newmann et al., 1996). Newmann et al. explored "Authentic pedagogy" in terms of four standards of best practice:

Construction of knowledge

Standard 1. Higher order thinking. Instruction involves students in manipulating information and ideas by synthesising, generalising, explaining, hypothesising or arriving at conclusions that produce new meaning and understandings for them.

Disciplined inquiry

Standard 2. Deep knowledge. Instruction addresses central ideas of a topic or discipline with enough thoroughness to explore connections and relationships and to produce relatively complex understandings.
Standard 3. Substantive conversation. Students engage in extended conversational exchanges with a teacher or his peers about subject matter in a way that builds improved and shared understanding of ideas or topics.

Value beyond school

Standard 4. Connections to the world beyond the classroom. Students make connections between substantive knowledge and either public problems or personal experiences.

We believe that teachers need a broad repertoire of teaching skills to promote student learning and the Pedagogic Profile we designed (Appendix 1) allowed school leaders to audit then develop the level of skills that teachers have in a student-centred, cooperative learning classroom environment

The true measures of pedagogic leadership are changes in teachers' pedagogic practices and, as a result, improved student learning. There is a vast array of strategies that pedagogic leaders use, but there is never a one best pedagogy, or a one best strategy to generate pedagogic change. Schools are complex and diverse communities. Accordingly, pedagogic leadership at the Bronx School is not transferable in a pure form to Greenfields School. Pedagogic leaders need a multi-faceted repertoire of skills and knowledge. It is only through the widespread development of this pedagogic repertoire that *Procrusteanism* will finally be put to rest.

General comment on chapter

We believe that education in schools is at a cross-road. If we accept that the various international testing regimes are singularly valid and reliable measures of what is important in students' learning, then local jurisdictions will need to re-evaluate what students learn and how teachers teach. This being said, it is important to remember that schools are also designed to socialise the next generation of citizens. A narrowing of the curriculum and moving teachers' pedagogic roles to improve testing results will make schools even less tenable and will damage further the views of society that students take into their adulthood.

A further concern is the failure of those accrediting universities that give pre-service teachers entry into the teaching profession to teach the craft aspect of teaching. In professional golfing it would be the equivalent of a golfer learning the physics and financial aspects of golfing, and as a result rarely hitting a golf ball. Teaching is not a theoretical exercise of study, but a living, breathing, doing pursuit that is also about relationships, presence, skill, knowledge and beliefs. Furthermore, the pedagogic hit-and-miss experiences that pre-service teachers have in schools experiences are uncontrolled, unprofessionally directed and an indictment of not only the universities but also the employers who accept these dubious accreditations.

References

Brady, L. (1985). *Models and methods of teaching.* Sydney: Prentice-Hall Australia.
Cuban, L. (2004, Spring). Whatever happened to …? The open classroom. *Education Next*, 4(2), 69–71. https://www.educationnext.org/theopenclassroom/
Cuban, L. (2009). *Hugging the middle: How teachers teach in an era of testing and accountability.* New York: Teachers College Press.
Curriculum Council of Western Australia (1998). *The curriculum framework for kindergarten to year 12 education in Western Australia.* Osborne Park, Western Australia: author.
Dickens, C. (1854/1996). *Hard times.* Koln, Germany: Konemann.
Fogarty Foundation (2017). EDvance Case studies. https://fogartyedvance.org.au/case-studies-booklet/
Knight, J. (2015). *The impact cycle: What good instructional coaches should do to foster powerful improvements in teaching.* Thousand Oaks, CA: Sage.
Newmann, F.M., et al. (1996). *Authentic achievement: Restructuring schools for intellectual quality.* San Francisco: Jossey-Bass.
Spillane, J.P. (2002, April). Local theories of teacher change: The pedagogy of district policies and programs. *Teachers College Record*, 104, 377–420.

9 Distributed leadership in modern schooling contexts
Delegation is not distributed leadership

The citizens of Western societies intuitively value the Utopian, democratic, egalitarian and visionary leadership and that is applied ubiquitously to both individuals and organisations. However, such is the power of *leadership* that *management* is now relegated to a far lesser status in literature on the subject. Leadership is a complex equation that considers the aspirations of the parties, and some authors and organisations simplistically believe that leadership can be learned. For example, the Australian military proudly advertises that the Royal Military College Duntroon is "Where Leaders are Made" (Australian Army Television Advertisement, 2015). If only *leadership* were that simple!

OUR BELIEF 18

> It is better to be a leader among leaders than a leader of followers.

Our understanding and definitions of leadership have changed profoundly since the days of the Knights of the Round Table, and the era of royal prerogatives.

Joanne Ciulla (2003) in her developmental description of leadership showed how leadership changed to a modern description incorporated in a mutual purpose equation. She argued that the perception of leadership has significantly altered from a 1920s perspective as the ability to impress one's will on those led and induce obedience, respect, loyalty and cooperation through to a more recent position of leadership as being a transformational and influential relationship between leaders and followers who intend real changes that reflect their mutual purposes (adapted from Ciulla, 2003). It is important to note that often ignored concept of moral altruism (improving students' life options) plays an important part in the mutual purpose equation for teachers and school administrators.

Such is the attraction of leadership studies that writers often develop different appellations of leadership styles using a variety of adjectives to categorise the concepts. Consequently, terms such as autocratic leadership, bureaucratic leadership, charismatic leadership, command and control leadership, coercive leadership, democratic leadership, distributed leadership, facilitative leadership, hero leadership, instructional leadership, laissez-faire leadership, moral leadership, servant leadership, situational leadership, transactional leadership, transformational leadership, visionary leadership have become common-place in the literature on the subject over time. Leithwood, Louis, Anderson and Wahlstrom (2004, p. 6) warned of the dangers of leadership by adjective:

> The lesson here is that we need to be sceptical about the "leadership by adjective" literature. Sometimes these adjectives have real meaning, but sometimes they mask the more important underlying themes common to successful leadership, regardless of the style being advocated.

Revisiting distributed leadership: All hands to the lifeboats

Distributed leadership in schools is seen as a sign of organisational maturity, however, with the warning of a looming conflict in school administration between what can be termed the forces of darkness and the forces of light. Both forces are seen to be at work in the dynamic equation of teacher and school accountability that influence the progress of distributed leadership in schools. *The Forces of Darkness were associated with those seen as the high-stakes testers and cynics who see teachers as piece workers on a production chain and who perceive the need to teacher-proof the curriculum. Conversely, the Forces of Light see teaching as a noble and moral profession predicated on a professional teaching workforce that has the skills and ability to develop each student to his/her full potential.*

High-stakes testing and the concept of good in education

Athletes training for the Olympic Games know that their preparation for the main event will change over time and their coaches try to ensure that their wards reach that optimal physical state at the time of the actual event. Athletes peaking too early, or too late, means that they are not at their competitive best for their event. This has often resulted in and a range of expert medical and technical analyses being used to supplement the advice given to coaches and teams. Likewise, school staff and students move through similar, but less scientific, stages of development within the contexts of normal effectiveness growth, which may also be influenced by the external measures of high-stakes testing.

Because school leaders are generally hierarchically positioned as middle-level managers, existing within systems with line managers based in district or state or national offices, they often operate in the entwined world of leadership and management. Consequently, the attributes of leadership and management vary according to the task. It is recognised that school leaders cannot exist without both complementary abilities in the performance of role expectations held of them.

Management, in a line-management context, as an important element of a school's operations, assumes that the leaders' focus ought to be on functions, tasks and behaviours associated with extant expectations. It provides the core structures under which the school community operates.

In this context management generally focuses on maintaining current organisational procedures effectively and encompasses the daily routines that are incorporated in schools, including the methodologies and pedagogies utilised for curriculum delivery, expectations regarding teacher timetabling, defining of learning and teaching objectives, evaluating of performance; right through to directing what records need to be kept within the school. The manager then, as stated by Everard, Morris and Wilson, is "less concerned with being a resource than with using resources" (2004, p. 5).

School management can be clustered primarily into three domains:

1 Human
2 Material
3 Financial

The human domain includes, but is not limited to, job design, career planning, curriculum development, performance management, training and project work. The material domain is concerned with purchasing, the control of stock and asset management. Finally, the financial domain would include such activities as budgeting, cost control and fund-raising.

School leaders who primarily manage and are focused on manipulating these three domains of management, can be effective in attaining the school's goals. Yet, it is important to note, that well-managed does not, by default, lead to a school that is well led. Bennis and Nanus (1985) best describe this when they state:

> The problem with many organisations ... is that they tend to be over managed and under led. They may excel in the ability to handle the daily routine, yet never question whether the routine should be done at all. (p. 109)

OUR BELIEF 19

Many schools are over-managed by a school leader, but under-led.

Further to this, while management ensures that a school is running effectively, it does so under the assumption that the school is a static organisation. Schools, however, are not immobile or unchanging, and their environments are continually changing, as too are their contexts. In this regard, a management model alone for schools is fundamentally flawed.

School management, or managerial leadership as it is sometimes referred to in current literature, has been the primary focus of school leaders throughout the previous century; however, within the last two decades there has been a shift from a management bias in schools to more of a pedagogic leadership model as school communities come to the realisation that management alone will not, and does not, guarantee a school's future outcomes success.

School leadership: The importance of a school leader's beliefs

Leading or *leadership*, as described by Cuban (1988, cited in Bush, 2007), is associated with influencing the actions of others in evoking change. Leadership is concerned with individuals shaping the motivations, actions and goals of others; with the overall purpose of engendering change and development. Bennis (1994, as cited in Dembowski, 2006, p. 3) distinguished leadership from management, by proposing that while "... management is getting people to do what needs to be done. Leadership is getting people to *want* to do what needs to be done".

In examining school leadership, we should consider Cuban's (1988) definition that connects it with influencing the actions of others in bringing about change. Gardner (1990) and Tosi (1982) similarly define leadership as a persuasive or influential process, whereby a leader, or leadership team, induces others to pursue common goals and objectives. The role of leaders within a school is to initiate change, to improve, innovate and transform; achieving current goals and setting new ones. Ultimately, leadership influences the actions of others to a desirable end.

The issue put simply is, if we do what we always have done then we get the results that we have always got. As an example, a shift in the overall decision-making processes in implementing a consensus approach can impact significantly on school management practices, for in some schools this concept may be a contentious one as there will always be individuals or groups of individuals on staff who are change adverse. This simply could be due to the fact that the staff members are uncomfortable in making the change either through a lack of knowledge, understanding or they simply desire to maintain the status quo. Furthermore, despite the overall promotion of *Collaboration, Consensus* and *Shared decision-making* and the need to move away from top-down decision-making, in the final analysis the end line accountability rests entirely with the school leader. This would appear to be counterproductive, to say the least, in that if an individual is going to be held accountable it should be as a result of the structures he or she has put into place, not the response of the cohort group to the proposed systemic changes.

School leader comment:

> I wanted teachers to use a variety of pedagogies to facilitate students' learning (cognitive, social, affective and kinaesthetic). I wanted to see students voluntarily and passionately engaged their learning. I wanted to see that each child's educational opportunity is maximised. I wanted to see parents and the community strongly supporting the students and the school.

With top-down management there can be no ambiguity of the expectations and or decisions being made. They come from the top, and as such are the foundations on which the senior leadership team build accountability structures for future development. It is when a staff accepts the articulated vision and demonstrates commitment not compliance to it that a school's leader can move from a management paradigm to a more authentic leadership role.

Distributed leadership

Distributed leadership is a slippery concept that means different things to different people and it needs to be re-examined because it has progressed to an iconic status. Unfortunately, the term distributed leadership itself has become corrupted over time with some writers confusing the term with that of delegation partly because there has been a variety of attempts at defining or describing *distributed leadership* in practice.

OUR BELIEF 20

> Delegation is not distributed leadership in schools, or in any organisation.

We argue that it is important to recognise here that there is a significant dichotomy between the concepts of delegation and distributed leadership. Where delegation refers to the assignment of responsibility or *authority* to another person (typically from a line manager to a subordinate) to carry out specific activities, distributed leadership on the other hand is enmeshed in the ideal of sharing the leadership function and as such is best seen as being context specific. In a purist sense, a distributed leadership scenario is characterised by a leadership culture where collaboration exists within the school as an organisation, underpinned by both respect and trust between the individuals involved. To this extent a distributed perspective means seeing leadership activities as a situated within a context of time, staff expertise, task complexity, organisational structure and staff stability. The fear is that distributed leadership has become a catchall for any attempt to define the sharing of the leadership function.

The appeal of a distributed perspective is the fact that it sits comfortably with the terms of democratic leadership, shared leadership, parallel leadership and collaborative leadership. However, there is a concern that the overlap of the terms can result in a serious misuse of the concept.

School leader comment:

> I looked for opportunities to allow staff ownership of the proposed change agenda empowering staff – really giving them opportunities to make meaningful decisions, you make your job easier; be firm in your beliefs but realise that those beliefs can change through your own professional growth [don't be inflexible]; spend a significant amount of time looking and listening when you arrive at your new school.

The advocates of distributed leadership often fall into the trap of failing to recognise that distributed leadership is not a universal panacea in

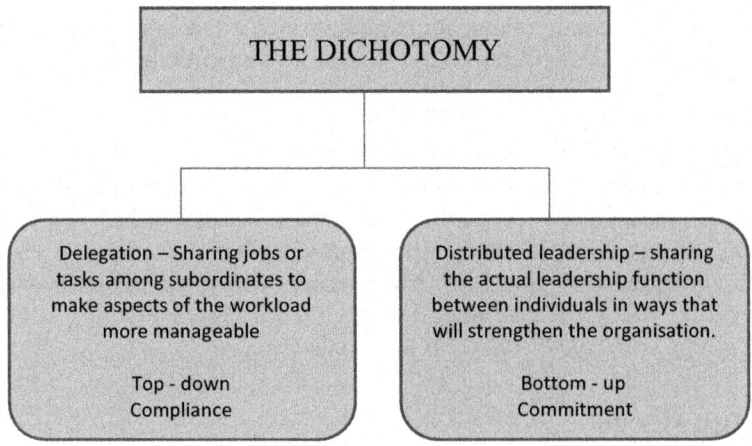

Figure 9.1 The distributed leadership – delegation dichotomy.

education. For example, a failing school that is dominated by a toxic culture does not encourage and foster an ethos conducive to a distributed leadership model because of the negativity that accompanies such a working environment.

When teams, organisations or schools are created the leadership/management requirements change according to the personnel and contextual variations. Leadership and management are never static in schools as the internal and external contexts are in constant flux. Using the Lester, Parnell, and Carraher (2003) *Organisational Life Cycle* model of organisational development (OD), the role of school leadership/management will be required to make necessary contextual changes as the organisation grows or declines.

- Stage 1: Existence.
- Stage 2: Survival.
- Stage 3: Success.
- Stage 4: Renewal.
- Stage 5: Decline> Demise.

In each of these five stages school leaders with a wide repertoire of skills will adjust their leadership/management styles, or the school will import a school leader with skills that meet the specific developmental needs of the school at that time. In medical parlance, the leadership/management divide is between the general practitioners and the specialists. However, bearing in mind that distributed leadership requires a specific set of necessary and sufficient conditions to flourish, the real question remains, "Where in this stylised Organizational Life Cycle does distributed leadership sit?"

One external education agency view of school leadership

The Australian Professional Standards for Principals (AITSL, 2015) states that it sets the standards that school leaders are expected to know, understand and do, to achieve excellence in their schools. It is claimed that "research and an evolving body of knowledge inform the leadership requirements" and professional practices that underwrite these so-called standards. Naively, AITSL (2011, p. 2) makes an ideological claim that "leadership is distributed and collaborative with teams working together to accomplish the vision and aims of the school led by the principal". Unfortunately, such a statement does not account for the myriad of contexts in which distributed leadership will not work. A school leader immersed in a toxic culture needs to be in control. It is a concern that in such a situation powerful, *negaholic* cliques will welcome the idea of democratic processes and distributed leadership because the school leader is rendered powerless.

Distributed leadership and our take on it.

It is a major concern for school-based school leaders that many writers who help form understandings of the collective wisdom of school leadership and management think of distributed leadership as a *silver bullet*; a goal that must be applied in all school situations. The point that we make in this book is that such thinking is naïve and demonstrates a poor understanding of developmental situations that occur in many schools. In some situations, distributed leadership is not possible, and as Hobbes (1968) observed in *Leviathan*, the leaders' (of schools) lives could be "solitary, poor, nasty, brutish, and short".

The elephant in the room in relation to distributed leadership is *power*, or more specifically *positional power*. Power is even more of an issue when the accountability of high-stakes testing is considered, because the accountability issues always come back to the school leader. So, the distribution of power in distributed leadership is conditional, and any continuation of that situation remains dependent on the school leader's decision. Distributed leadership can never be a permanent agreement as it is influenced by a vast array of dynamic conditions that affect a school's operations.

School leaders who have actively encouraged a distributed leadership style in their schools have indicated that it has proved to be both personally rewarding and a remarkable stress reliever. Basically, it is about having confidence in your staff abilities within a school that you can let go. Distributed leadership for us is captured in the aphorism – a team of horses runs faster when you let go of the reins. It is about trust and respecting those with whom you have confidence, and empowering staff so that they are empowered in their roles as facilitators of learning within the school.

References

Australian Institute for Teaching and School Leadership (2015). *Australian professional standard for principals.* www.aitsl.edu.au/australian-professional-standard-for-principals

Bennis, W. & Nanus, B. (1985). *Leaders: The strategies for taking charge.* New York: Harper & Row.

Bush, T. (2007). Educational leadership and management: theory, policy and practice. *South African Journal of Education*, 27(3), 391–406. www.sajournalofeducation.co.za/index.php/saje/article/viewFile/107/29

Ciulla, J.B. (2003). *The ethics of leadership.* Belmont, CA: Thomson.

Dembowski, F. (2006). The changing roles of leadership and management in educational administration. http://cnx.org/content/m14280/latest/Dembowski.pdf.pdf

Everard, K.B., Morris, G., & Wilson, I. (2004). *Effective school management* (4th ed.). London: Sage.

Gardner, J.W. (1990). *On leadership.* New York: The Free Press.

Hobbes, T. (1968). *Leviathan.* Ringwood, Australia: Penguin Books.

Leithwood, K., Louis, K.S., Anderson, S., & Wahlstrom, K. (2004). *How leadership influences student learning.* New York: The Wallace Foundation. https://www.wallacefoundation.org/knowledge-left/Documents/How-Leadership-Influences-Student-Learning.pdf

Lester, D.L., Parnell, J.A., & Carraher, S. (2003). Organizational life cycle: A five stage empirical scale. *The International Journal of Organizational Analysis*, 11(4), 339–354.

Tosi, J.J., Jr. (1982). Toward a paradigm shift in the study of leadership. In J.G. Hunt, U. Sekaran, & C.A. Schriesheim (Eds.), *Leadership beyond establishment views* (pp. 222–233). Carbondale: Southern Illinois University Press.

10 Schools as learning organisations

Growing organisational, professional and personal capital

> Human resources are like natural resources; they're often buried deep. You have to go looking for them, they're not just lying around on the surface. You have to create the circumstances where they show themselves.
>
> Ken Robinson

In education it is our experience that many school leaders have tried to cushion themselves and their schools from the corporate, political and managerialist thrusts into education. This may explain why so many question as to why many educationalists so readily reject the change paradigms being put to them.

Unfortunately, at the graduate and postgraduate level studies of educational administration, present-day university students, except those with courses in the schools of business, use texts which do not draw widely on business organisation experiences and their associated leadership and management practices. This can be partly explained by a belief held by many school executives that schools as teaching-learning organisations have little in common with the business sector, particularly with its profit motive orientation. Yet, schools like their business counterparts, are concerned with people management, and efficient and effective practices to achieve desired outcomes.

The failure of schools, as organisations, to accept the corporate business paradigms on offer is identified as one significant drawback to them becoming balanced and proactive learning organisations, receptive to the ever changing social and political environment within which they operate.

It is the authors' intention to revisit the concept of the school as a learning organisation and then to offer a perspective of organisational change which may result in a Damascus Road conversion for the unbelievers. Be warned, however, some of the good ideas we share come from the business sector!

The concept of the *learning organisation* may cause a degree of cognitive dissonance in some educational circles. This is because some educators may believe that their schools are automatically learning organisations given that they are involved in teaching and learning. This is in fact not the case as teaching may not be learning, and similarly, teaching may not be education.

While the material on learning organisations was developed at the turn of the Millennium, the concept is still highly relevant. Hargreaves and Fullan's (2013) work on *professional capital* has breathed a new reality into learning organisation, as did the Human Capital Management (HCM) theory, which challenged Human Resource Management to optimise the organisation's human capital assets.

It is important to recognise that while schools have an administrative management aspect to them, they also have a more important pedagogic imperative as well, which centres on the delivery of the curriculum to its students. A learning organisation culture will influence both. in a developmental sense, we are advocates of a performance focused organisation because it fits the learning organisation model well, and describes a necessary change in the focus of school administration.

Change is a fact of life and the *educational corpus* has suffered severe strain because the current models of schooling are ill-adapted to change in a rapidly changing and increasingly technological society. Marquardt puts the situation rather provocatively:

> The large dinosaur organisations with pea-sized brains that flourished in the past cannot breathe and survive in this new atmosphere of rapid change and intense competition. The survival of the fittest is quickly becoming the survival of the fittest-to-learn. (Marquardt, 1996, p. 1)

Table 10.1 The locus of control dichotomy in organisations

Control-focused organisations	*Performance-focused organisations*
• Organisation pyramids value control.	• Focus is on the customer above all else.
• Organisations are inward looking.	• Organisations are outward looking.
• Predictability is valued.	• Improvements are always being sought.
• Whole departments are created for control purposes.	• Responsiveness is valued.
• To lose control is to lose everything.	• There is reduced or eliminated dependence on inspection.
• As long as we are in control who cares what else is happening.	• To give control is to get control.
• External controls are emphasised.	• Focus is on service and contribution to the whole.
• There are rules (which are inflexible).	• Self-control is emphasised.
• 'No surprises' leads to the illusion of control.	• There are guidelines (which allow flexibility).
• All learning is preceded by ignorance, followed by surprise.	• Surprise is essential to high performance.
• People avoid individual responsibility.	• It is surprise that develops energy and motivation.
• Performance assessment is from above.	• People act as if it is their business.
• We feel our survival is in the hands of others.	• It is appreciated that in reality we know it is not possible to accurately plan and predict.
	• Our survival is in our hands.

(Napoli, quoted by Whiteley, 1995, p. 125.)

Defining a learning organisation

We begin our examination of what a learning organisation by exploring the developing definition of the concept. The British Training Commission in outlining its interpretation of a learning organisation subsequently employed this as a definition:

> A learning organisation is one which facilitates learning and development of all its employees, whilst continually transforming itself. (Beck, 1989, p. 22)

Such a definition implies that underpinning a learning organisation is the concept of internal transformation as a key to successful, lasting change. The key concepts identified in this perspective are further replicated by Pedler et al. (1992).

In their introduction it would appear that Pedler et al. prefer the term learning company to learning organisation because for them the term was more convivial. And in a similar vein, Garvin's (1993) definition developed the learning aspects of such an organisation further by indicating that:

> A learning organisation is one skilled at creating, acquiring and transferring knowledge, and at modifying its behaviour to reflect new knowledge and insights. (Garvin, 1993, p. 80)

In the United States, however, it was Peter Senge, author of the influential work *The Fifth Discipline* who offered a deceptively simple definition of the learning organisation as "an organisation that is continually expanding its capacity to create its future" (Senge, 1995, p. 14). And, re-asserting the human aspect of the learning organisation he noted it was a place "where people continually expand their capacity to create the results they truly desire, where new and expansive patterns of thinking are nurtured, where collective aspiration is set free, and where people are continually learning how to learn together" (Senge, 1995, p. 3).

From these early works we have been able to identify five, common, inclusive elements that have particular relevance to schools as learning organisations. A learning organisation:

- is always about growing human creativity;
- facilitates and promotes learning at all levels;
- transforms the organisation and individual's practices;
- demonstrates organisational and individual improvement; and
- is able to adapt to, and lead change.

We maintain that unless all these elements are present, a learning organisation does not exist.

What learning organisations look like

By examining the environment, the type of management and leadership in evidence, and the role of staff in learning organisations a more succinct statement about the environment within the learning organisation can be framed. Consequently, we have identified eight characteristics of a learning organisation:

- a perspective of staff as being the organisations greatest asset (organisational capital), valuing its people, including their feelings and emotions, in learning;
- an emphasis on internal motivation through staff empowerment;
- active reflection on existing practice, and a culture of problem solving is grown;
- a conscious ongoing evaluation of the organisation's goals, norms and values;
- a culture of experimentation, risk willingness and inquiry leading to new approaches to action;
- a culture of fostering the use of team and whole of staff learning, which develops the organisation's professional capital;
- a commitment to the enhancement of general overall organisational efficacy, inclusive of individual self-esteem, self-discovery and self-directedness;
- one that fosters continuous professional learning.

Leadership in a learning organisation

As to be expected the role of the school leader as a pedagogic leader is contextually different in many respects in a school as a learning organisation as opposed to the business sector. Not surprisingly, the three roles that Senge described for learning organisations fit schools well: leaders as designers, stewards and teachers (Senge, 1995, pp. 341–357).

Pedler confirmed this highly practical, *hands-on* role of the leader/manager, which complements the instructional leadership model well:

1   Do it yourself. You are always engaged in learning something...
2   Share and demonstrate your new learning...
3   Make learning normal, legitimise it and encourage other to do it ... (Pedler et al., 1992, p. 129)

The implications of this view for the school leader as a pedagogic leader are significant within a school setting as it portrays a picture of the leadership role as one that many school leaders will have difficulty relating to due to its adversarial, hierarchical nature. The chicken-and-egg argument is raised when the question arises as to whether the school leader can move to a leadership style more in line with that expected within a transformative learning culture, and particularly if the staff haven't reached the level of development conducive to accepting such a school-wide approach. The authors response to this dichotomy is that the school leader and the staff must ideally develop together towards the shared vision of the school being a learning organisation based on mutual trust and associated risk-taking.

Consequently, the learning organisation has to win the hearts and minds of staff and as such, the school culture would need to be one where:

- staff at all levels are able and willing to undertake the various teaching and learning role expectations held for them;
- staff are pedagogically able and encouraged to be creative and think beyond existing boundaries;
- resilient staff at all levels who have a balanced, rather than stressed, approach to their responsibility within a learning and teaching culture.

Critics may think that this is a very Utopian view in the sense that it is an ideal and may not fully achieved. We believe that in this case Utopia is achievable and the seeds of which lie within every teacher and school leader.

There have been occasions when as school leaders we may have seen elements of a learning organisation in operation, but perhaps not recognised them as such. We argue that the more efficacious and reflective school leaders are able to appropriately audit the school characteristics within the framework offered by a learning organisation and check them against their most successful experience, and then put these snapshots, which may elicit a warm glow, into a theoretical context. Staff will then be able to recognise the practices that made the experience successful and try to replicate them in the future.

Schools as learning organisations

There is a dearth of material being written about schools as learning organisations. Senge et al . (1999, p. 484), identified some examples of innovatory practices in schools but they seem to have been fitted to the learning organisation *ex post facto* (or retrofitted as engineers are want to say).

OUR BELIEF 21

> The school as a learning organisation is an organisation that is skilled at creating, acquiring, and transferring knowledge, and at modifying its teachers' behaviours to reflect new knowledge and insights.

Holly and Southworth's book, *The Developing School* (1989, reprinted 1993), replicated the one of many texts about school development that emanated in the 1980s and 1990s. However, of interest to school leaders in the context of what we now know about schools as learning organisations, is the fact that these authors have not referred, or quoted at least, apart from Schon's learning system any of the material on learning organisations, yet they write authoritatively about "The Learning School":

> Essentially the Learning School is a place that works for both children and adults; it is a place 'designed for learning'. We have borrowed the term from 'Ten Good Schools: A Secondary School Enquiry by the HMI'. We would argue, however, that it is a pertinent phrase for all developing schools ... (Holly & Southworth, 1993, p. 3)

The fact that Holly and Southworth have serendipitously described a learning organisation, demonstrates to school staff that theory (of learning organisations) and practice can already be seen in some cases of best practice in our schools.

These authors then go on to present five characteristics of a learning school and then set out the roles of the key players in such an organisation:

- the focus is on children and their learning;
- individual teachers are encouraged to be continuing learners themselves;
- the group of teachers (and sometimes others) who constitute the 'staff' is encouraged to collaborate by learning with and from each other;
  - the school (i.e. all those people who constitute the 'school') learns its way forward.
  - the school as an organisation is a 'learning system'... the head teacher is the leading learner. (Holly & Southworth, 1993, pp. 3–4)

We believe that the school needs to be convinced of the theory and practice of the learning organisation, make public declarations to that end, obtain support, do a cultural and core values audit, then set about changing the school culture to be that of a learning culture by developing practices in this genre.

OUR BELIEF 22

> Continuous school improvement and renewal requires a commitment to learning. Therefore, the first step for the school leader is to foster an environment that is conducive to that learning, noting that not all learning comes from staff reflection and self-analysis. Sometimes, the most powerful insights come from looking outside one's immediate school environment in order to gain a new perspective on teaching and learning.

Implementing practices that characterise the learning organisation at the school level

The most difficult change to effect in any organisation is a macro-cultural change. Clearly, opening a new school with personally selected staff is the easiest route to establishing a learning organisation culture in a school community. However, school leaders are rarely this fortunate!

In an established school, the school leader as the agent of change needs to ensure the processes of cultural change are correct and acceptable. Alma Whiteley (1995) offered excellent advice to in this respect, for she identifies the core values as one approach to successful change.

> The core values model is a practical model for building or renewing culture in an organisation. It is built on the philosophy that every person, every human resource in an organisation, is able to construct a personal reality of the organisation to whose success he/she contributes. The model seeks to bring together sets of reality so that a holistic identity can be formed. (Whiteley, 1995, p. 42)

In everyday practice, what she implies is that the shared vision and values are the vehicle to progress change. Seemingly, a small point but in reality, an enormous undertaking for school leaders and staff who have existed in cultures so different to that of learning organisations most of their working lives.

The question facing the school leader and other stake holders is whether to implement a totally new start or undertake a re-culturation through incremental changes? We suggest that most school leaders and stakeholders will find the second, incremental alternative more attractive because it allows small changes to start with; a building on the school's best practice. Let's face it, it is extremely difficult to change the way people interact and do things, quickly. Within school communities there are at least five sets of stakeholders each with their own set of values which in turn influence the core values of the school:

- students
- parents/community
- teachers
- administration team members
- the employing body.

Getting started is probably easier than sustaining the change over an extended time. Probably the greatest threat to the process of change is that the drivers of change simply run out of energy and the desired renewal hasn't been planned or undertaken. *The Fifth Discipline Field Book* (Senge, 1995) shows the way to continuous improvement and renewal-networking, dialogue and support groups all externalise the commitment. However, embedding the learning organisation model into their schools' strategic plans and operations is the key to bringing about long-term, meaningful change.

The school as a learning organisation, which involves all of the school staff, puts a different spin on the way individuals relate to each other and gives the school more of a corporate sense of direction. The biggest challenge is to

Table 10.2 Environmental changes as the learning organisation evolves

All from an organisation environment that:	To an organisation environment that:
Has many different and often conflicting goals.	Has a common vision shared by everyone.
Punishes mistakes, high or rationalises problems.	Openly discusses problems, sees defects as opportunities to improve.
Following long established policies is rewarded.	Rewards risk-taking and creative thinking.
Short-term problems drive and dominate activity.	Focuses on long-term continuous improvement.
Relies on inspection to catch and mistakes.	Improves processes to prevent mistakes.
Gives management full authority.	Trusts and empowers employees.
Tolerates turf battles.	Facilitates and rewards cross functional cooperation.
Makes decisions arbitrarily.	Decisions based on data.
As a negative or indifferent self-image.	Feels and looks like a winner.

ensure that the learning organisation remains educationally, vision oriented and is not subverted into another school-based industrial forum.

OUR BELIEF 23

In the absence of ongoing learning, school staff simply repeat previous practices and therefore, changes remain cosmetic, and student outcome improvements are either fortuitous or at best short-lived.

General comments on chapter

This chapter has bought together some of the thoughts of leading players in the transformation of organisations today. Their views provide a variety of lenses through which the concept of the learning organisation can be better understood and mastered.

Firstly, the term *learning organisation* is an anthropomorphic metaphor that is used to model the development of *professional capital* within a professional-economic collective. Without drawing attention to the link between learning organisations and professional capital, Hargreaves and Fullan (2013) redirect the curious to the human-professional dimension of organisational growth. At the school level we worked to develop of staff's professional capital through high levels of professional learning and developing supported Communities of Practice. As Tucker (2018, p. 171) warned, our job as leaders is to understand how to manage talent to ensure success.

Secondly, there is no doubting that building a learning organisation will require a significant paradigm shift for educators in terms of how they think and interact. Developing a school culture that is based upon the learning organisation paradigm will require a vision that is *grounded* in reality, and a significant element of entrepreneurial activity tempered with a strong element of curiosity on the part of the school executive.

The authors believe that learning organisations and the active promotion of professional capital may be a dynamic vehicle to grow substantial sustainable changes on the path to school improvement.

References

Beck, M. (1989, May–June). Learning organisations – how to create them. *Industrial and Commercial Training*, 21, 21–28.

Garvin, D.A. (1993, July–August). Building the learning organisation. *Harvard Business Review*, 78–91.

Hargreaves, A., & Fullan, M. (2013, June).The power of professional capital. *Journal of Staff Development*, 34(3), 36–39. www.michaelfullan.ca/wp-content/uploads/2013/08/JSD-Power-of-Professional-Capital.pdf

Holly, P., & Southworth, G. (1993). *The developing school*. London: Falmer Press.

Marquardt, M.J. (1996). *Building the learning organisation*. New York: McGraw-Hill.

Pedler, M., Burgoyne, J., & Boydell, T. (1992). *The learning company*. London: McGraw-Hill.

Senge, P.M. (1995). *The fifth discipline: The art and practice of the learning organization.* New York: Doubleday.

Senge, P.M., Kleiner, A., Roberts, C., Ross, R.B., & Smith, B.J. (1999). *The dance of change: The challenges of sustaining momentum in learning organizations.* New York: Doubleday.

Tucker, E. (2018). Secrets to success: Human Capital Management strategy. *Strategic HR Review*, 17(4), 170–175.

Whiteley, A. (1995). *Managing change: A core values approach*. South Melbourne: Macmillan Education Australia.

Robinson, K. (2010). Bring on the learning revolution. *TED Talk*. TED2010. https://www.ted.com/talks/sir_ken_robinson_bring_on_the_learning_revolution/transcript?language=en

11 New school leadership
Jettisoning the comfortable present

As jurisdictions drift away from the centralist conformity based on the economic rationalist influences of the bureaucracy, Neoliberalism and New Public Management (NPM) there is a need to implement the changes from *school systems* to *systems of schools* as one template of schooling does not fit or cater for the needs of differently situated communities of learners.

We are convinced that it remains in the wider communities' best interests to have a viable, responsive, world-class government education system that built on strong local support and ownership. This change we maintained would require strong, diversified and credible school leadership. Bureaucratic models of school administration dominate contemporary school systems, and more entrepreneurial lenses are required when exploring leadership as it applies to a more empowered public-school paradigm.

The wild, non-conformist characteristics of entrepreneurial school leadership

Rules exist to prevent failure and apportion blame, and Silcox's (2003) research showed that the wild dispositions of non-conformity and risk-taking, driven by a moral imperative of getting the best educational outcome for students (often in spite of systemic restrictions), are the key to creative, future leadership. Silcox reported:

> Renewal behaviours were positively related to the personality trait of dominance, being self-confident and motivated by daily challenges and tangible results. These behaviours were negatively associated with the traits of patience and conformity. In addition, these behaviours positively related to proactivity and were strongly associated with willingness to take risks.

Important support for this thesis is offered by Randall White and Sandra Shullman (2010, p. 94), who observed that in new models of leadership the leaders need the skills to be "comfortable navigating ambiguous situations" in complex, competitive organisations. Furthermore, these authors identify three main leadership models: command and control; participative an empowered; and learning (p. 96). Our renewal model fits the third model of learning organisation leadership. Independence, risk-taking and tolerance of ambiguity are strong contextual requirements for these principals to operate well, and they cannot exist in schools with supervisors micro-managing school operations.

Overlapping the Independent Public Schools and Charter schools movements, attempts to realign schools and school leadership with the changing world has been a growing public mistrust of internal "self-assessments", which have the contaminated validity of all internal investigations. For example, in Australia the AITSL Professional Standards for Principals (2015), a government-initiated reform, is a simple, in-house example of what middle-class people associated with the education industry think that "good" principals should be and do. Unfortunately, there is some disconnect with this level of discussion or assessment, which is not seen as being central in the thinking to both public and private school board members.

The only data that counts in the eyes of the public these days are the independent, external measures such as national and state testing and the various school 'League Tables' that appear annually in the media. Clearly, there is a growing mis-match between what educators and the general public think are the important indicators of school and principal effectiveness. The school boards are not inherently interested in **the how** principals get their school to perform, they are interested in **the what** of the measures of success. Such is the impact of these external measures that globally in the case of public schools in particular where there are extant enrolment boundaries there is growing evidence that parents try to purchase houses in the boundaries of the higher performing schools.

The world of school evaluation has also undertaken a seismic shift in recent years (see Table 11.1 below) and if the current trends continue in the future it would appear that only "hard" data will count and assuage the outcome expectations of the school's client-base. Furthermore, as school boards comprise a mix of members, some that come from industries outside education, they may have different views of what in fact counts as data, and success.

OUR BELIEF 24

> An empowered school is one in which individuals have the knowledge, skill, desire and opportunity to personally succeed in a way that leads to improved student outcome success.

In is inevitable that the future Independent School leadership models will be multileveled with each school leader responding in different ways, in different circumstances, to different levels of accountability.

138 New school leadership

Table 11.1 The phases of development of independent schools

	Traditional schools	Moving towards independent status	Independent
Macro control	System/Departmental	Mixed evolving	School board
Principal Performance Management	Directors/ Superintendents Education Secretariat (Hierarchical)	Mixed Evolving	School Board/ Employment agencies
School Accountability	Directors/ Superintendents to CEO / Director General	Evolving	School board to external body representing Legislative responsibility
Principals ability to work independently of external supervision	Weak	Developing	An essential requirement
Workforce Planning	Central bureaucracy Driven	Evolving	School principal
Sustainability	Centralised template of schooling	Evolving	School board and principal
Strategic Planning and target setting	Principal to line manager	Developing	Principal to school board
School review	Principal to line manager	Developing	School board and principal self-review of school to external body representing Legislative responsibility

Formal performance management of the principal

We believe that a principal's performance management should be seen as a continuous process of reflecting, negotiating, developing, reviewing and making decisions about performance in achieving mutually agreed upon organisational goals. Effective management of a principal's performance by the school board, a board nominee or line manager is one approach employed systemically to improve educational outcomes for students. However, in order to achieve the most benefit from the process initially it must be made clear to the principal involved what are the required outcomes that are being sought, when they are to be met, and how they are to be delivered.

We know that it is the quality of a principal's leadership that can make a significant difference to what is achieved by a school in terms of student and staff learning and teaching outcomes, and then how the school is subsequently viewed and judged by others. However, the success of principal performance management as an activity is itself very dependent on the quality of the relationships that he or she has with key stakeholders involved in the processes, and the credibility of the persons involved, particularly in understanding the role expectations. Consequently, these relationships will need to be underpinned by a sense of openness, providing opportunities to recognise and celebrate achievement along with a willingness on the part of the principal to demonstrate their accountability.

An effective performance management process allows for the provision of informed and sensitive feedback to the principal on performance and, if done well, it also provides an ideal opportunity for them to reflect on, consolidate, plan and review their overall work performance. From our experience principals have generally adopted a responsible attitude to their performance management taking the opportunity provided to demonstrate and be accountable for their performance in relation to the implementation of negotiated goals. Furthermore, we maintain that performance management needs to be a collaborative venture that encourages and supports ongoing principal leadership development and allow individuals to take responsibility for their own performance.

Ideally then, a performance management review for the school principal would therefore need to encompass:

- A clear understanding of the board's expectations (and an articulation of key performance indicators) for the principal against which they will be audited.
- An evaluation of the principal's contribution to the school's strategic objectives as articulated in school planning documentation (value-adding).
- An indicator of desired student learning and development outcome targets for the principal to aspire to attain.
- An evaluation of the principal's achievements against pre-determined systemic/Board derived and agreed upon professional standards.

From this contractual statement, the key performance indicators (KPIs) which are negotiated, then become the yardstick by which a principal's effectiveness will be measured.

So, what is different, and how should we respond to this new paradigm of school leader's performances?

First and foremost, while school boards rarely contain education experts per se, there is a developing realisation among its members of their increasing role and influence in setting school plan targets and articulating desired outcomes both aspirational and realistic. Based on a required, thorough, self-review process and student performance data, Board members are able to establish and endorse the strategic direction of school's learning and teaching programme. The school principal, while remaining the pedagogic leader in the school now reports to the school board on issues of student learning, school performance efficacy and resource allocation and usage.

Secondly, with school boards assuming a greater role in principal selection the traditional bureaucratic model of school administration and its associated role parameters of the position of school principal are now evolving to a more entrepreneurial and locally responsive perspective of school leadership. Consequently, the school principal in the independent model does not fit into an educational hierarchy that describes the bureaucratic model of school administration of the past. In this new paradigm of schooling the principal develops a relationship with the school board that is different to that which was had perhaps with directors and superintendents or line managers, and it is more akin to the role of CEO of a company. Finance and student performance outcomes become the main drivers of conversation in this new relationship.

Thirdly, the potential dissonance between the school and system's interests no longer exists with the school's leadership responding to local board expectations and resource constraints. An education department or district in such a scenario relinquishes much of its macro management of a school's learning and teaching endeavour and, therefore, becomes more of a support and resource avenue for the school boards.

Fourthly, by separating the resourcing from the accountability of schools, opportunities are provided to external agencies to examine and report on a school's effectiveness, efficiency and efficacy in meeting established targets and agreed student performance outcomes. This enables more realistic comparisons of school performance and leadership to be presented in the public arena

Fifthly, the principal takes a much more significant role in conjunction with the school board in areas associated with succession planning and ongoing sustainability through target setting, workforce planning and resourcing. This involves a greater strategic and coordinated approach to educational developments and planning in the school.

As previously indicated a pedagogic focus to the change agenda is consistently evident in schools where curriculum and cultural renewal is an ongoing endeavour. Collaborative cultures in those schools undergoing renewal are seen to evolve through principals adopting an approach that has them initiating changes within the school environment that challenge the status quo, and as staff gain in confidence with the changes, the desired collaboration ensures.

As the principal of a primary school indicated:

> I realised that I could not bring about a renewal in learning and teaching by myself.
> I had to engage staff as they were at the coalface and it is there that the pedagogical changes had to occur. I used every occasion to provide learning opportunities for staff and the community to gain an understanding of best practice scenarios and to work collaboratively on classroom activities.

Once the seeds of renewal were planted it was then a matter of engaging in conversation with staff and community about what was happening and how the changes would have a positive impact on student learning outcomes.

A perceived danger is that the principal, in articulating a vision for school renewal, will focus on doing what is already being done in terms of learning and teaching practice, although perhaps with an eye to fine-tuning and continuous improvement of what already exists.

Building capacity for achieving effective implementation of a school renewal agenda, for achieving desired change, however, might require that principals do some quite different things equally as well, particularly in terms of introducing changes in the way to make staff think about their teaching, and build shared ownership in the process. It must be recognised by principals that, ultimately, for the renewal agenda to be embodied as part of the school's beliefs about learning and teaching, staff and community commitment and participation are seen as prerequisites.

OUR BELIEF 25

> Empowerment within a school context is a process of enabling staff to adopt new desired pedagogic behaviours that further their individual aspirations and those of the school in general.

We maintain that as the desired culture of trust evolves through implementation of the change agenda, staff participation will increase and resistance will be reduced. And further, that by renewing the school with an emphasis on the development of a collaborative culture among teachers it is possible for the principal to positively alter the dynamics of individualism and balkanisation that may have been previously in evidence in their schools.

Finally, professional learning for the principal becomes the prime responsibility of the school leader. This will no longer be determined externally for the individual but will be more reliant upon a realistic personal self-review and evaluation of performance in the role and those expectations associated with it.

Typically, standards established at system, district or department levels for school leadership, as currently presented, tend to be colourful, clichéd example of what may have been expected of principals in the past where their schools remained under more of centralist, hierarchical control. However, the world of school leadership as we are indicating has undergone significant transformational changes, particularly in respect to school governance, and these principal leadership standards, as presented, are seen as no longer being truly reflective of the principal's role that has evolved in the new paradigm of school leadership.

Most principals will recognise that the standards have existed in a reality of answering to a school board's set key performance indicators. However, for the majority of school principals, the new school board reality is slowly arriving as the more centralised system controls fall away.

Concluding remarks on chapter

A good school is one blessed with credible professional educators in both teaching and leadership roles across it. Ideally, we don't want our schools to be just good schools; we want them to be great schools. For this to occur the principal needs to engage with the community to ensure that it is meaningfully integrated into the life of a school. When there is synchronicity between the community and the school with its goals and aspirations, only then can true excellence be fostered. Within a school it should always been an aim of leadership to develop a purposeful community, one with the collective efficacy and capability to develop and use available assets, both intellectual and resource based to accomplish excellence in student outcome attainment.

To become the great school to which every school staff should aspire there is a need to harness this collective community efficacy through the articulation of a vision of great possibilities. To this extent among the school's fundamental aims must be the development a sense of community pride in it and what it is achieving in terms of student outcomes.

Pride is the foundation of excellence. Each time that a school communicates with its community, using the opportunity to celebrate and to build pride in what is being achieved, it is in fact developing pride within the community. Therefore, it is important that the perspective a principal has of the community the school serves and the readiness to engage in debate, reflection and to progress, the *can-do* attitude that is part and parcel of the learning and teaching culture to which the school aspires will ensue that the held perceptions of reality are both shared and grounded. When engaging the community in partnerships, the importance of having the consistent message reinforced gives credibility to the school's endeavours.

References

Australian Institute for Teaching and School Leadership (2015). Australian professional standard for principals. Retrieved from www.aitsl.edu.au/australian-professional-standard-for-principals

Silcox, S.B. (2003). An investigation of the roles of school principals in leading school renewal in a Western Australian school district (Doctoral thesis). Curtin University, Western Australia.

White, R.P., & Shullman, L.S. (2010). Acceptance of uncertainty as an indicator of effective leadership. *Consulting Psychology Journal: Practice and Research*, 62(2), 94–104.

Wittmann, E. (2006, April–June). Reducing school administration to a technicality? Philosophical reflections of senior German school administrators in the context of New Public Management-based vocational school reform. *International Journal of Leadership in Education*, 9(2), 111–128.

12 Value-adding and student voice

The commercial world is inclined to see *value-adding* as stages by which value is added to an intended outcome or product in a *value chain*, commencing at the raw materials stage and finishing at the point of acceptance according to market demand.

For schools, the metaphor of a value chain asks important questions about the educational, social and intellectual capital that a child brings on entry to the schooling experience (the raw material) and the extent to which the school has designed the experience as an authentic response to the contemporary societal, political and economic contexts (the market demand). In the real world of school education, as opposed to how education is perceived within the corporate metaphor, the relative values to be found in the raw material and their connection to outcomes at the end of the value chain, cannot be asserted as paradigmatic; nor can the relationships between process and product always be regarded as quantitative or behavioural.

At its most elemental point, what is considered to be of value in the value chain of schooling is subject to the vagaries of certain debates involving the teaching profession, government policy makers and ever shifting community points of view. Parents may well have genuine aspirations for their child, but finding the school within the marketplace which will realise those aspirations through the character of its perceived or reputed value-adding process, is highly problematic because defining or measuring the value-adding process claimed by the school might be actually elusive or by trying to anticipate market demand, actually platitudinous.

Despite all this, however, the various professional associations have supported the pursuit of a valid instrument for measuring value-adding. It believed then that measuring value-adding would empower teachers by providing procedures which enable the gathering of information about the performance of their students and programmes in a range of agreed areas. If this data were validated and aggregated, school leaders could then be provided with reliable information about the performance of their students using measures that show the extent to which the school has added quality to the educational outcomes of its students. This would enable schools to build on their strengths and overcome perceived identified weaknesses. It could well re-describe what has been long argued, if somewhat vaguely, about how we could recognise a *successful school*. That is, one that adds value optimally to the educational and social raw material of its pupils' capabilities on entry.

OUR BELIEF 26

> When school leaders put the priority on adding value to the schools' learning and teaching culture improved student achievement outcomes follow.

In more recent times a general consensus about the relevance of value-adding as a criterion for understanding school effectiveness is developing. A quick examination of Internet sites via a Google search term such as "value adding schools" will indicate that the concept is strongly endorsed within the professional literature but with apparently little explanation of methodology or techniques of measurement. Not unexpectedly, sites describing the context in the commercial business world when considering value-adding far outnumber that of the world of schools.

In schools, notwithstanding the paucity of empirical data, the key issue appears to be to develop an agreed set of indicators and benchmarks for measuring the character of the student experience at certain sequential stages until they exit the school. This data, when collected in a non-intrusive and sensitive manner would consequently provide a means for a school to know how individual students, teachers, schools and indeed education systems are performing. The extent to which value-adding for an individual student, in terms of growth in academic and non-academic domains, could be attributed to the actions and quality of the learning and teaching approaches of a school was the impetus behind a four-year school-based research project undertaken in 2009–2012 (Silcox, 2012). The study findings contended that much of the data for measuring value-adding needs to come directly from students and how they describe their personal schooling experiences. The student is after all, a key stakeholder in the process.

Additionally, value-adding recognises that students begin at different stages along a developmental progression scale. Progress is therefore measured by establishing base line data and then measuring the difference in performance over time. Consequently, value-adding ideally should be an ongoing longitudinal study capable of detecting transformation in the student. This longitudinal research validated just how valuable it is also to have qualitative data to support student outcomes information and hence to give a balanced scorecard in respect to a school's overall performance.

Much of the data collected in schools is data collected about the student through the auspice of instruments and assessment rubrics that are applied to them to obtain a quantitative score (SAT test scores, ATAR, etc.). Quantitative benchmark information is valuable to a point as it can be used to indicate progress along a scale of improvement with the focus on attainment in absolute scores. Judgements about student improvement may be verified through the use of a number of measures in the same domain (i.e. mathematics, literacy) with no one measure being totally adequate.

Measuring value-added

Bennett (2001) indicated that as easy as it is to state assessment of value-added, it is difficult to undertake because of a variety of considerations. Inherent in these considerations is the additional difficulty of making comparisons between schools within any device for measuring value-adding. They included the facts that:

- Value has many dimensions and as a school is not trying to develop a single capability in students but more an array of capabilities, any measure must therefore accommodate these different dimensions of value.
- Schools are all different (one template does not fit all situations) and consequently they do not all seek to add the same kind of value to a students' development.
- Value-added needs to be assessed against a school's identified operations as articulated in its vision and purpose statements. Any attempt to rank schools along a single values continuum is therefore flawed.
- The impact effect of a school's education may take many years to unfold and therefore it may require a long-term longitudinal study to ascertain.
- Measurement of value-added is complex and expensive in terms of both time and resources.

While it is recognised that a value-added measurement approach is the best way to assess student learning at a system level, there is not a similar commitment to developing reliable measures of the most important dimensions of a school education. Quantitative measures (league tables, comparative test score data, etc.) can conceal the nature of the qualitative transformation that a school fashions in its students.

The more recent new emphasis on quantitative performance data of the form of system sponsored literacy and numeracy testing and, tertiary entrance exam results, to hold schools accountable gives rise to concerns that schools cannot be judged fairly in the absence of supporting qualitative value-added data as well. Qualitative data has allowed for the exploration of the existence and interplay between two factors; the attitude of the community of learners which the school caters for, the beliefs about learning and teaching (and when this at an optimum) held by staff and, the ongoing relationships between persons in the school, its learning and teaching culture.

OUR BELIEF 27

> Value can be added to a school in different ways, such as through changes to pedagogy, the learning environment and relationships with and between stakeholders.

146 *Value-adding and student voice*

The role of schools is to ensure that learners fully participate in and contribute to the learning process in such a way that they become responsible for creating and evaluating the outcomes attained. That is, they are both at the centre of the process by which their learning is evaluated while also being at the centre of the learning process itself as it unfolds. Student voice, therefore, is the critical component of any amalgam or formula that purports to describe value-adding.

Assumptions underpinning value-adding in an educational context

We argue that meaningful comparisons between schools cannot be made if the factors that constitute the idiosyncratic, holistic experience of each of the schools are discounted.

A site-specific procedure, as opposed to a systemic model, for measuring value-adding has certain fundamental assumptions supporting it and which need to be identified within the context of the school:

- That the school will have a complete statement of aims and objectives or school purpose, from which it will be possible to deconstruct its precise expectations of what it seeks to achieve for each of its students.
- That objective assessment systems will be in place in the school through which it is possible to chart a student's academic achievement record from entry to exit.
- That the hopes and expectations of each of its students can be collected as qualitative data at certain stages of the student's school journey but only as they are consistent with the school's statements of purpose.
- That each student's goals and aspirations during a school career will shift because of the impact of maturation, peer socialisation and evolving student and parental priorities.
- That qualitative and quantitative measurement will be utilised in data collection for value-adding. One will be seen to complement the other not to replace it or be mutually exclusive to it.
- That students will enter the school with individual levels of social, educational and intellectual capital and any attempt to understand those levels will need to be done at the start of the school experience.
- That ongoing professional development of teachers will be necessary both in terms of data collection and shaping constructive responses to the data. The professional legitimacy of teacher prediction will be endorsed and reflected in the model.
- That the school sees its exit procedures as having a direct relationship to its commitment to maintain high standards of pedagogy and assessment. In terms of school renewal, value-adding is a formative assessment exercise for the school rather than an exercise in marketing.

At its core, the definition of value-added applied in this book is the growth that students achieve (in respect to knowledge, skills and other attributes) as a result of their experience in their school. It is a measure of the extent to which the educational experience has enhanced both their academic and affective development.

Research tells us that successful, effective schools share a number of key identifiable attributes that includes strong, effective leadership, a common vision with learning the highest priority, teachers who engage in informed, successful practices, effective and transparent accountability processes, and parent involvement.

The significant questions asked when evaluating a school's value-adding would consequently entail:

- What is the perceived impact that the school; and in particular the quality that pedagogy has on the engagement and learning outcomes of students?
- Is a school a successful learning community where staff are valued, leadership is evident and student outcomes are maximised?

OUR BELIEF 28

> Leadership within a school that is predicated on value-adding can best be understood as an amalgam between a value creation mindset and leadership intent with behaviours that are necessary to translate that mindset into quality learning and teaching endeavours.

A school as a community of educators will recognise that learning is not a defined piece of content that can be taught, but rather it is a state of mind, a value that is modelled in everyday pedagogy by teachers. Strong relationships underpin effective teaching and give substance to the rhetoric of lifelong learning. Teachers model lifelong learning through their own actions and behaviours. The values and attitudes held by a learning community collectively are transmitted to students through each teacher's demonstrated commitment and meaningful engagement with the learning process.

General comments on chapter

By far the most clearly articulated proposition is the importance that student and teacher relationships play in the learning and teaching endeavour. In each year of the longitudinal study referred to above students were keen to indicate through their feedback that the relationship they had with their teachers was a key factor in their engagement with the curriculum and the life of the school in general. This correlated well with feedback gained from interviews with parents as well. Further, a number of qualities exhibited by teachers perceived as being of excellent value could be readily distilled from the research. Specifically, the research identified that:

- Effective teachers were relationship builders and excellent communicators. Students appreciated those staff who took an interest in them at a personal

level and who were able to articulate at a whole of classroom level behavioural boundaries. These teachers exhibited curriculum credibility, compassion and were identified as being relaxed in their teaching while at the same time in control of their learning environment and classroom processes. It was evident that teachers who exhibited friendship and understanding tinged with a sense of humour were respected by students.
- Teachers who held high expectations for their students and were able to engage them appropriately in their respective learning processes were those seen to employ a range of pedagogies in their classroom. Such teachers were identified as passionate about their teaching, highly motivated and self-reflective.
- Teachers who were accepting of student diversity, in particular their familial backgrounds, aspirations and interests, were in return highly respected and acknowledged by students.
- The importance of executive and teacher leadership in the school and the impact that this has on morale and the health of the overall learning.

The work of John Hattie involving meta-analyses of influences on student learning in a global research context showed the significant impact of effective pedagogic practices on student learning. For the first time classroom teachers had access to an evidenced based statistical process that had the capability of demonstrating the size of performance improvement. However, Tom Guskey (2019, p. 273) warned,

> Nearly every discussion about educational improvement today refers to "effect-sizes." Education organizations compare effect sizes in planning professional learning programs. District and school leaders consider effect sizes when selecting the strategies to include in school improvement initiatives. Even classroom teachers evaluate effect sizes in deciding what practices will be most effective in helping their students learn.

John Hattie (2013) states that an effect size of 0.4 approximates to a one-year gain, which is often interpreted as a measure of value-adding.

References

Bennett, D. (2001). *The school of the future: Key issues for school leaders.* Nottingham, UK: National College for School Leadership. www.ncsl.org.uk/mediastore/image2/kpool-evidence-bennett.pdf

Hattie, J. (2013). *Visible learning: A synthesis of over 800 meta-analyses relating to achievement.* Thousand Oaks, CA: Corwin.

Guskey, T.R. (2019). Interpreting average effect sizes: Never a centre without a spread. *NASSP Bulletin*, 103(4), 273–280.

Silcox, S.B. (2012). *The Ballajura Community College value adding project: A report on a four year value adding assessment study 2009–2012.* Perth, Western Australia: Swan Print.

13 Profiling school leaders' leadership standards

The identification and profiling of the standards of school leadership were initially developed in the work of Leithwood and Montgomery (1986) and later by Begley (1990) and then by Begley and Murray (1993). However, the recent prominence of school renewal as a particular type of educational change provides us with an appropriate context to explore and analyse school leader leadership behaviours and, subsequently, their overall willingness to engage in school renewal processes.

The profile instrument developed by Leithwood and Montgomery (1986) used a technique that essentially was an application of a curriculum analysis procedure employed at the time to the descriptive tasks that a school leader performs in the course of their leadership of a school. The profiling instrument they used actually evolved from the effective school research of the time, along with associated instructional leadership practices. Leithwood and Montgomery (1986) confirmed in their framework on school leader profiles the traits identified earlier by DeCharms (1968) as key dimensions of school leadership. They supported the proposition that more effective school leaders derived substantial personal enjoyment from issue discovery and problem-solving activities and, partly as a consequence of this, were more proactive in dealing with school related problems.

In the school context, we have discussed how effective school leader behaviour is influenced by their personal role efficacy, the belief in their capacity to perform the roles and responsibilities associated with the leadership position they hold. We have then gone on to advocate the view that improving school leader pedagogic leadership effectiveness will ultimately contribute to an improvement in overall school effectiveness, and improved student learning outcomes. Therefore, improving school leader effectiveness can be viewed as one of many possible inter-dependent strategies within a comprehensive framework for planned and managed change within schools. Those school leaders who choose to be more actively involved with the school's pedagogy appear to have a greater, more significant impact on student learning outcome attainment and the achievement of the school's vision. This predisposition to action and involvement in managing school change processes both of a renewal and programme dimension, are identified as desirable behaviours on the part of the school leader.

The Principal Profile, as designed by Leithwood and Montgomery (1986), was defined as a multidimensional, multilevel description of beliefs, intentions and actions which were broadly referred to as principal behaviours. Their profile defined those dimensions of principal behaviour considered critical in determining a principal's impact on the school's learning and teaching culture. They employed a rubric which outlined alternative patterns of behaviour within these dimensions, ordered from least to most effective.

Of importance in profiling school leader behaviours is the significance that stakeholder perception of the school leader's leadership role has in relation to such things as the way innovation and vision are implemented across the school; also, how change processes are managed. It is recognised that judgements about a principal's effectiveness in respect to these points depend very much on which outcomes are indeed valued the most within the school community.

Begley's (1990) profile work which built on the Leithwood and Montgomery material incorporated implicit growth and development strands in its composition. These strands were developed in a dichotomous format which included leadership tendencies toward reactive responses as opposed to proactive ones, and from rigid adherence to fixed procedures to procedural flexibility. The major value of this later profile development lay in its identification and description of the characteristics of leadership achievement and therefore, it is not perceived as a deficit model which describe the shortcomings of a failing school leader.

OUR BELIEF 29

> The selection of the right people for school leadership positions is of critical importance as leaders have such a significant impact on overall teacher effectiveness and in turn the overall organisation's performance and success.

A set of decisions, which represent categories of school leader action most likely to be critical to the achievement of an effective school scenario are identified in the Principal Profile Questionnaire that Begley and Murray (1993) developed which he refers to as dimensions of behaviour. The dimensions of behaviour as identified in the Begley Profile are the:

- self-dimension (which refers to the personal knowledge, skills and disposition that the school leader brings to the leadership role);
- process dimension (which refers to sets of school leader behaviours or actions that impacted on the educational growth of the school community); and
- outcome dimension (which links specific school leader actions that are considered effective (high order) to particular educational outcomes (products)).

Each of these dimensions, then, is differentiated further into sub-dimensions, each representing key school leader behaviours as shown in Table 13.1.

Within each sub-dimension of the Leadership Profile alternative forms of school leader behaviour are described. These alternatives, ordered in terms of effective school leader practice, are referred to as stages in line with the schema adopted by Leithwood and Montgomery (1986). For example, as shown in Table 13.2, the school leader as a visionary had the following staged development within the Principal's Profile.

The Profile represents a two-dimensional matrix arrangement that describes growth in school leader behaviour within selected dimensions from relatively less effective (non-implementation) to more effective and efficacious behaviours (full-implementation).

Many of the sub-dimensions identified in the Begley (1990) profiles are also recognisable in the Drake Predictive Profiling Instrument (2001) we used to categorise behaviour traits of a large school leader sample cohort. The Drake Predictive Profiling Instrument sub-dimensions included similar categories of

Table 13.1 Principal Profile sub-dimension behaviours (Begley & Murray, 1993)

- Visionary
- Monitor
- Effective communicator
- Change agent
- Problem solver
- Goal setter
- Team builder
- Programme evaluator
- Expectation holder
- Staff developer
- Human resource manager
- Community facilitator
- Time manager
- Financial resource manager
- Cultural leader
- Acknowledger of achievement

Table 13.2 The Administrator as a Visionary Leader (Principal's Profile, Begley, 1990)

Pursues a personal view.	Imparts a personal vision of school purpose.	Pursues a community vision of school purpose.	Imparts a community vision and commitment to the school.

behaviours as identified in the profile instrument of Begley (see Table 13.3) and was influenced by the work of both Goleman (1998) and Lanyon (1999). These authors identified six leadership styles or behaviour groups in respect to the emotional intelligence of leadership. They were represented as:

- Coercive, where the leader demands compliance. (Do what I tell you.)
- Authoritative, where the leader mobilises people towards a vision. (Come with me.)
- Affiliative, where the leader creates harmony and builds emotional bonds. (People come first.)
- Democratic, where the leader forges consensus through participation. (What did you think?)
- Pacesetting, where the leader sets high standards for performance. (Do as I did, now.)
- Coaching, where the leader develops people for the future. (Try this.)
(Goleman, 1998, pp. 82–83)

Goleman (1998) argued that two of the six styles negatively affect organisational climate and, in turn, the performance and commitment of subordinates.

Table 13.3 Profile Dimensions (Drake Predictive Profiling Instrument, 2001)

Business and individual skills profile:
- Vision
- Change agent
- Flexibility
- Management of routines
- Preparation
- Teamwork profile
- Relationship building
- People focus
- Conflict management
- Professional and technical profile
- Reporting
- Issue discovery
- Procedures
- Management and coaching considerations
- Coaching style
- Team style
- Job mobility
- Promotion adaptation

These were the coercive style and the pacesetting style. All four of the other leadership styles have a significantly positive impact on an organisations climate and overall performance. Underpinning the authoritative, affiliative, democratic and coaching styles is high emotional intelligence. Low emotional intelligence is seen as the hallmark of coercive and pacesetting leaders.

Goleman (1998) maintained that a group of characteristics based on personality and behaviour play an important role in job success, especially at the higher levels of organisational leadership. Goleman's (1998, pp. 82–83) emotional competency characteristics are collectively termed Emotional Intelligence. The component aspects of Goleman's Emotional intelligence thesis are outlined in Table 13.4.

OUR BELIEF 30

Improving emotional intelligence in the school workplace can have a direct and positive impact on:
- The effectiveness of the school's leadership and management
- Staff morale and retention
- Communications and relationship building
- Client satisfaction and student learning outcomes.

Fullan (2001) supported the propositions of Goleman (1998) by reworking his leadership behaviour domains associated with Emotional Intelligence under the two headings of personal and social competence as shown in Table 13.5. Here it is noted that there is an important link between the concept of

Table 13.4 The Components of Emotional Intelligence (Adapted from Lanyon & Goodstein, 1998)

Dimension	Description
Personal Insight	The capacity to accurately recognise and understand one's own emotions as they occur and to base personal self-confidence on an accurate assessment of one's own abilities. (Accurate self-assessment is a trait clearly identified in studies by Bandura (1997) relating to efficacious behaviours).
Self-Discipline	The capacity to delay gratification when pursuing goals, to speak carefully and to control negative impulses.
Drive	The capacity to pursue goals energetically, to relentlessly seek self-improvement and to persevere despite obstacles or disappointments.
Interpersonal Insight	The capacity to understand the emotions of others, to adjust one's own style to interact well with others and to empathise with alternative perspectives.
Social Agility	The capacity to be at ease in almost any social situation, to prevent or resolve conflict, to cultivate rapport and build lasting relationships.

Table 13.5 Fullan Leadership Behaviour Domains (Fullan, 2001)

Personal competence:

- Self-awareness (knowing one's internal state preferences, resources and intuitions)
- Self-regulation (managing one's internal states, impulses and resources)
- Social competence
- Motivation (emotional tendencies that guide or facilitate reaching goals)
- Empathy (awareness of others' feelings, needs and concerns)
- Social skills (adeptness at including desirable responses from others)
- In a manner similar to Goleman, Stein and Book (2000) named five realms of emotional intelligence:
- Intrapersonal (self-awareness, actualisation, independence and self-regard)
- Interpersonal (empathy, social responsibility)
- Adaptability (problem-solving, flexibility)
- Stress management (stress, tolerance, impulse control)
- General mood (happiness, optimism)

self-esteem and performance within the work environment, particularly where it was seen to relate to a sense of power, competency, autonomy and influence; which relate to the Goleman (1998) dimensions of personal insight, drive and self-discipline.

Effective leaders accepted and readily admitted their personal responsibility for success or failure and actively seek feedback on their performance by encouraging their staff to give their perspective on certain issues while openly soliciting recommendations for programme or policy improvement. They are leaders who exhibit motivation towards risk-taking and goal-setting behaviours.

Earlier we identified efficacious school leaders as being those most predisposed to action particularly in response to initiating a change agenda in their school, as opposed to those who would rather wait for something to happen or for a situation to develop. Likewise, Silcox (2003) confirmed this as "an individual's disposition toward proactive behaviour" (represented diagrammatically as Figure 13.1).

Self-assessment issues in profiling leadership behaviours

Accurate self-assessment is identified as a competency in which an individual has a more realistic and grounded view of themselves. These individuals see their strengths and weaknesses and know their limitations, a characteristic that Bray et al. (1974) termed self-objectivity in his research on management competencies. Our premise is that school leaders who possess accurate self-assessment and high leadership efficacy behave in certain ways in their schools. They are able to describe and evaluate the effectiveness of their own performance in particular situations with considerable accuracy. Their

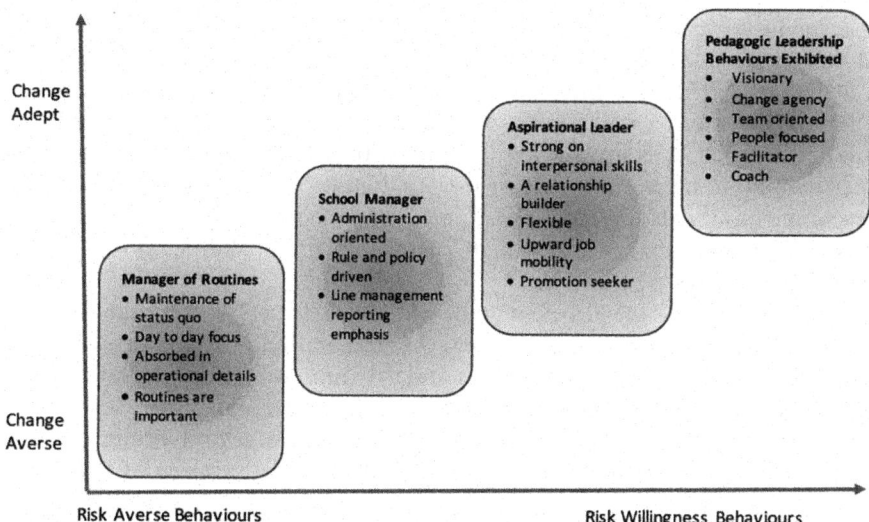

Figure 13.1 Principal leadership styles and change and risk willingness.

strengths are not aggrandised or overestimated, they are discussed in the context of admitted personal limitations or weaknesses. It follows, therefore, that school leader with accurate self-assessment exhibit behaviours that have a positive correlation between their accurate self-assessment and their self-efficacy beliefs.

It is desirable for school leaders to have a realistic view of their strengths and limitations (accurate self-assessment); particularly when engaging and initiating school change related activities. Without this realistic view school staff and the community in general would see the school leader as a threat to their integrity, or at best as a marginal player. Stakeholder responsiveness to the school leader's approach to school leadership can severely limit the school leader's ability to influence and direct the sense of vision within the school community context and, hence, diminish significantly their ability to engage and oversee a whole-of-school change orientation. At the same time, it is not easy for school leaders to get a realistic view of their own strengths and limitations without collaborative relationships in which there is honest and realistic interpersonal communication.

OUR BELIEF 31

> Effective school leaders have the skills to manage their personal emotions and moods, and to influence the emotions and moods of other people to attain the best possible educational outcomes.

Silcox (2003) established a link between leaders' accurate self-assessment of their personal effectiveness within a school as being intricately linked to their overall organisational effectiveness. School leaders who possess accurate self-assessment behave in certain ways and are able to describe and evaluate the effectiveness of their performance in particular situations. In a similar vein, Bray et al. (1974) identified accurate self-assessment as a competency in which people have a realistic or grounded view of themselves and their capabilities. Further, it is argued that leaders with accurate self-assessment identified, sought help and undertook activities (networking, professional development, mentoring, coaching, etc.) to remedy their perceived weaknesses. The accurate self-assessment of one's own capabilities is seen to be related to effective performance.

The rewrite of the Professional Standards for Educational Leaders (National Policy Board for Education Administration, 2015) gave American school leaders a comprehensive 10-standard framework for measuring their performances. This metric was supported by the development of key indicators that expanded each standard, which then gave school leaders a tight description of what their job entailed, according to the creators of PSEL.

Profiling professional growth using the Professional Standards for Educational Leaders (PSEL)

What is really useful to school-based leaders is a personal exploration of what the standards mean, and then plotting the personal ratings resulting from regular, personal performance reviews. Using a similar process to that used by MacNeill and Silcox (2006), school leaders and aspirant school leaders can create the two axes describing the leadership act (as in Table 13.7).

The challenge then comes with the writing of what Below Standard, At Standard, Above Standard and Excels looks like in schools across the district or system. This exercise is best done with trusted colleagues, and the discussion and brain-storming is excellent professional learning. Remembering that this Professional Profile is *Work-in-Progress* it is important to complete the four levels of performance for all of the standards, and descriptors, as can be seen in Table 13.8.

We found that the creation of the content items was the source of excellent professional discussion, and then when the working model of the Principal Profile was completed each of us used the ratings for self-assessment and professional improvement.

General comments on chapter

In this chapter we have explored the concepts of school leader leadership behaviours, and these have been explored with particular reference to the context of whole-school renewal and change. Particular emphasis has been directed at exploring behaviours associated with a leader's predisposition to engage in school change activities. The impact of a leader's behavioural drive and personal efficacy on the initiation and development of a school renewal

Table 13.6 Dimensions of Pedagogic Profile of Principal Leadership (Silcox & MacNeill, 2007)

Dimensions of pedagogic leadership	Type 1 (capable, hands-on teacher)	Type 2 (Teacher team leadership, hands-on)	Type 3 (Competent manager, hands-on. Teaching and leading)	Type 4 (Effective leader, transitional hands-on to facilitative)	Type 5 (Executive leader, facilitative)
1. Discharges of moral obligations to students and society					
2. Commits to a shared vision and sense of mission					
3. Has expert knowledge about pedagogy and schooling					
4. Leads change					
5. Facilitates the engagement and empowerment of staff					
6. Distributes multiple levels of leadership					
7. Balances administrative roles with pedagogic roles					
8. Creates and shares knowledge					
9. Develops a sense of community					
10. Applies of a re-culturing approach					
11. Gains commitment by expecting high standards					

Table 13.7 The Creation of a Professional Profile using the PSEL Metric (Structure) Part 1

Standard (PSEL)	Descriptors	Below standard	At standard	Above standard	Excels
1. Mission, vision and core values	Mission				
	Vision				
	Core values				

Table 13.8 The creation of a Professional Profile Using the PSEL Metric (Content) Part 2

Standard (PSEL)	Descriptors	Below standard	At standard	Above standard	Excels
1. Mission, vision and core values	1a. Mission statement	Lists the word "Mission".	Mission is "improving students' learning".	Mission has five parts: 1. Are clear. 2. Are specific. (What exactly are students supposed to learn?) 3. Are measurable. (How do we know students have learned?) 4. Provide for failure. (How do we respond when students don't learn?) 5. Future-oriented.	Mission statement has five parts and it was created by the school community.
	1b. Vision	Mentions word "vision" but no demonstrated elaboration.	Discusses vision and future.	Discusses vision and future. Examines what the world will look like when students finish schooling.	Examines what society and work will be in 20 years' time. Changes curriculum to meet those challenges.
	1c. Core Values	No understanding or elaboration of core values.	Lists a set of core values, and shows commitment.	School publicly proclaims its values, and these can be seen in every newsletter.	School staff and students **live** the core values.

agenda and the capacity to effect change in the school's learning environment becomes a self-evident truth. What we like about this process is that it can extend personal introspection beyond the mandated line-management criteria to issues that school leaders feel they need to examine, without showing their cards to observers making external judgements about their performance.

References

Begley, P. (1990). A matrix for principal development (Unpublished manuscript). Centre for Educational Leadership, Edith Cowan University, Faculty of Education, Perth, W.A.

Begley, P., & Murray, P.E. (1993). *School leadership in the NWT: A profile for the 90s.* Yellow Knife, NWT: Department of Education, Culture and Employment (Canada).

Bray, D.W., Campbell, R.J., & Grant, D.G. (1974). *Formative years in business: A long term AT and T study of managerial lives.* New York: John Wiley & Sons.

DeCharms, R. (1968). *Personal causation: The internal affective determinants of behaviour.* San Diego, CA: Academic Press.

Drake International (2001). *Drake P3 behaviour assessment survey.* Drake Predictive Performance Profile, Inc.

Fullan, M. (2001). *Leading in a culture of change.* San Francisco: Jossey-Bass.

Goleman, D. (1998). *Working with emotional intelligence.* New York: Bantam.

Lanyon, R.I. (1999). The Drake P3 Profiling Instrument. Research monograph for the Drake P3 System Communication Survey. Drake Predictive Profiles Inc.

Leithwood, K.A., & Montgomery, D.J. (1986). Obstacles preventing principals from becoming more effective. *Education & Urban Society,* 17(1), 73–88.

MacNeill, N., & Silcox, S.B. (2006). Leading Learning: The essence of successful change in schools. https://www.academia.edu/32156514/2006_Leading_Learning_The_essence_of_successful_change_in_schools

National Policy Board for Education Administration (2015). *Professional standards for educational leaders.* Reston, VA: author.

Silcox, S.B. (2003). An investigation of the roles of school principals in leading school renewal in a Western Australian school district (Unpublished doctoral dissertation). Curtin University, Western Australia.

14 School leaders and psychological resilience and mental health

> You don't have to practice being miserable.
> (Grossman & Christensen, 2004, p. 128)

Education is generally a contested issue fought over in many state and national elections, which means that the public is continually made aware of perceived shortcomings that need fixing by newly elected governments resulting in schools, teachers and school leaders constantly being in the spotlight. As Glickman (1998) rightly argued:

> Once-respected public institutions established to respond to government needs and protect the government trust are today being scorned. One of our most comprehensive institutions – the government school system – is being attacked continuously, with some calling to replace such government schools with privatization. By some strange inverse logic then the term private is now seen as better than government. Downsizing, deregulation and other great efforts to swell the economic efficiency and productivity are now the greater goals for society rather than the healthy growth and development of our citizens. (Glickman, 1998, p. 1)

In a pointed attack, Heather-Jane Robertson in her book, *No More Teachers, No More Books* (1998) stated:

> From a political standpoint, making schools responsible for every societal problem is clearly expedient. Better that schools take the blame than politicians and their friends. And it is so much easier to scapegoat education than to examine economic and political realities.

We acknowledge that education can never not need improving! *Ipso facto*, there will always be something we can do better. The combination of an unrelenting push for improvement in education, accompanied by ever increasing accountability will continue to change the education milieu in which we operate. By way of example, high-stakes testing has generated a number of stressors for school leaders. Hazel (2018), in a Times Education

Supplement, also warned that high-stakes testing and a narrowing of the curriculum had also "contributed to an explosion in pupils' mental ill-health. Student suicide in a now more frequently reported statistic in education".

OUR BELIEF 32

> Public scrutiny of schools and the education enterprise will only increase with time, not decrease.

Lessons on resilience from a military context

Conflict and violence are becoming far more common in our schools, and on occasions schools can look like war zones, and the traumatic events that involve conflict and fear in civilian and military contexts may elicit the symptoms of what is now known as post-traumatic stress disorder (PTSD) in those affected. During the First World War the public became aware of this condition known as shell-shock, battle fatigue, traumatic war neuroses. Probably, as a consequence of PTSD some 266 British soldiers were executed for cowardice; however, they were all posthumously pardoned in 2006.

The catastrophic consequences of the Vietnam War saw PTSD recognised as a psychological condition, and brought into the public domain. Lieutenant Colonel Dave Grossman (1996) observed:

> If we accept that we need an Army, then we have to accept that it has to be as capable of surviving as we can make it. But if society prepares a soldier to overcome his resistance to killing and places him in an environment in which he has to kill, then that society has an obligation to deal forthrightly, intelligently, and morally with the psychological event and its repercussions upon the soldier and society ... this has not happened with the Vietnam veterans. (p. 284)

The factors that exacerbated PTSD in Vietnam veterans were primarily the failure of the home nations to support their troops during the war; the nature of the warfare experiences (Who is the enemy?); the lack of unit support when individuals flew home; the personal attacks on individual service men and women on their return by the violent anti-war elements; and finally, society rewarded those who protested loudest, as many became the next generation of state and national politicians.

What we are now seeing is that PTSD did not disappear with the Vietnam veterans, and nations' involvement in a variety of conflicts since then has continued to generate new PTSD cases, even among elite troops. The American military complex quickly realised that they also had a growing responsibility in terms of occupational health and safety in respect to this issue and they adopted programmes designed to promote psychological resilience in their military. There is an identified huge personal cost to those afflicted by

PTSD. Dao (2012) reported in *The New York Times* that a diagnosis of PTSD could cost the government $1.5m for the term of the soldier's life. Dao's (2012) article goes on to suggest that the American military is going so far as to label some soldiers with "Personality Disorder" to circumvent future PTSD claims.

Martin Seligman, a professor of psychology at the University of Pennsylvania, developed a preventative course of action to ameliorate some depressive behaviours in the civilian population. The American military recognised the potential of Seligman's work and they worked on developing a new programme called "Comprehensive Soldier Fitness: Strong minds, Strong bodies", which addressed physical, emotional, social, family and spiritual training among its troops. A RAND meta-analysis (Meredith et al., 2011) indicated that since 2007 there has been a growing interest in the development of military resilience "... as an effort to shift the culture within the military away from an illness-focussed medical model of care to a model that focuses on psychological health" (pp. 6–7). The aim of Comprehensive Soldier Fitness is "... a long-term strategy that prepares the Army community – including all Soldiers, Family members and Department of the Army (DA) Civilians – not only to survive, but also to thrive in the face of protracted warfare and everyday challenges of Army life".

A major change in Comprehensive Soldier Fitness is that the Non-Commissioned Officers (NCOs) have a strong educative and mentoring role in ensuring each soldier's mental fitness, as they take on the roles of Master Resilience Trainers (MRT). While the training skills are variations and extensions on what good officers and NCOs would already do, the training package gives a research-based approach to enhancing positive thought and extending consequential resilience at squad and family levels.

Secondly, a variation on the overt trauma of military operations is the impact of long-term (40+ days) combat, where operatives can be reduced to a vegetative state.

Thirdly, it would be a mistake to consider PTSD in the dichotomous terms: you either have PTSD or you don't have PTSD. A better conceptual model is to think of PTSD in terms of a continuum, and the early precursors are important signs that carers must watch for, and address.

As life gets tougher for teachers in some situations, we believe that some of the characteristics of battle fatigue, combat exhaustion and PTSD are transferable to the teaching experience.

The lessons for education

Flow is a state of euphoria that can occur when individuals or teams (athletes, swimmers, soldiers, artists, fire fighters or writers) achieve high levels of success in a challenging, defined task. It is interesting that school leaders in tough schools rarely experienced high levels of flow while carrying out their duties, and this becomes problematic when considering their mental health.

Psychological resilience and mental health 163

Flow in its pure state exhibits nine characteristics:

1 Challenge-skills balance
2 Action-awareness merging
3 Clear goals
4 Unambiguous feedback
5 Concentration on the task in hand
6 Sense of control
7 Loss of self-consciousness
8 Transformation of time
9 Autotelic experience. (Jackson and Csikszentmihalyi, 1999, p. 16)

The school leaders from the challenging schools who took part in MacNeill's research (2012) noted that they could never relax from the state of hypervigilance to enter the euphoria experienced by long-distance runners and elite athletes because "You never know what is coming through the door next". The major lesson for school systems and organisations is that the abrasive effects of continued stress on school leaders (and staff) will eventually take a toll. Grossman (1996, p. 44; quoting Swank and Marchand, 1946) explained the effects of combat exhaustion on troops' efficiency over time, as shown in Figure 14.1.

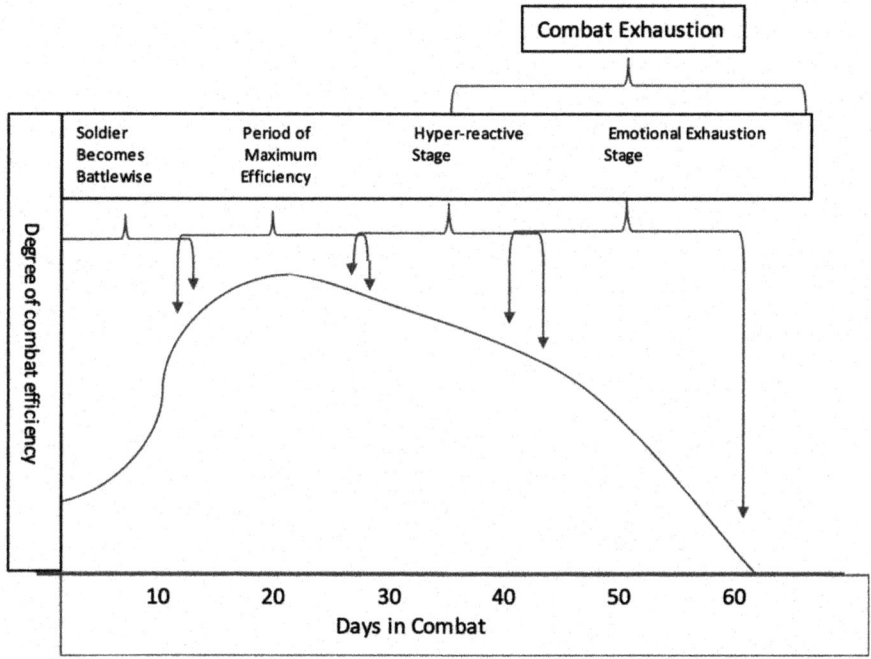

Figure 14.1 Efficiency as a factor of days in combat.

Each educational jurisdiction has psychological support mechanisms available for staff afflicted by trauma. However, an educational equivalent of the Comprehensive Soldier Fitness programme appears to be necessary under an employer's duty of care but also in terms of improving the delivery of a stable educational environment in every classroom. School leaders, like military NCOs, take on the overt role of Master Resilience Trainers (MRTs), which includes a role that is more encompassing than the actual school site. Teachers, paraprofessionals, and school administrators are the intellectual capital of a school, and they need to be managed and supported to enable them to deliver high-quality educational programmes.

OUR BELIEF 33

> School leaders in renewing schools will need to understand that they have a significant role in growing the intellectual and resilience capacity of all staff, including themselves.

In the three-term school years of thirteen- and fourteen-week semesters and terms, it is clear that teachers became tired and less efficient (similar to combat exhaustion), especially during the hotter months. An attempt has been made in some jurisdictions to ameliorate this issue by breaking the school year, equivalent to forty weeks into four terms of ten weeks. It has even been suggested that perhaps a redistribution of the year's teaching load over a different configuration would lessen teacher stress by dividing the forty-week school year into eight terms of five weeks which would then spread the workload more evenly, take out the long summer holidays (children no longer have to help with the summer harvest), and importantly, such an initiative may overcome the phenomenon of *summer forgetting* for students.

Obviously, a new supportive school culture needs to be developed to support those experiencing a large degree of stress. The concept of *group absolution* is an important inoculum in preventing traumatic stress and the social cohesion of staff members in really tough schools is always stronger than in the more genteel schools, and staff support each other through their daily crises.

A secondary school leader remarked:

> I didn't doubt my skills and competence; however, my resiliency has certainly been tested at times. I have a strong belief in my skills and ability to apply them in a variety of contexts and I didn't doubt myself in what I was trying to achieve or why.

Resilience in staff is developed through empowerment at the ground level where staff have some degree of involvement in decisions that affect their teaching. Furthermore, a sense of ownership is evident in schools when its teachers are able to either individually or collectively solve problems that matter to them, and particularly those which have an impact on their classroom teaching activities.

We argue in a similar way that it is important for the management structures of an organisation to not get in the way or retard desired work practices. The Swedish academic Gunnar Berg (2004) described what he called the *invisible contract* that has existed in schools, and this contract culturally enforces the separation of teachers from administrators. However, with recent developments in school pedagogic leadership, Berg concluded "An activity responsibility school leader rooted in the multi-professional school is on the other hand, a suitable professional actor to lead such a process". Within an educational context the primacy of quality learning and teaching needs to be supported by appropriate leadership and school structures that empower teachers as facilitators of student learning and which do not impede practices.

OUR BELIEF 34

> An effective school staff concentrates on their core business: the quality of its learning and teaching programmes.

A concern raised by Fullan and Stiegelbauer (1991) is that micro-management approaches to supervision by a school's leadership can stifle teacher willingness to become more professionally engaged in a learning and teaching culture that is providing empowerment and devolved decision-making. In many respects the micro-management processes mirror some of the controlling and restrictive practices evident in systemically derived policies in respect to school operations and accountability demands on the school leader. That same sense of frustration that is felt when we are micro-managed is felt by teachers as well when school practices and decision-making is disenfranchising.

The problem is further complicated by the paradox that while teachers and their associated pedagogy are the targets of school change (whether renewal or reform) they are also its implementers. We found that a key aspect of the process of engaging staff in reflective practice and pedagogical change is creating a culture that is purposeful and which encourages fellowship by which teachers are empowered through increased access to school decision-making. We maintain that a transformational leadership style encourages such an ethos of engagement among teachers. Such a style is built upon a leadership disposition that values and encourages the fairness, openness, honesty, loyalty and integrity in relationships across the school. Figure 14.2 clearly shows the relationships between school leader credibility, receptiveness to a renewal agenda and school leader resilience. The outcome of a High-High rating is Optimal Efficacy and it describes risk-willing, resilient leadership.

The principles of resilience training are applicable in all uniformed services including the police, prisons, fire and ambulance, and other stressful professions. Post-Traumatic Stress Disorder is a price that families, schools and society should not have to pay.

166 *Psychological resilience and mental health*

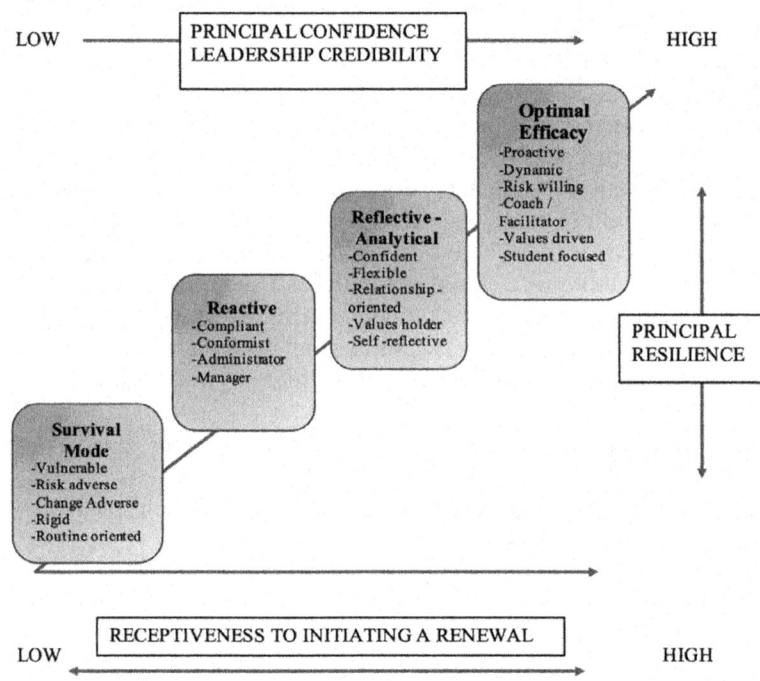

Figure 14.2 Confidence, credibility, resilience and receptiveness to renewal.

Taking the roles of the Resilience Trainers and embedding them into the school leadership teams we believe will bring about a change of direction that most school leaders in tough schools through necessity are already looking to put into place. These changes need to be supplemented by cultural changes to encourage team support. What needs to happen is that the training for the trainers needs to be accompanied by a resilience strengthening program for all school staff. In this case we can learn from the military about surviving in tough environments.

Structural changes to the school year may be worth looking at in terms of spreading the workload. Teaching is becoming a series of pedagogic sprints, and is no longer a series of gentle marathons. Therefore, the concept of shortening of the school terms makes good sense in developing staff resilience. The heavy losses to school staff through stress is not acceptable in terms of a leaderships duty of care, the tragic imperilment of teachers' family lives, and the loss of intellectual and practical capital to our school systems.

School leaders dealing with a range of mental health issues presenting in schools

Many schools have embedded in its ethos and beliefs statement a comment that all students can be nurtured to achieve their best in terms of learning outcomes. The significant challenge for all school leaders has been in forming a learning and teaching environment that does not allow any student to fall through the gaps. The aim, of course, is to ensure that failure is not an option in our classrooms. A school culture that is characterised by the professionalism, endeavour and continued exemplary commitment of staff in meeting the learning needs of all students is indeed a positive and powerful workplace in which to engage.

OUR BELIEF 35

A school leader's mantra should be that failure is not an option.

We have stressed throughout this work that it is the quality of learning and teaching that makes or breaks a school. Teachers who enjoy their teaching are infectious. They are the shot in the arm that inspire both students and their colleagues alike. We know from both personal experience, supported in educational research literature, that quality teachers make a difference to the lives of students and to those with whom they work and interact.

We also recognise that the teaching profession is very demanding, particularly in terms of the high expectations held of the school's staff, and the time demands placed upon teachers by an increasingly time hungry learning community. Furthermore, we recognise that how an individual feels about their role as an educator, their attitude to teaching (the whether the glass is half empty or half full perspective) influences the quality of learning and teaching that occurs in the classroom and therefore in the school as an entity. While altruistically every effort should continue to be made by the school's administration to enhance the learning environment and to recognise and value the contribution that each member of staff makes to the ethos and culture of commitment, we must also be realists, knowing there will be times when frustration, uncertainty and breakdowns in communication may impact upon us all. These times require collective understanding and support. This position is further compounded when the range of mental health issues present and enter the mix.

Increasingly, schools have to deal with a greater spectrum of ever increasing mental health issues, not only from among the student body but often from the teaching and parent body as well. Mental health is a prevalent issue that in more recent times has manifested in a variety of ways both within schools and also in the wider community. For example, many of the mental health parental issues tend to spill over into the school which is seen as a responsive agency that is accessible and understanding; even though not resourced to accommodate the variety of needs identified or the raft of issues that present on a daily basis.

Consistently the school sector is seen to be adversely disadvantaged through the lack of appropriate funding for mental health staff training and student support, often making it extremely difficult for them to cater for often severely alienated and at times an extremely violent strata of the student population. Schools by necessity have become a safety net in terms of dealing with issues associated with aberrant manifest mental health behaviours.

OUR BELIEF 36

Schools will increasingly have to risk-manage aberrant mental health issues.

Alarming statistics that have been generated in relation to the Adverse Childhood Experience research reveal the shocking number of students affected by trauma. Awareness of childhood trauma is often discussed by school staff who are concerned about the impact on their students. In 1998, Felitti et al. had coined the term *Adverse Childhood Experiences* (ACE) to describe these traumatic experiences traumatised children had faced. Furthermore, these authors found that "(b)ecause adverse childhood experiences are common and they have strong long-term associations with adult health risk behaviours, health status, and diseases, increased attention to primary, secondary, and tertiary prevention strategies is needed" (p. 254).

To help quantify the ACE data Felitti et al. (1998) developed the ACE survey and the data for Adverse Childhood Experiences survey revealed the dimensions of this issue, with the American data (Sacks, Murphey, & Moore, 2014, p. 1) claiming that 46% of American children have experienced an ACE. This data is recognised as being conservative. When translating the statistics to the current school student populations primary and secondary, conservatively staff can be dealing with a significant number of students with a mental illness or trauma of one kind or another in their classrooms on a daily ongoing basis. Statistical data at a school level concerning interventions related to mental health issues confirm these figures.

The large numbers of such students presenting with significant mental health problems in our schools and the subsequent ability of staff to respond to their needs with the appropriate level of support they require is proving to be a near impossible task given current school resource parameters.

Mental health issues impact significantly on class sizes, curriculum offering, staff morale, resilience and well-being, resources availability and on teacher and support staff time and can be seen as presenting through various behaviours at the school and classroom level including:

- Increased violence (from both students and parents)
- Oppositional defiance
- Truancy
- Social withdrawal
- Low energy levels and depressed behaviours
- Emotional distress and high anxiety
- Avoidance behaviours

- Physical manifestations (well-being – wellness).

While the perception of schools, seen as the panacea for many community issues is a fact of life, realistically schools are increasingly ill equipped to handle the complexities associated with the higher end mental health issues that present. Given the aspirations held for schools along with the greater public accountability and scrutiny they face and the many associated tasks they perform particularly when catering for students with aberrant mental health behaviours it is first necessary for governments to give due recognition to the impact that such behaviours are having on student learning outcomes in general.

The requirement for school leaders to deal with identified quite difficult behaviours without resource provision or the availability of alternative effective respite education environments is now becoming evident in a decline in staff morale, resilience and injury statistics. The follow-up rehabilitation of abused staff and the ongoing need to ensure their overall well-being and then guaranteeing their safety is not only very stressful for school leadership but also time consuming and resource intensive as well. The significant increase in workers' compensation costs in recent years bears witness to the problems of non-trained and ill-equipped teaching staff dealing with problematic mental health issues.

CASE STUDY 7

Disruptive student – school incident reports

Record taken from a school file

An 11-year-old student had accumulated nine critical incident reports in a fortnight, for behaviours including assault and battery, verbal and physical abuse of teaching staff and threats and intimidation of fellow students, vandalism (including continually smearing faeces over toilet blocks and school facilities), burglary with violence. There was no system appetite to become involved preferring instead to leave the problem at the school leader's office for him to take action. The parents, one of whom was constantly in and out of prison, openly indicated that they had no control over the child and the school leader was reluctant to suspend the student, as this would only create significant and greater issues within the wider community. In-school suspension and supervision were therefore the only alternative available. Assigned supervision of the student had an adverse impact on staff morale.

American schools and universities live in trepidation of the next student shooting. Shootings recording more than five deaths/injuries include Roseburg (Oregon), Parkland (Florida), Santa Fe (Texas), Flint (Michigan), Marshall County (Kentucky) and Los Angeles. By way of example, an examination of the case of Adam Lanza and the dreadful Sandy Hook massacre of young students and school staff, poses the question that all school leaders and staff face, could more have been done to identify and re-socialise students who will potentially fall into the same trajectory as Adam Lanza. In Australia, Martin Bryant who committed the Port Arthur massacre, provides an excellent cross-cultural comparison to Adam Lanza.

The moment a new student arrives at the classroom door the perceptive teacher will predict whom that student will befriend, or be befriended by, and the student's appearance (clothing, haircut, language and behaviour) and that of his/her parents signal the overt tribal markers of identity to everyone watching. However, there are some key behavioural markers that quickly raise the red flags of alarm within the schools, and the schools then rush to engage their counsellors for expert opinions about how the new students will fit into the school context. Many of the students who exhibit extreme Tier 3 (top 5%) behavioural predispositions barely fit the school cultures and they bump through thirteen years of not quite fitting modelled expectations.

In the teachers' lounge, students' future life trajectories are hypothesised over morning coffee, as teachers share their collective experiences and wisdom. In these collegial discussions the longest serving teachers' trump cards are the stories of the rambunctious students who have come to very sticky ends.

The growth of mental health problems in schools

In education, teachers perceive an increase in student mental health issues and Kieling, Baker-Henningham, Belfer, Conti, Ertem, Omigbodum, Rohde, Srinath, Ulkuer, and Rahman (2011) stated that mental health problems now affect an alarming 10–20% of children and adolescents worldwide. The situation in the United States is similar, and in examining mental health in American schools, Adelman and Taylor (2006) also sounded the alarm bells noting that 12–22% of students require support for mental and behavioural problems. However, considering the undiagnosed and unreported emotional and learning problems, these authors claim over 50% of students are affected.

Richard Tremblay (2012) is an acknowledged Canadian authority on childhood violence. Tremblay's longitudinal research deprived environments of Montreal examined generations of family aggression and violence. As a result, in 1985 he initiated a programme to support families at risk, and this demonstrated that early intervention could deflect children away from adult criminality. This important research underwrites the need for a focused communal intervention to break the cycle of violence. Tremblay's work showed the factors that influence children's inability to regulate physical aggression in early childhood included having mothers who exhibited antisocial activity at school, mothers who get pregnant at a young age, mothers who smoke during pregnancy, and mothers who have low income parents who have problems living together.

The programme of intervention undertaken by Tremblay, Vitaro, Bertrand, LeBlanc, Beauchesne, Boileau, and David (1992) included specific training for the parents and it touched on classroom strategies used by teachers.

In relation to schooling, Tremblay warned teachers that the early childhood years are the first time many new students meet society's behavioural expectations. Assessing the policy implications of aggression in childhood, Tremblay made two points, and both are relevant to school-based policies:

1 The early childhood years have the greatest potential in helping children who are at risk of becoming severe aggressors because most children are exposed to a different set of expectations in relation to behaviour and aggression.
2 Most children have used physical aggression during early childhood, and most will continue to use violence unless they are taught alternative strategies.

The conclusions from a three-country study, in which Tremblay took part, reinforced the second point, and there are dire consequences for society if this childhood demonstrated aggression cannot be changed.

The American case of Adam Lanza

On 14 December 2012, the 20-year-old Adam Lanza murdered his mother and then drove to Sandy Hook Elementary School (Newtown, Connecticut), which he had attended as a child, and he then murdered twenty first-graders and six staff members. In the Report of the Child Advocate (Connecticut), thirty-seven key findings were made, and these findings attempted to show how Adam Lanza slipped through the education and health systems of Connecticut, and how his medical/psychological needs were not adequately addressed for a variety of organisational and familial reasons.

With the advantages of hindsight, the possible danger signs for teachers included:

1 **The experience of schooling**.
2 Lysiak, in his book "Newtown", reported that Adam Lanza's time at Sandy Hook Elementary School was characterised by progress despite being socially awkward. Lysiak also reported that Adam Lanza's family saw encouraging signs in his development at Sandy Hook. The moves to Intermediate and then high school, accompanied by the effects of bodily maturation, saw a massive change in Adam Lanza's behaviour as his environment became more uncontrolled.
3 **A variety of psychological problems**.
4 It appeared that the delicate structure that held Adam Lanza's mental state together began to disintegrate and formal schooling became

untenable to Adam's mother, so she withdrew him from school. Violent computer games became an obsession for Adam and in that anonymous world he developed a persona of bravado, Lysiak, observed. A problem would arise when the virtual and real worlds collided for Adam Lanza.

5   **Familial circumstances.**
6   The familial structure became more problematic when Adam's parents divorced. In looking for reasons for Lanza's murderous behaviour, Emily Miller (2013), an editor at the *Washington Times*, pointed her finger squarely at Adam Lanza's mother saying that gun control, the failure to obtain adequate mental health support, and video games cannot be held responsible for Lanza's behaviour. Instead, she said that Lanza's mother should have pursued better medical support and ensured that the medical advice was followed.

The Australian case of Martin Bryant

The Port Arthur massacre that took place in the south-east corner of Tasmania, in April 1996. Thirty-five people were killed by the 29-year-old Bryant, and twenty-three people were injured in this murderous rampage. However, the seeds for this infamous act may have been set long before April 1996. Bryant's ancestry on his mother's side included two convicts (Eliza Fitzgerald, 1834; Richard Cordwell, 1825) transported to Van Diemen's Land (Tasmania) for life.

Wainwright and Totaro (2009) identified recurrent themes that characterised Bryant's behaviour:

1   **Cruelty and hurting others**
2   A school report in August 1977 said of Martin's behaviour:

> He is not interested in participating in class activities, excursions. He prefers to slide on the floors, chase other children and often ruins an otherwise excellent outing. The most disturbing and worrying aspect of Martin's behaviour is his violent nature. He kicks and torments (another child) in particular, often reducing him to tears. He often hurls objects around the room … (W&T, 2009, p. 67)

(A)   A sign of his dislike of the other students are the two reports of Martin urinating on others (W&T, 2009, p. 65 and p. 100).
(B)   **Vengeance**
(C)   As a youth Martin made seashell mice that he was trying to sell to tourists however, he was chased from the Broad Arrow café by an older man who was selling the same things in his souvenir shop. "Ordered away, Martin Bryant never forgot the encounter …" (W&T, 2009, p. 103).

(D) **Hunting, love of guns and killing**
(E) Martin Bryant had a fascination with guns and hunting. Even though he did not have the appropriate licences he purchased military grade weaponry and hundreds of rounds of ammunition.
(F) **Schooling** is problematic/medications/ Psychologist and school intervention.
(G) Martin Bryant was said to be three years' behind chronological progress when he was placed in a special education class at high school (W&T, 2009, p. 95).
(H) **Lack of friends**
(I) In a psychiatric report prepared for his trial Bryant described his childhood behaviour as "aggressive, destructive and very difficult with other children" and referred to "records of Mr Bryant torturing and harassing animals and tormenting his sister" (Blake, 2015).
(J) **Fascination with pain**
(K) As a child Bryant was injured while playing with fireworks and at the local hospital, he was asked by a television journalist if he would be more careful next time? He cheerfully answered, "No." (W&T, 2009, p. 94). After burning himself by lighting petrol, Wainwright and Totaro (2009, pp. 103–104) observed that Martin "seemed impervious to emotion, physical discomfort – or pain- often swimming in the dead of winter with snow on the ground".
(L) **Not seen as "normal" in school**
(M) Martin had trouble speaking when he went to school; and testing at the end of primary school showed that he was "three years below his chronological age in spelling and word knowledge, and two years below his mathematical understanding" (W&T, 2009, p. 95). The other children referred to him as "Silly Marty".
(N) **Energy levels**
(O) Martin's energy levels were excessive, and in his early years his parents moved to give him lots of room to play, and his father would take him for long walks to tire him out.
(P) **Family situation**
(Q) Bryant's relationship with his mother was difficult, and she had not bonded with him when he was born. Martin's father worked hard in providing suitable housing environments and exercise for Martin, but he died three years before the Port Arthur massacre.
(R) **Where will this student be in the future?**
(S) While Martin Bryant's future is sealed (life in gaol without parole), his teachers at primary and secondary school, as caring people, would have been concerned for him. However, none could have predicted this scenario of the extreme violence for the younger Martin Bryant.

Systemic early identification and risk management

The early, broad identification of students who appear to have the potential to develop problematic behaviour as they move into adulthood is possible. And, while such programmes need to be sensitively developed, it is a multifactored issue that the country cannot ignore. The Connecticut Office of the Child Advocate's Report provides an excellent overview of how schools fit into this demanding task of risk management:

In education:

- There needs to be a system that integrates schools with mental health support systems, which will promote mental health in schools.
- Support organisations such as occupational therapy and behaviourist services need to be built into school funding.
- Schools need to be required to report on, and seek support for perceived areas of social-emotional concern, even when there are no concerns for students' academic performances.
- In terms of identifying and working with students' disabilities schools need to take a broad view and look beyond the "primary disability". It is argued that in cases like that of Adam Lanza that the broad picture of multiple disabilities would have given a more accurate picture.
- Home bound/ Home schooling needs to be constantly audited and students' needs assessed.

Post-secondary readiness, with a focus on skills wider than academic skills, needs to be put into place, to facilitate students' independent living options.

General comments on chapter

Richard Tremblay (2012) and his colleagues have shown that early, interventions can change endangered children's life trajectories, and in so doing, make the children's lives better, and our communities better, and safer places. However, without the establishment of strong, multi-agency support teams that have the personnel and resources to make a sustained difference to people's lives, nothing will change. Clearly, this pressing problem needs a strong, coordinated determination to make a difference in identified families.

In American society, where human rights are constitutionally guaranteed by the Bill of Rights, potentially dangerous students can slip through the system, and these students' life trajectories remain unchanged despite the warnings signalled by perceptive school staff. School staff continue to act as society's "first responders" in identifying students at severe risk, but in many cases the support for these early warnings are piecemeal. Targeted governmental and nongovernmental interventions are desperately needed to ensure that all the relevant agencies form a combined taskforce approach as can be seen in the English *Troubled Families Programme* (Longfield, 2019), which is a large-scale model of what Tremblay previously experimented with in Canada twenty-five years earlier. Such a coordinated approach will lessen future threats to our schools and communities; and it will make teaching more successful for many students.

Distilling recent literature on the topic of mental health we can make the following observations:

- Most students behave well, but the small minority who don't have a significant impact on the other (5%).
- 15 to 20% of a given school student population is realistically likely to have mental health problems; 5% of this cohort likely to have aggressive/conduct disorders.
- Depression is the second highest reason for a teacher to make a doctor's visit in Australia.
- Support for teachers and schools is often too little too late with not enough coming after an incident.
- School leaders and teachers don't want to hear. "If you get the pedagogy and curriculum right, behaviour problems will disappear." Pedagogy and curriculum impact on behaviour in a very positive way – but a more comprehensive perspective of aberrant mental health behaviours is required.
- Parents need to accept responsibility for their children's behaviour. Work done at school can be largely undone in the home.
- Bigger and better punishments are not the answer. A getting tough syndrome is not the answer. One of the weakest ways to change behaviour is punishment. However, the public mood is for toughness – they want schools to get tougher.
- Changes in behaviour are best achieved through positive reinforcement.
- There are some students whose behaviour does demand an alternative placement. While concept of *sin bin* doesn't work – it must be recognised that there is a small percentage of students who do require resources not in schools.
- Students from single parent families are more likely to be affected by lower economic status, move more often and be at a health disadvantage.
- There continues to be an increase in evidence of students with mental health issues (i.e. ADHD and Oppositional Defiance syndrome, etc.) that will become manifest in classroom student behaviours. It is becoming increasingly difficult for schools to handle these issues.

Many teachers and school leaders have experienced the behaviours of students with Foetal Alcohol Syndrome Disorder (FASD), but the numbers of students with behavioural and learning problems is not lessening. The IDEAL research (Smith et al., 2015) and Neonatal Abstinence Syndrome (NAS) research (Oei et al., 2017) alert us to issues that are already in our schools, but not identified or properly supported.

The increasing frustration of school leaders to focus on teaching and learning in dealing with mental health issues adds exponentially to the growing and saddening cynicism of teachers with their increasing workload and working environments. It is recognised that a valued and effective education system is a key component of any functioning democracy as it ensures the respect and support of all students as they develop into effective future citizens.

References

Adelman, H.S., & Taylor, L. (2006, May-June). Mental health in schools and public health. *Public Health Reports*, 12(3), 294–298. https://www.ncbi.nlm.nih.gov/pmc/articles/PMC1525289/

Berg, G. (2004). To lead or to be led – That is the question: From unprofessional to multi-professional school organisation. In J. Lee, L. Lo, & A. Walker (Eds.), *Partnership and change: Towards school development*. Hong Kong: Chinese University Press.

Blake, S. (2015, 5 December). Martin Bryant's sister, the former Lindy Bryant, says she has changed her life and name to escape her past. *The Daily Telegraph*. www.dailytelegraph.com.au/news/national/martin-bryants-sister-the-former-lindy-bryant-says-she-has-changed-her-life-and-name-to-escape-her-past/news-story/5705315d53124bb496192b6c3ec32fd2

Dao, J. (2012, 24 February). Branding a soldier with "Personality Disorder". *The New York Times*. www.nytimes.com/2012/02/25/us/a-military-diagnosis-personality-disorder-is-challenged.html?_r=1&pagewanted=all

Felitti, V.J., Anda, R.F., Nordenberg, D., Williamson, D.F., Spitz, A.M., Edwards, V., & Marks, J.S. (1998). Relationship of childhood abuse and household dysfunction to many of the leading causes of death in adults: The Adverse Childhood Experiences (ACE) Study. *American Journal of Preventative Medicine*, 14(4), 245–258.

Fullan, M., & Stiegelbauer, S. (1991). *The new meaning of educational change*. New York: Teachers College Press.

Glickman, C.D. (1998). *Renewing America's schools: A guide for school-based action*. San Francisco: Jossey-Bass.

Grossman, D. (1996). *On killing*. New York: Back Bay Books.

Grossman, D., & Christensen, L.W. (2004). *On combat: The psychology and physiology of deadly conflict in war and peace*. PPCT Research Publications.

Hazel, W. (2018, 28 March). Tests and narrow curriculum behind 'explosion' in mental ill health, says union. *Times Educational Supplement*. https://www.tes.com/news/tests-and-narrow-curriculum-behind-explosion-mental-ill-health-says-union

Jackson, S., & Csikszentmihalyi, M. (1999). *Flow in sports: The keys to optimal experiences and performances*. Champaign, IL: Human Kinetics.

Kieling, C., Baker-Henningham, H., Belfer, M., Conti, G., Ertem, I., Omigbodum, O., Rohde, L.A., Srinath, S., Ulkuer, N., & Rahman, A. (2011, 17 October). Child and adolescent mental health worldwide: Evidence for action. *Lancet*, 378, 1515–1525.

Longfield, A. (2019). *A manifesto for children*. London: Office of the Children's Commissioner. https://www.childrenscommissioner.gov.uk/wp-content/uploads/2019/09/cco-a-manifesto-for-children.pdf

Lysiak, M. (2013). *Newtown: An American tragedy*. New York: Gallery Books.

MacNeill, C.N. (2012). An examination of Csikszentmihalyi's concept of flow in Western Australian school leaders' work and learning (Unpublished doctoral dissertation). Curtin University, Bentley, Western Australia.

Meredith, L.S., Sherbourne, C.D., Gaillot, S., Hansell, L., Ritschard, H.V., Parker, A. M., & Wrenn, G. (2011). *Promoting psychological resilience in the U.S. military.* Santa Monica, CA: RAND.

Miller, E. (2013, 25 November). What would have prevented Lanza from mass murder at Sandy Hook? *Washington Times.* https://www.washingtontimes.com/news/2013/nov/25/adam-lanza-shooting-sandy-hook-elementary-school-n/

Oei, J.L., Melhuish, E., Uebel, H., *et al.* (2017, February). Neonatal Abstinence Syndrome and high school performance. *Pediatrics,* 139(2). DOI: https://doi.org/10.1542/peds.2016-2651

Robertson, H.J. (1998). *No more teachers, no more books: The commercialization of Canada's schools.* Toronto: McClelland and Stewart.

Sacks, V., Murphey, D., & Moore, K. (2014, July). Adverse childhood experiences: National and state-level prevalence (Research Brief). *Child Trends.* https://childtrends-ciw49tixgw5lbab.stackpathdns.com/wp-content/uploads/2014/07/Brief-adverse-childhood-experiences_FINAL.pdf

Smith, L.M., Diaz, S., LaGasse, L.L.*et al.* (2015). Developmental and behavioral consequences of prenatal methamphetamine exposure: A review of the Infant Development, Environment, and Lifestyle (IDEAL) study. *Neurotoxicology and Teratology* 51, 35–44. doi:10.1016/j.ntt.2015.07.006

Tremblay, R. (2012). The development of physical aggression. *Encyclopedia of Early Childhood Development.* www.child-encyclopedia.com/aggression/according-experts/development-physical-aggression

Tremblay, R.E., Vitaro, F., Bertrand, L., LeBlanc, M., Beauchesne, H., Boileau, H., & David, L. (1992). Parent and child training to prevent early onset of delinquency: The Montreal longitudinal-experimental study. In J. McCord & R.E. Tremblay (Eds.), *Preventing antisocial behaviour: Interventions from birth through adolescence* (pp. 117–138). New York: The Guilford Press.

Wainwright, R., & Totaro, P. (2009). *Born or bred? Martin Bryant: The making of a mass murderer.* Pyrmont, NSW: Fairfax Books.

15 Catalytic teachers and the X factor of teaching and learning

Over the last few decades, successive theories of school change have focused on the nature and quality of leadership in schools. In the late 1970s the school effectiveness movement dominated school leadership theory and practice. When this movement had run its course, theorists began to focus on the role of school leaders to bring about mandated changes, usually in the form of school reforms. In the United States, particularly, this led to a focus on instructional leadership, which risked narrowing perceptions of what school leaders should do. In Britain, New Zealand and Australia, New Public Management (NPM) dominated perceptions of leadership from the late 1980s to the present, generating the myth of the hero leader. As Campbell, Kyriakides, Muijs and Robinson (2003) observed in relation to the school effectiveness movement, student performance is more heavily dependent on classroom factors than school factors (2003, p. 350). School change depends heavily on teachers' willingness to adopt new teaching practices, which in turn raises the question of how teachers themselves learn.

Impacting on teachers' abilities to bring about change in classrooms is a phenomenon that is now called *work intensification*. Wang, Pollock and Hauseman (2018, p. 74) reported:

> The increased expectations for Canadian school principals involve the number of short- and long-term tasks they are expected to complete, the amount of time they are given to complete those tasks, and the growing workload that prevents them from keeping up with their daily routine.

Likewise, in secondary schools, research is supporting reports of work intensification. Lawrence, Loi and Gudex (2019, p. 196) found:

> Reports of moderate to substantial increases in workload suggest that work intensification has been a feature of secondary teaching in recent years. Responses indicate strong dissatisfaction with non-teaching-related workload and, conversely, moderate satisfaction with teaching-related workload.

These factors all affect staff change acceptance.

OUR BELIEF 37

Growing staff skills, by providing appropriate resources, authority, opportunities, motivation, as well as holding them responsible and accountable for outcomes of their actions, will contribute to general staff competence and satisfaction.

How teachers learn and accept changes to their practice

We argue that the popular differentiation between deep and shallow student learning also applies to teacher learning and associated professional development. It is now widely recognised that the billions of dollars spent across the world on one-day courses for teachers' professional development have resulted in shallow learning, at best. Too often experienced staff are subjected to presentations that are of dubious quality or attend courses that leave participants with a sea of notes, but with little direction or support to change or grow professionally.

In transforming the school's approaches to teaching, particularly with a renewal agenda in mind, its leadership must first define what constitutes better learning and teaching practice. However, as Tom Guskey (1989) noted, it is primarily observing in-classroom practice itself that changes teachers' attitudes. Guskey argued that teachers must actually try these new practices with the students for whom they believe the practices are problematical. If the new practices succeed with those students, teachers then have the opportunity to reflect on their values and attitudes, and on the changes to them that are required as a result of this experience. Guskey found that teachers who were able to use certain practices successfully "expressed more positive attitudes toward teaching and increased personal responsibility for their students' learning" (Guskey 1989, p. 444).

There are a number of phases through which school staff progress in their acceptance of the change or renewal agenda. First, they gain knowledge of, and experience with, the changes proposed and/or required of them in terms of pedagogic and curriculum practices. These desired changes are articulated by the school's school leader, usually in the form of a sense of direction or personal vision for learning and teaching in the school. Staff then form a positive or negative attitude towards the renewal agenda based on their personal perceptions of its impact on their personal experience of teaching.

The school leaders' communication and people skills are crucial at this point as their ability to persuade, coach and mentor staff is seen to impact on the teachers' decision to adopt the proposed changes. Once a decision has been made to implement the change agenda at the classroom level, staff will often seek confirmation from the school leader about their choice and critically important feedback on their endeavours.

Catalytic teachers and teacher leadership

Often, in implementing desired change, a school leader will use staff whom we have identified as catalysts in the implementation of a renewal of a school's pedagogic practices. These *catalytic teachers* are identified as teachers who are themselves either fully engaged or willing to engage in pedagogical and curriculum renewal at the classroom level.

Catalytic teachers are often seen as leaders in their own right within the pedagogic profession. They often share insights with other teachers; they take part in distributed leadership when opportunities are provided within the school context; they are ground-breakers in terms of learning and teaching practice, and have internal and, sometimes, external credibility as well. Credible school leaders have no trouble in identifying those staff with the desired pedagogic knowledge, skills and efficacy predisposed to change. They are those members of staff who are receptive to new ideas. They question and even challenge existing practice, and they think about their teaching and ways to improve their own, their colleagues' and students' performances.

It is quite interesting that the concept of the *Expert Teacher* was promoted in the educational literature, but the point that we make is that a catalytic teacher is an *Expert Teacher+*. Lachner, Jarodzka and Nuckles (2016, p. 197) divided effective teaching knowledge bases into three types:

1. Deep understanding of the content matter.
2. General pedagogic knowledge about the nature of teaching and learning.
3. Content knowledge of how best to explain subject matter to students and anticipate problems.

And, the expert teachers have greater knowledge and this is organised around specific cases into higher-order structures called curriculum scripts, which

> are higher-order knowledge structures which integrate the subject-matter knowledge to be conveyed together with pedagogical content knowledge, such as suitable representations of concepts or students' potential misconceptions, and with general pedagogical knowledge about learning processes and instructional strategies. (p. 198)

For us, the catalytic teacher is an expert teacher in the classroom, with an important leadership tenacity to be able to lead others by proselytising, demonstrating and supporting expert pedagogic practice.

Catalytic teacher leaders can be seen as a variant of the teacher leader definitions. DeLawter in the Kappa Delta Pi Blog (2015) lists seven characteristics of teacher leaders: work ethic; teamwork; leadership; openness; vision; positive effect; and risk-taking. This is a description of general leadership, and it too, does not pick up the nuanced characteristics of catalytic leadership.

We see catalytic teachers as opinion leaders in the school, and are an important ingredient in establishing the critical mass for change. Such staff can become great allies to the school's leadership in challenging and helping to change existing staff attitudes towards the learning and teaching function in a whole-of-school context, becoming an important ingredient in the teaching mix to facilitate an effective change reaction in learning and teaching quality. In some scenarios it is the school leader, in the role of change agent and pedagogical leader, who initially adopts the role of catalyst for renewal in their school.

Catalytic teachers appreciate and engage with the opportunity to see desired teaching practices in operation. We believe that being creative in fostering opportunities for such interactions of staff with these catalytic teachers is a most effective way to bring about change in pedagogic thinking within a school.

Successful strategies for school renewal and change in general often require school leaders to maintain the impetus for that change and to challenge the existing school culture until staff and community beliefs move to be more in line with what is wanted or required. Promoting a journey of change, conversation, dialogue and discussion about learning and teaching and the outcomes desired are important elements that must be fostered by leadership in this respect.

The most important measure of a true pedagogic leaders is not where they stand in moments of comfort, but where he or she stands at times of challenge, change and controversy. School leaders who hold an unshakable belief in and high expectations for the ultimate success of their staff and students gain far better results than those who do not hold such beliefs. Getting staff on side with the change process is a significant challenge that every leader has faced at one time or another. The use and active involvement of identified catalytic staff who have demonstrated a change-willing orientation is one of the most successful strategies for school leaders to employ.

The role of the school leader, when implementing a renewal agenda, is described best as "comforting the afflicted", those who are uncertain of the impact of the changes proposed, and "afflicting the comfortable", those who are reluctant to alter existing pedagogical and curriculum endeavours. Recent educational literature in the area, Fullan (2001) by way of example, support the contention that strong team building, and people skills are desirable leadership behaviours in overcoming individualism in teaching approaches.

OUR BELIEF 38

> School leaders are the advocates in every school for optimising every student's learning capacity, and their catalytic teachers are the enthusiastic leaders who get this done.

School leaders need to focus on people within a renewal scenario, and this is demonstrated by their ability to connect with others easily and frequently. Hence, there is evident a *team style,* which is motivated by a preference for participation in team activities. This team style is seen to extend beyond the confines of the school and include colleagues and line management.

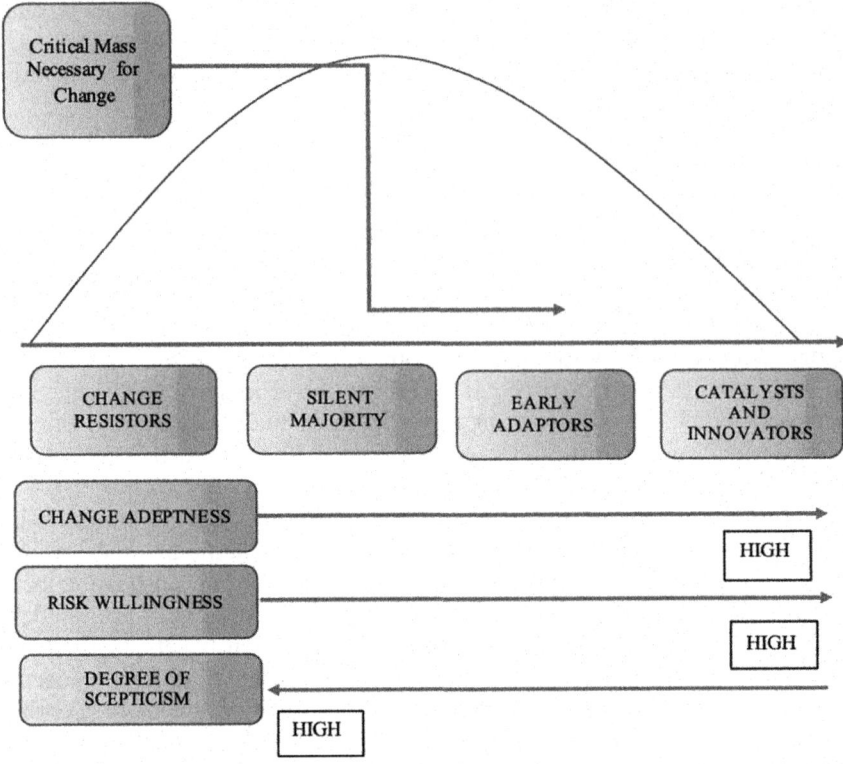

Figure 15.1. Critical mass of staff required for change to be initiated.

A variety of leadership behaviours will need to be successfully demonstrated by the school leader in engaging stakeholders in the change process, inclusive of communication strategies employed, coaching and training styles, relationship building activities, flexibility and team building (relationships) approaches influenced stakeholder attitudes.

OUR BELIEF 39

> A school leader engaged in school renewal will need to possess excellent communication and people skills, and be prepared to coach and mentor both new and existing staff.

It is proposed that by a school community engaging in change there will be a corresponding reciprocal influence on the school context and disposition, and also on school leader behaviours. This is because, as the change agenda is progressed, staff and community attitudes alter as the changes are adopted and gain general acceptance within stakeholder groups and required different behavioural emphases at various stages of implementation. For example, in the initial phases of change behaviours associated with motivating and stimulating stakeholder interest would be required inclusive of visioning, change agency, communication. These leader behaviours will alter as the renewal agenda becomes embedded in the school to encompass more of an orientation that is focused on relationship building; that is behaviours more conducive to a coaching, team building and nurturing style.

A school where teachers see themselves as drivers of the learning programmes in their classrooms and where the school's leader and teachers have a strong sense of efficacy towards their teaching and hold high aspirations and expectations for student performance outcomes as the basis of school renewal.

A mix of explicit teaching and cooperative learning in teams that engage students in their learning is evident in a renewing school with teachers working collaboratively to achieve the desired learning ethos. Such a collaborative organisational culture emphasises a web of relationships, and points to the important role of the leader in defining and stimulating effective teamwork among teachers.

The characteristics of a catalytic teacher

We know that the most important part of the classroom environment is the quality of the teacher. According to students the best teachers are stronger leaders, happier, friendlier and understanding' organised, espousing high but fair standards, and being professionally approachable.

Developing communicative relationships between students and teachers is perceived as beneficial to student engagement and subsequent learning outcome achievement. Efficacious teachers maintain open discourse as a method of empowering students with opportunities for negotiating their learning, participating in assessment, engaging in collaborative and open-ended inquiry with fellow students and participating in reconstructing the social norms of the classroom. A teacher's own behaviour can have a significant impact on student learning and outcomes attainment, and Fraser (2001) provided a brilliant example of a teacher's reflection:

> I've come to a frightening conclusion that I am the decisive element in the classroom. It's my personal approach that creates the climate. It's my daily mood that creates the classroom climate. As a teacher, I have a tremendous power to make a child's life miserable or conversely, joyous. I can be a tool of torture or an instrument of inspiration. I can humiliate or humour, hurt or heal. In all situations, it is my response that decides whether a crisis will be escalated or de-escalated and a child humanised or dehumanised.

Paradoxically, it is not surprising that a number of studies have indicated that teacher behaviours are an important aspect of learning environments and that these interpersonal behaviours strongly relate to student outcomes.

Information about the efficacy of teacher behaviours is useful because of the potential role it has in assisting teacher reflection about how they operate within their classroom environments. Environments that promote and sustain quality relationships between students and teachers make critical differences in student learning.

It is important that a school leader is aware that teacher factors are an important consideration when looking to initiate pedagogic cultural change in schools and classroom learning environments. Therefore, the engagement of teachers, through the auspices of the articulated renewal agenda, and further, by sharing the vision for the proposed change becomes crucial to a leaders' efforts at re-culturing the schools' learning and teaching activities.

Build the capacity

One often neglected responsibility of school leaders is to build capacity amongst their staff. And there is really only one way to do this: make space for them to grow professionally and personally by giving them the opportunities, provide the training and professional development whenever necessary, and always acknowledge their achievements so that they are encouraged in their endeavours.

School leaders will often bemoan the fact that they are unable to bring about lasting change for improvement because of the inability of those with whom they work to either commit to the change process or undertake the new responsibilities asked of them as part of the re-culturation aspects of the proposed agenda. Perhaps it may be conceded that they were already working beyond their level of competence when the changes were introduced. Our experience would indicate that a school leader will more often than not have to confront the reality of a less than perfect team. So, one key task for the school leadership is to look at the available skills and abilities of those on staff, identify how to take advantage of each of their talents, and develop opportunities for those talents to be used to advantage of the wider school learning and teaching endeavours.

The fundamental purpose of leadership is professional and personal growth – growth in the teachers and support staff in their professional capabilities; growth in the students in their academic, social, physical and emotional well-being; and growth in the wider community in their ability to enhance the life chances of their children. So, school leadership is a personal journey that embraces a commitment to care for (and about) all others in the school community, and will therefore, require the use of inclusive processes to engage them in a learning journey that is future focused. There is a level of uniqueness in this exercise too – uniqueness that is created because of the individuals who comprise the school community who provide the context for the leadership journey, and the people who will participate in that journey, will always be the most important considerations in determining the nature and outcomes of that journey.

Catalytic teachers and the X factor of teaching and learning

When watching people perform and teams play, occasionally we see an act that is really outstanding. If the person doing this outstanding act can replicate the action over time, and particularly if that performance galvanises the team to win, then we may anoint the brilliant player or performer as having the X factor. The term X factor was popularised with television talent programmes of that name being shown around the world.

In business and in education there is now a strong push to identify potential and talent, as can be seen in World Bank Group (Kraay, 2018) background paper on the World Bank Human Capital Index. It is interesting that talent identification in sport is far more advanced than in business and education, and this is because physical sport talent identification is far more linear.

If we were to back-track our current crop of catalytic teachers, we can see that as new teachers they had a good work ethic, good teaching, and excellent, professional relationships with their students, but most didn't have the *Wow!* or *X Factor*. That came later, as they developed credibility with their peers, who then ask them for pedagogic advice. When the X factor teachers become respected resources for the other teachers, then they reach the status of catalytic teachers.

References

Campbell, R.J., Kyriakides, L., Muijs, R.D., & Robinson, W. (2003, September). Differential teacher effectiveness: Towards a model for research and teacher appraisal. *Oxford Review of Education*, 29(3), 347–362.

DeLawter, K. (2015, 21 February). 7 qualities of a teacher leader. *Kappa Delta Pi Blog*. https://blog.kdp.org/2015/02/21/7-qualities-of-a-teacher-leader/

Fraser, B. J. (2001). Twenty thousand hours: Editor's introduction. *Learning Environments Research: An International Journal*, 4, 1–5.

Fullan, M. (2001). *Leading in a culture of change*. San Francisco: Jossey-Bass.

Guskey, T.R. (1989). Attitude and perceptual change in teachers. *International Journal of Educational Research*, 13 (4), 439–453.

Kraay, A. (2018). Methodology for a world bank human capital index. Policy Research Working Paper 8593. Development Research Group. World Bank Group. https://documents.worldbank.org/en/publication/documents-reports/documentdetail/300071537907028892/methodology-for-a-world-bank-human-capital-index

Lachner, A., Jarodzka, H., & Nuckles, M. (2016). What makes an expert teacher? Investigating teachers' professional vision and discourse abilities. *Instructional Science*, 44(3), 197–404. doi:10.1007/s11251-016-9376-y.

Lawrence, D.F., Loi, N.M., & Gudex, B.W. (2019). Understanding the relationship between work intensification and burnout in secondary teachers. *Teachers and Teaching*, 25(2), 189–199.

Wang, F., Pollock, K., & Hauseman, C. (2018). School principals' job satisfaction: The effects of work intensification. *Canadian Journal of Educational Administration and Policy*, 184, 73–90.

16 Accountability and public confidence

Accountability can be either internal (personal) or externally focused. In this chapter we examine external accountability, which is a key, strategic issue in most school systems, as quality assurance is a factor of public confidence. We recognise that quality cannot be installed like new technology or air conditioning units into our schools, nor can it be simply proclaimed by well-intentioned school leaders or externally based officials. Each school must choose its own path to quality attainment and accountability. Around the world this path to quality is to a large extent invested in the various accountability measures that have been negotiated with key stakeholders both within and external to the school as an entity. What has become evident, particularly in more recent times is the type and rigour of accountability to which schools are subjected is inversely proportional to public trust and satisfaction with the education system.

OUR BELIEF 40

> The levels of accountability required of schools are directly a measure of public trust.

This relationship can be represented in graphical form (Figure 16.1).

While recognising that accountability is a notoriously imprecise term, nonetheless, many educational writers on the topic have tried to establish working definitions of it. The difficulty arises, however, when the concept is applied to the core business of education, specifically, improving student learning. This is because the problem that emerges relates to identifying the schools' actual value-added component.

Within the general school context, our definition of accountability is:

> The duty or obligation of those given responsibilities and resources to explain and justify how they have used (or applied) those responsibilities and resources in the achievement of agreed objectives. This definition acknowledges the traditional concepts of accountability, such as stewardship, ethics, quality leadership etc., with the added focus of outcome

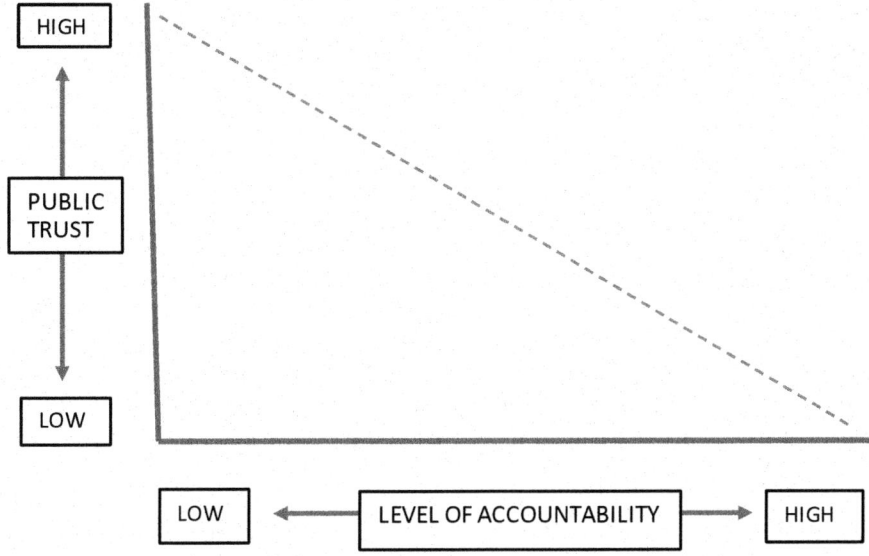

Figure 16.1 Level of accountability versus public trust.

achievement. Such a perspective we have summarised in terms of what we have termed accountability principles which provided a greater sense of direction for school leaders:

- As schools exist to enhance the education of children, then accountability processes must be focused on improving student learning outcomes.
- Accountability is a continuous school process of negotiation, self-reflection, review and adjustment rather than a focus on a singular inspection event.
- It is a way for schools to effectively communicate, in an informed way, the extent to which school programmes are meeting stated targets and outcomes.
- A credible accountability process strengthens community confidence in the school by providing feedback on a range of performance indicators.

Generally, accountability definitions are seen to incorporate a publicly demonstrated responsibility dimension, and such an orientation sits comfortably within the context of a school system. In education the accountability process changed as schools moved away from direct supervision by superintendents. Until the advent of New Public Management (NPM)/ Neoliberalism school superintendents were selected because they were expert school leaders. Superintendents' experiences were such that they could support developing school leaders, but also pass judgements on their performances. In many cases the untidy mix of the coaching and umpiring roles were not conducive to facilitating school leaders' professional growth. New Public

Management changed that equation almost overnight, and as a result, struggling school leaders were left floundering because to ask for help publicly signalled a weakness that was often better concealed.

The tightening "loose coupling" relationships in schools

The relationships between school leaders and teachers have been predicated on the untouchable insularity of teachers' professional status, protected by the four walls, closed doors of the classrooms, and strong Unions, which Berg (2004) referred to as the *invisible contract*. In such situations, Weick (1976) had described this relationship between school leader and teacher as *loose coupling*, which was compared with the tight coupling seen in military units. An insightful Richard Elmore (2002) warned that loose coupling forces school leaders into the invidious position of protecting the teaching, over which they have little control:

> Administration in education, then, has come to mean not the management of instruction but the management of the structures and processes around instruction. That which cannot be directly managed must, in this view, be protected from external scrutiny. Buffering consists of creating structures and procedures around the technical core of teaching that, at the same time, (1) protect teachers from outside intrusions in their highly uncertain and murky work, and (2) create the appearance of rational management of the technical core, so as to allay the uncertainties of the public about the actual quality or legitimacy of what is happening in the technical core. This buffering creates what institutional theorists call a "logic of confidence" between public schools and their constituents. Local board members, system-level administrators, and school administrators perform the ritualistic tasks of organizing, budgeting, managing, and dealing with disruptions inside and outside the system, all in the name of creating and maintaining public confidence in the institutions of public education. Teachers, working in isolated classrooms, under highly uncertain conditions, manage the technical core. This division of labour has been amazingly constant over the past century. (p. 6)

With the publication of national and state testing results as a part of the accountability process, *buffering* has become more difficult for school administrators, and the cloak of anonymity is being peeled away from teachers and schools' performances.

Considerable comment has ensured in more recent times about accountability particularly as schools have moved through evolutionary stages into a more self-management paradigm. School leaders have always been responsible for both the educational and financial management of their schools, but there is now the demand for a more formal, publicly demonstrated accountability, one based on student outcomes, not processes or inputs.

Again, by way of example, one of the major problems that schools face is the often-encountered *dichotomy of obligation*. Public schools are responsible to two master: the district or system, and the educational community the school serves (parents, students, citizens). This dichotomy of obligation imposes upon the school two sets of formal accountability requirements. The challenge for school leaders is to ensure that there is a high level of correlation between the internal and external accountability requirements and results. It would be problematic if the external accountability were used to damage a school where there was a high degree of satisfaction with a school at the local level simply because of a mis-match of accountability requirements.

In the United States *accountability* first appeared in the *American Education Index* in 1969. By 1976 outcomes focused education had been replaced in the United States by one that held schools accountable against a standards frameworks.

The British experience was significantly influenced by the economic recession of the 1970s and the resultant budgetary cuts to education at that time. British schools came under closer scrutiny as the public purse tightened and felt strong pressure to justify their limited share of public funding. Consequently, the British education authorities demand for accountability tended to focus on total schools' operating costs and the resulting growth in marketable knowledge and skills.

While the link between autonomy and accountability is recognised, it is rare to get academic confirmations of this relationship. Esther Klein (2017), a German academic, observed that schools serving a low socio-economic clientele often have accountability retribution applied when the students' results aren't up to expectations. She noted: "For instance, high-needs schools might be governed more tightly by the external administration, have the perception that structural restraints give them less room to manoeuvre, or receive additional funding that increases their autonomy" (p. 589). Such an observation is cause for concern, and obviously such perspectives of accountability requirements must acknowledge the diversity in education and recognise the importance of collecting accurate contextual information.

OUR BELIEF 41

> Accountability is recognised as a dynamic and heuristic process. It is part of what a school is, not something it does. Each school will need to identify through its planning processes its own path to improvement and then as a collaborative and inclusive exercise, it then becomes a part of everyone's responsibility.

Linda McNeil (2000) in her book, *Contradictions of School Reform*, warned of the inexorable links between accountability, standardised testing and then what she refers to as the inevitable standardisation of teaching.

The model of public accountability that we have seen evolve in recent times is based upon an important consideration that its focus must be on the system or District School Board as the schools' school leader client. This may explain why various education jurisdictions have responded to the call for greater school outcome accountability by employing a more devolved system of schools, however, with external system oversight of accountability measures.

We acknowledge that school accountability needs to be focused on improved student outcomes, and therefore, can also be regarded as a continuous process of open negotiation, review and adjustments. This as opposed to processes that are more focused only on an annual testing event. Our position requires that both schools and school systems are encouraged to recognise that the accountability processes that need to be tightened are those in respect to the community dimension. We advocate a position in line with the community school covenant or charter process.

A variety of policy and research papers has been created over time on school planning for improvement as a further response to this accountability thrust. The overall perspective of this accountability from the system perspective is that accountability can be taken to mean the school's ability to account for the extent of its achievements related to the objectives stated in its planning documentation. The implications of this position for a school's leadership is that from this system perspective:

- School accountability needs to be focused on improved achievement outcomes because schools exist to enhance the education of its students.
- Accountability must be seen as a continuous process of open negotiation, review and adjustment.
- The school facilitates and negotiates its own accountability dimensions with all relevant stakeholder groups as it incorporates both school-based and system priorities into its planning.

The school leader's role, and a function of their position in the school, is to demonstrate how the school's educational learning and teaching programmes and management organisation have made an impact on student learning. To this end systems require that schools demonstrate that they are performing effectively and economically in terms of the education programme students are receiving. Consequently, in such a paradigm of accountability the school leader is held responsible for monitoring the students learning outcomes as specified in planning documentation. The challenge confronting the school leader is to seek to achieve an improvement in these outcomes. Schools planning for learning outcome improvement and curriculum reforms, and in particular the consultative processes employed by the school leader in identifying desirable student outcomes, therefore, should become an integral part in any accountability discussions and further, is intricately linked to change initiatives employed by the school leader.

OUR BELIEF 42

Teachers are more willing to accept the accountability demands required of them if the leader to whom they are accountable has creditability.

As educational leaders, we should examine the concepts of both internal and external accountability, because if the internal accountability is convincing then public trust in schools will rise, and the destructive drive of current one-stop accountability through standardised testing and the rise of standardised teaching can be curtailed.

To begin with, it needs to be recognised that currently schooling is undergoing a significant shift in accountabilities as it responds to the drivers of change often outside its control. In many jurisdictions, schools are struggling to break free of the old paradigm of mass education, to move into the new paradigm of meeting the specific needs of students, who will exist in a global economy.

Very few educators actually engage in a debate about the future developments of the accountability argument in the context of a widespread belief that school systems are failing. Schools have been unable to convince governments that standards are being achieved, consequently more intrusive and controlling accountability processes have been progressively initiated. It is unlikely that politicians are going to be seen to be pouring good money after bad into education if the public's support for schools is antipathetic.

CASE STUDY 8

Sample of newspaper headlines on perceived school failures

How are America's public schools really doing? *The Washington Post* **(16 October 2018)**
How are America's public schools doing? The question is a fundamental component of any contemporary education policy discussion. Yet it is also notoriously difficult to answer. With nearly 100,000 schools spread across roughly 13,000 districts, the scale of the enterprise is beyond what any set of individuals can see and experience.

Despite this challenge, one answer has emerged over the past 40 years: American schools are failing. Beginning with the "Back to Basics" movement of the 1970s and reaching a fever pitch with the 1983 publication of "A Nation at Risk," rhetoric about public school performance grew progressively more negative until it hit its stride during the No Child Left Behind (NCLB) era. Today, pessimistic policy talk is now so standard as to constitute a form of truth. The crisis in public education is seemingly self-evident.

English schools are broken. Only radical action will fix them. *The Guardian* **(9 August 2018)**

> There is now widespread recognition of the drear reality: inadequate multi-academy trusts failing thousands of pupils, parents increasingly shut out of their children's education. Crisis can be an overworked term in politics, and our schools are good examples of public institutions, subject to years of poor political decisions, that continue to do remarkable work. Ultimately, an education system which is failing our children. Not only do our schools have a funding crisis, but subsequently a recruitment and retention crisis too. Years of under inflation pay rises and excessive workloads are driving teachers away and deterring new recruits. Teachers are being asked to do more, with less, for less, for longer. The crisis in teacher recruitment means that whilst schools are struggling to fill vacancies, large numbers of pupils are being taught by teachers who do not have a relevant qualification in the subject, and class sizes are growing.
>
> **The Current Education System is Failing our Students:** *Ed Surge* **(9 March 2018)**
> The educational system was built with a bias; bias in deciding where to direct funds, bias in the material we teach, and bias in where the school is located. It makes all the difference in the world if your neighbourhood is wealthy or poor. The bias is dependent upon "the have and have nots" mentality, and this bias determines student success.
>
> **While individual schools might shine, PISA results show our education system is stagnating:** *The Sydney Morning Herald* **(6 December 2019)**
> While individual schools might shine, the results of international tests, released earlier this week, suggest our education system as a whole is stagnating. For the first time, Australia failed to exceed the OECD average in maths, and the nation's results in reading and science have declined since

The extent to which schools are failing around the world is a matter of some conjecture. However, this is not a new phenomenon, but it is one that has in recent times gathered a momentum of its own, particularly overseas. Significantly, standards debates are evident in the United Kingdom particularly in relation to OFSTED (Office of Standards in Education) activities and in Australia with respect to PISA results. The leader of the National Association of Head Teachers in the United Kingdom claimed, after a series of teacher suicides, that school inspections are the modern equivalent of the Spanish inquisition and have ceased to fulfil a useful purpose. He argued:

> Nobody denies that schools should be accountable and should stand up to scrutiny, but a system more suited to the Spanish inquisition must give way to something that more readily meets the needs of this century. It is surely time to take stock of what we know and use that knowledge to build rather than continue to condemn. (Tavistock, 2002)

Greater devolution of responsibility to schools places a premium on accountability, and changes the purpose school evaluation in terms of the checking and balancing processes that are in place. People have different views of how things should be done and so, accountability and validation practices appropriately conducted increases the credibility of each school's operation and planning and reduces potential for error and conflict. School performance reviews and reporting at a school level is seen as a function of the school's leadership and as such cannot be delegated. It requires school leadership to commit to the process, and consistent ongoing visible support for staff. It further requires a school to systematically document its operations to ensure that those responsible for certain functions are trained and know what is expected of them. While this may appear to create a paradox between the roles performed by the coach and the umpire, it is essentially the role of leadership. Leadership, therefore, requires both intent and action in terms of demonstrating accountability for performance.

CASE STUDY 9

Beyond the emperor's new clothes: Improving public education

Many of us owe the foundation of our formal learning to the dedicated and inspiring teachers in public schools. In this life, a rule of thumb that has guided us is that we should leave the world in a better condition than we found it, but in the field of education, it seems that, organisationally, these endeavours have been unsuccessful.

As school leaders we can remember that at an education executive meeting the participants were presented with a series graphs which indicated that if current enrolment trends continued, there would be as many students in private schools as in the public-school system. The tipping point, participants were warned, was but a couple of years away. Now in hindsight, the figures presented were overly pessimistic, but the mutation that Brian Caldwell (2000), an astute futurist, saw happening to school systems was that by 2020 public schools could simply be reduced to what he termed "safety net schools". In other words, people who were prepared to pay money for a private school education would walk away from the public-school system. To some degree Caldwell is right, perhaps not to the drastic levels that were then being predicted.

If in private industry, the dire prediction of future trends would have rung alarm bells, but this was not the case for schools, and it was business as usual. In education, nothing changed. In the following years there were a number of system-initiated self-congratulatory messages about how teaching and learning was getting better in schools, and there even comparative statements showing excellent results in the "national testing". However, school leaders and their staff knew that things were not right, and in

> education there was a need to look at the past, reflect and acknowledge mistakes, in order to then move forward.
>
> The first truly national testing results were in fact, shocking. An examination of the cause identified that in both government and private schools there was a problem with the teaching, and the curriculum that was being taught. The ideological add-ons of whole-language; no rote learning of tables and combinations; choice about hand-writing styles; students' self-generated spelling lists; no professional discussions between teachers and line-managers about the programme of the content to be taught; the reduction of the "significant adult" in the classroom to the role of a *facilitator*; and the *negotiated curriculum*, all added up to an anarchic, nihilistic mess. The result, was as one parent quipped, "that her child had studied dinosaurs four times in primary school and could spell *stegosaurus*, but not *because*."
>
> We had long argued that the traditional paradigm of schools needed to change and move towards a system of schools, not a school system.
>
> This we argued could be achieved by adopting curriculum change, where successful informed world-class syllabus practices that accommodated mastery of the essential learning, with associated creative extensions. And secondly, by empowering school leaders to lead school-based changes that would more appropriately engage students in their learning. This would require school leaders accepting a pedagogic leadership role in their schools ensuring that teachers used a full range of pedagogic processes to engage students in learning, and avoiding the looming, reactive push back into total didacticism. For this re-culturation process to become viable it was necessary for schools to be able to select its own staff. A further, important consideration for school leaders in bringing about successful changes to pedagogy in their schools was the unstated requirement that they had to tackle, poor performance, quickly and efficiently.

This very downbeat analysis of the loss of student numbers from the public to the private sphere led the authors at that time to pen an obituary for public schools

In Memorandum
The Demise of the Public-School system

The community sadly acknowledges the passing of the Public-School system. The once vibrant and revered part of this country's life was barely missed with its passing into obscurity and obsolescence. The Public-School system, once a champion of academic rigour, social justice, equity and fairness began the painful road to oblivion as those charged with maintaining its honour sought comfort in the arms of expedient, centralist and corporate managerialist actions through the facile maintenance of their fragile status. The death knell was the loss of contact with its core business, learning and teaching, in favour of expediency and inappropriate cost cutting measures. With leadership lacking and a loss of public confidence, the once prized edifice of the public good has slipped into a terminal sleep.

The change to New Public Management began the marked decline of the Public-School system with its overt politicisation of education. Public schools never recovered from this blow. The untimely demise of the Public-School system cannot be attributed to governments alone, the Teachers' Union with its unquestioning desire to protect the interests of poor performing teachers along with general public apathy helped to condemn and euthanize government school rigour, the lifeblood of a vibrant system. Attacks upon principals who dared to raise questions about poor performance, inappropriate curriculum responsiveness and denigration of those who dared to lead were characteristics of the final moments of Public-School system.

Like a cancer, ongoing policy and curriculum debacles and lack of vision from leadership caused considerable angst among the last remnants of school leadership left in schools. Unfortunately, early warning signs were not heeded, and the Public-School system exhibited rapid decline from this point onwards.

A further indication of the demise of the Public-School system was its inability to recruit leaders with credibility who were suited and committed to its ethos of excellence, equity and care. Local school responsiveness was killed by bureaucrats who could see a potential loss of power and influence and resisted change. Little progress was made to rectify this setback in treatment, allowing the disease to become more widespread through the body corporate.

In desperation, quality staff and leadership have abandoned the ailing system resulting in the deterioration of the quality in learning and teaching endeavour generally. The resulting transfusion of ineffective managers into the once vibrant and healthy system resulted in the quick spread of inappropriate policies, centralised ineffective practices, inducing a further rapid decline.

A last resort solution through the politically driven leadership agenda proved to be ineffective in halting the decline. The Public-School system's failure to recognise the problems of decline in school morale along with leadership tensions began its downfall. The system's subsequent failure to recognise problems when they were identified simply consolidated the risk.

It is with regret that the community marks the passing of this once much-loved institution that enabled so many to realise their potential.

Private memorial services will be held in schools across the state.

No flowers please.

OUR BELIEF 43

The commitment to excellent public schooling underwrites our entrenched beliefs in democracy, equity and social mobility.

In standardised testing, schools are judged against other schools by a crude system of analysis that would be laughable in its naiveté, if it were not used as a stick with which to beat the school systems. To a large degree the standardised test and associated league tables are a way of publicly shaming some schools into improvement, or enticing them with cash rewards.

The states of New York and Florida are good examples of different approaches to the accountability issue in schools. Pushing further in its drive for accountability and tougher standards, the New York State Board of Education voted to publicly grade every school in the state based on scores on the new state-wide tests, rewarding or punishing schools according to where they rank. After the grades are assigned, the system would consider what rewards or penalties to assign to each level.

One of the most surprising things about the spate of extremely negative school criticism between 1980 and now is that the general public supports the rating of schools, so interest has remained consistently high. However, even with negative publicity about schools, survey evidence shows the public rating of local public schools actually has been positive. Ironically, people rate their own local schools significantly higher than they rate schools in general across the nation.

The accountability demands have meant that schools are required to their monitor performance against the key performance indicators (KPIs) in the school plan and also against national pre-determined benchmarks. Typically, schools then use the school plan for self-monitoring and self-improvement with the school's board given an account of its performance against the plan's targets. The accountability journey for schools that has evolved over time has been interesting to say the least.

A fair-minded and just concept of accountability begins with a clear sense of who is accountable to whom, and for what. There is no denying that schools need to be accountable, however, a case could be made for the premise that this accountability should not be to corporate entities, remote educational experts, or some restless national audience created by mass media, but rather to their local communities, which then could be encouraged to engage in ongoing negotiations with the school about what it means to be an effective, responsible local citizen.

We believe that such an accountability paradigm should be negotiated between the school and the local community and clearly articulated in an agreement beforehand. It is impossible to understate the strategic concern over quality assurance and accountability in system level administration. The very future of schooling is dependent on public confidence in the quality of education being offered at the local level. Unless government gets accountability right, the public-school system will become a system of second choice and a safety net for those who cannot afford a private schooling pathway.

While accountability requirements need to acknowledge the diversity across schools and recognise the importance of collecting contextual information, at the same time both schools and the system must recognise that the accountability processes that need to be tightened are those in respect to the community dimension. It is this contextual information that is often lost in media translation and reporting of performance data, through the league table reporting exercises.

Governments require that schools demonstrate that they are performing effectively and economically in terms of the education programme students are receiving. Consequently, the school leader is rightly held accountable for monitoring student outcomes being achieved by the school. The challenge confronting the school leader is to seek to achieve an improvement in these outcomes.

The public has lofty the expectations for education, giving schools responsibility for much of their children's welfare, values, skills and knowledge. One expectation is that schools can correct such social ills as crime, teenage pregnancy, mental illness and adolescent rudeness. There is also the expectation that schools will provide self-fulfilment education, ranging from employment skills to personal happiness. Schools, then, are seen as a source for both problems and possible solutions.

Education is an essential community service and as educators we must be open with the community about the outcomes being achieved by our students. This is crucial to building community support for and confidence in schooling. As well as ensuring that every school's performance is open to scrutiny, accountability mechanisms should ideally help the school to improve its performance. This will occur as schools engage in a thorough self-examination identifying their strengths and weaknesses as a basis for their planning for improvement. Collective reflection, analysis and commitment to improvement will ensure that the effort schools put into demonstrating accountability will add real value to their educational work.

Critics of schools are easy to find as people are not bashful about noting school problems, but will disagree over what is wrong, who is responsible, and what should be done to remedy the issues or change schools accordingly. We maintain that criticism of schools is fully consistent with an open democracy. Of all social institutions in a democracy, the school should be willing to submit to examination and be open to critical assessment and reassessment that flows from such an activity. This does not mean that all criticism of schools and schooling is justified. Some critics espouse simplistic, mean-spirited or wrong-headedly arrogant perspectives not grounded in factual evidence. But some of the criticisms are well founded, thoughtful and cogent. Although some unjustified criticism can be detrimental to education in a democracy, open debate can permit the best ideas to percolate, to be developed and revisited, and to be evaluated.

Venomous accountability

There are so many variables that can be inserted into a school or classroom accountability programme that it becomes impossible for the denizens to cover every option. So, a venomous accountability process can always list ten areas for improvement, and knowing this vulnerability causes great stress to school-based staff. In the United Kingdom the OFSTED school inspections have been directly linked to staff suicide.

It is interesting that David Weinberger (2007) writing for the *Harvard Business Review* coined the phrase *accountabalism* to describe venomous accountability processes. He stated that accountability "… has become *accountabalism*, the practice of eating sacrificial victims in an attempt to magically ward off evil". And, he notes that this practice has spread into our schools at multiple levels:

> Accountabalism is uncontrolled accountability and it bureaucratizes and atomizes responsibility. While claiming to increase individual responsibility, it drives out human judgement. When a sign-off is required for every step in the work-flow, those closest to a process lack the leeway to optimise or rectify it. (Weinberger, 2007)

Because accountability suggests that there is a right and a wrong answer to every question, it flourishes where we can measure results exactly. It spread to schools where it is eating our young, as a result of our recent irrational exuberance about testing, which forces education to become something that can be measured precisely. Accountabalism not only eats the young but devours the perfectionist teachers and school leaders who can make a difference in students' lives.

General comments on chapter

Schools are not neat laboratory experiments where all of the variables can be controlled. They are dynamic microcosms of the school communities that they serve, and as such any accountability process needs to be confined to the big picture issues of student learning, safety and happiness. The imposition of accountabalistic inspections and testing serves no good purpose, and those requiring a demonstrated accountability need to be realistic and fair.

References

Berg, G. (2004). To lead or to be led – That is the question: From unprofessional to multi-professional school organisation. In J. Lee, L. Lo, & A. Walker (Eds.), *Partnership and change: Towards school development*. Hong Kong: Chinese University Press.

Caldwell, B.J. (2000). A "public good" test to guide the transformation of public education. *Journal of Educational Change*, 1(4), 307–329.

Elmore, R.F. (2002). *Bridging the gap between standards and achievement: The imperative for professional development in education*. Washington, DC: The Albert Shanker Institute. http://www.shankerinstitute.org/Downloads/Bridging_Gap.pdf

Klein, E, (2017). Autonomy and accountability in schools serving disadvantaged communities. *Journal of Educational Administration*, 55(5), 589–604.

McNeil, L.M., (2000). *Contradictions of school reform: Educational costs of standardised testing*. New York: Routledge.
Tavistock Institute (2002). Review of current pedagogic research and practice in the fields of post-compulsory education and lifelong learning. *Final report: Submitted to the Economic and Social Research Council*. London: author.
Weick, K.E. (1976, March). Educational organizations as loosely coupled systems. *Administrative Science Quarterly*, 21(1) 1–19.
Weinberger, D. (2007, February). The folly of accountabalism. *Harvard Business Review* (Breakthrough ideas for 2007), 54. https://hbr.org/2007/02/the-hbr-list-breakthrough-ideas-for-2007

17 Introducing the universal five key steps to sustainable school renewal

We have proposed throughout this book that the essence of sustainable change in schools is often the serendipitous and conscious balancing of the rich and volatile mix of the school leaders' pedagogic leadership, change knowledge, risk willingness and skills to counter a coterie of inhibitors. Interest in this area of school administration is such that deeply embedded curriculum and cultural change, leadership and accountability are among the themes that dominate current educational research and writing on school leadership and change. We argue that these themes are intertwined. For example, it is impossible to have school leader leadership without change, because maintaining the status quo is managerial in nature, not leadership, and both forms exist in a climate of increased accountability.

Leadership by the school leader is seen as the ultimate goal in schools where school leaders are expected to manage and lead, as each situation demands. We have also recognised that leadership in schools is not the sole domain of school leaders and that leadership in a school can be effectively distributed. Therefore, it follows that multi-levelled leadership is necessary in its own right and should be facilitated for a variety of moral and practical reasons by the school leader.

Leadership of the change processes leading to improvement in schools can be exciting journeys as they have the capacity to engage teachers, students and parents in new levels of learning. Besides, leadership is a noble calling that actively solicits partners in change who wish to make teaching and learning better and so improve the learning community.

Leadership and change

Leadership and change are closely connected, and it is important to note that leadership is a relationship based on differential but increasing rewards for all parties. Individuals enter the leadership-followership equation in the belief that change will improve their circumstances. The leadership-followership equation, therefore, is dynamic, not static, and the old idiom that *one man's power is another man's impotence* is not true.

The five key steps to sustainable renewal 201

There are three constants in life: taxes, death and change. Change in society and schools is never ending, and teachers and parents will have noticed this being the case more often than not in their schools. A model of change that best describes what is happening in schools has become known as Hegel's Dialectic. The popular version of Hegel's Dialectic is the *thesis-antithesis-synthesis* triad. In schools we have seen a change introduced (the *thesis*), teachers develop an *antithesis* and then a new *synthesis* is formed. However, over time and with the change in circumstances the synthesis becomes accepted as the new *thesis* and then inevitably a new antithesis is developed. The Dialectic holds for both internal and external contexts, and as a consequence change never stops as people and organisations try to improve their situations, particularly when seen as a part of the school renewal process that builds on success.

OUR BELIEF 44

In any school renewal process the sustainability of a change is often difficult to determine as embedded change becomes the accepted way of doing things over time, and it then becomes the foundational base of the next iteration of renewal.

Change does not necessarily mean the things will get better for all of the actors in the change equation, and when a leader fails to provide change that improves the lot for the followership, the followers tend to drift away. The same holds just as strongly in schools. The school leader has to show that a change will produce a reward for the staff. While direct rewards inclusive of better pay or working conditions may be the more obvious examples as seen in various Enterprise Bargain Agreements (EBAs), indirect rewards can also be strong motivators and include a vicarious sense of achievement through actions that improve student achievement. Gleicher's formula, adapted by Dannemiller and Jacobs (1992), sets out a model of the conditions for successful change: $C = D \times V \times F > R$. In this formula Change = Dissatisfaction x Vision x First steps, and this needs to be more attractive than the pain of resistance (R).

The locus of operational control is a critical element in designing change, for without the engagement of staff any change proposed is doomed to failure. Throughout this work we have argued that school renewal, driven by staff and community from the bottom-up is a far better approach to change in schools because it has a better ability to engage stakeholders in what is about to happen.

We maintain that what it takes to ensure change is meaningful and lasting that an individual won't engage with the change process unless:

- They share a compelling reason to change.
- They have ownership of or in the change that is proposed.
- The leadership models that it is serious about the change agenda and its implementation.

- They have a picture of what the change will look like for them personally.
- They see tangible resource support for the change proposed.
- They can see benefits for the students and themselves.

Distributing the leadership

A key factor in building the pressure for change and then the pressure for embedding the change into teachers' pedagogic repertoires can be accomplished by the school leader through the development of a distributed leadership orientation among staff in the school. This is because the broader the base of the drive to change, the greater the likelihood of that change being implemented successfully. The presence of distributed leadership in a school culture is seen as a harbinger of teacher empowerment and engagement, and both are essential factors of profound change in schools. The question that often arises in discussions of distributed leadership relates to the identification of leaders or prospective leaders. In reality, there are a multitude of different tasks in modern schools within a context of competing time requirements, and it is highly unlikely, therefore, that the school administration, now and in the future, will be able to do everything.

The literature of instructional leadership is replete with the myths of the hero school leader riding into town, bringing about change, riding out again. What is not recorded is that the population then go back to doing things the way that they have always done them. Distributed leadership we maintain is the only known antidote to the myth of the hero school leader in schools.

OUR BELIEF 45

> A school renewal process never has just one leader, as positional power has little credibility if the renewal is going to be embedded in the practice of every classroom teacher.

The distribution of leadership without an accompanying synergistic cultural change that necessarily accompanies it will simply create another layer to the school's administration and will not facilitate the engagement all of the staff. The democratisation of distributed leadership empowers stakeholders and consequently, a shared vision of the future can be developed. Given the nature of schools as organisations the school leader holds the key to the distribution of leadership. Distributing leadership must not be seen as a single, stand-alone act, but as part of deep cultural change in the school. We argue therefore that multi-levelled school leadership is the key for embedding change in schools.

OUR BELIEF 46

> School leaders need to forecast what values, skills and knowledge their students will need in a society thirteen years in the future. And, we all need to be

cognisant of what the international testing is telling us about where we sit in what will be the new order.

A vision with a thirteen-year horizon

Developing a shared vision is a prerequisite for pedagogically focused school leader because it is the key to staff and stakeholder engagement, which aims at winning commitment, not compliance from staff. The literature on leadership is awash with notes on developing a shared vision. Given the nature of compulsory schooling in the Western world we argue that to make the vision relevant now and into the future it is important to develop the vision with at least a thirteen-year horizon (the length of time that a student typically spends at school).

We see a school's vision as being integrally linked with a school's mission; it is the destination of the journey along the effectiveness highway that school leaders aspire to achieve. A school has to know where it wants to get to before it can plan how to get there. Therefore it stands to reason that a school's vision, its mission and purpose must realistically provide a clear link between the aspirations of the school the capabilities of the school leader, its staff, its resources and the learning environment. If the mission of a school is the means by which it intends to achieve success in terms of its purpose, then consequently the school's vision will be a series of more precise statements that show how the mission is to be achieved over a given period of time.

Once the vision and direction of the school is established it then becomes the function of leadership to firstly align people and communicate a direction to all stakeholders, staff, parents and students, needs, values and emotions. In the sense that we have used the term *vision* in this book, it is not mystical or intangible, but means simply a description of something a school and its community aspires to in the future.

The vision of a transforming school leader may be a dream expressed in written form as simply as this: our school will be a centre for learning in the community, where every child will enjoy coming to school and will acquire the essential skills necessary to participate as a valued citizen in their community. Or, alternatively, the vision may be a more precise statement of mission: our students are presently performing below those in schools in comparable social settings on tests of basic skills; we aim to come in the top ten among these schools on system-wide tests of achievement.

The school leader as a pedagogic leader must assume the mantle of a shepherd of change and the key to achievement of desired outcomes as articulated through the school's vision.

Consequently, a major challenge facing a school leader's efforts in articulating a shared vision within the school context in the first instance is his or her own pedagogic credibility; getting people to believe the message. It is also recognised that many things contribute to a leader's credibility, inclusive of the track record of the person delivering the message in terms of both its strength and relevance to the situation at hand, along with the content of the message itself. So, consistency between the school leader's words and deeds are important.

It is our experience that at one end of the spectrum schools tend to adopt vision scenarios that simply repeat what has been done in the past, paying little attention or heed to the particular community aspirations and expectations that are held for the teaching and learning programme within a specific school setting. At the other end of the spectrum the field is littered with vision statements that have not made a difference. Simply making an elegant, comprehensive and well-articulated personal vision does not assume a successful teaching and learning programme will eventuate in the school.

However, it is the visioning, and the consequential planning, that have the potential to be the unique, unifying actions within a school.

Pedagogic leadership

When the school effectiveness movement faltered in the 1980s it was realised that the leadership of school leaders was essential to foster successful change. Instructional leadership was then developed as the great hope of education, in a time of growing cynicism about change and re-culturation in schools. The idea of instructional leadership was fine, but *instruction* was too narrow a vehicle on which to mount a campaign of change particularly if the aim was to change teachers' pedagogic practices comprehensively. We prefer the term *pedagogy* over *instruction* as it encompasses all of the aspects that constitute the teacher–student relationship in a learning-teaching environment, not just instruction. Secondly, it is now recognised that school leaders' pedagogic obsolescence is a major inhibiting factor to both instructional and pedagogic leadership. School leaders need to make strategic choices about what is important in schools, the learning and teaching, or the management.

Pedagogic leadership is predicated on the assumption that improving students' learning, through better pedagogy is the purpose of schooling. Table 17.1 sets down the parameters of pedagogic leadership by contrasting it with instructional leadership.

An extension of pedagogic leadership is leading *relational pedagogy* (Boyd, MacNeill, & Silcox, 2006). Relational pedagogy acknowledges that pedagogy is determined by the nature of the teacher–learner relationship and builds on this to overtly teach students the interpersonal skills and group work strategies necessary to enhance their social learning. Within the concept of relational pedagogy, it is argued that the school's purpose is to develop the whole child, while also giving recognition to the fact that there is increasing pressure for schools to concentrate on the cognitive aspects of the curriculum.

We have identified the four key aspects of relational pedagogy:

- It is based on the primacy of relationships in teaching and learning.
- It is about, and models, appropriate pedagogic interaction in the classroom.

Table 17.1 Pedagogic leadership and instructional leadership

Instructional leadership	Pedagogic leadership
Focus on teacher instruction	Focus on students' learning
Driven by mandated curriculum	Determined by the needs and interests of students
Classroom centred	Connected to examples drawn from real life/world
Test results seen as a goal	Test results seen as one aspect of learning and informative of level of student understanding of concepts explored
Predicated on teaching as a craft	Predicated on teaching as a profession
Hierarchical in nature	Distributed leadership
More about school management	More about building a professional learning community
School leader as an instructor of teachers	School leader as a leader of teachers' professional learning
Pragmatic in nature	Moral and facilitative in nature

- It acknowledges that social learning is just as important as cognitive learning.
- The development of relationships without improved student learning across all the dimensions of education is not good pedagogy or for that fact, good education.

In leading relational pedagogy, the school leader is expected to model the behaviours being taught in the classrooms. To bring about change that moves away from a default pedagogy that inhabits our schools with an over emphasis on didactic, explicit approaches will require teachers and school leaders to develop new language, concepts, skills and values in respect to teaching and learning. For example, the language of relational pedagogy includes such activities as think-pair-share, WIPS (whole class, individuals, pairs and small groups), mixed-pair-share, team building, think-write round robin, round table and team stand-n-share. The language of relational pedagogy needs to be shared in the sense of students becoming conversant not only with the language that supports this paradigm but also with the processes that are identified as effective learning tools to support curriculum delivery and ultimately enable concept attainment

The accountability context

As we have pointed out, the public trust of a school is the driver of the accountability demands placed upon it. What has become evident is that accountability to which schools are subjected is inversely proportional to public trust and satisfaction with what is being provided by schools and the system overall. The lower the public trust and satisfaction, the higher the levels of accountability required of the school system. The higher the public trust, the lower the expected levels of accountability. This highlights the importance of the relationship between public trust and levels of external accountability and the concept of earned autonomy.

We argue that earned autonomy enables and encourages schools to focus their attention, resources and expertise on addressing the community's expectations and in meeting organisational priorities associated with learning and teaching. Enhanced autonomy is enabling in that it removes bureaucracy, improves the schools focus on client needs and facilitates teacher responsiveness to them. It recognises that there is no one right design or structure that will suit all schools, further recognising that one template for accountability and compliance does not fit all school situations.

> **CASE STUDY 10**
>
> *Sorry Minister – You have got it wrong*
>
> When accountability becomes strident, those responsible for the accounting may attempt to fudge the figures. An excellent example where this has occurred with significant fallout can be seen in an Australian context, where a state Minister for Education at the time informed Parliament during question time that the state's student outcome results against government endorsed literacy and numeracy tests had improved significantly in the previous twelve months. This position was clarified a day later. To her severe embarrassment it was later indicated that the Minister's own department had lowered student benchmarks to get the improved result she had spoken about. This debacle eventually contributed to her later resignation. This remains an excellent example of the dangers of high-stakes accountability.

External accountability impacts heavily on leadership and change in schools because it influences the scope of leaders' actions, and affects the development of reflective, internal accountability processes. In terms of the leaders' moral development of doing good for students, external accountability limits leaders to the pre-conventional (Levels 1 and 2) and conventional levels (Levels 3 and 4) of Kohlberg's hierarchy (Galbraith & Jones, 1976). That is, external accountability works because of sets of rules and punishments, but in so doing inhibit the moral development underwriting the self-accountability development of school leaders. Table 17.2 demonstrates the links between the stages of moral development and accountability.

The consequences of heavy external accountability are low trust and low levels of self-accountability. The growth of the moral component of doing the right thing for students and the educational community requires demonstrated trust from all parties. However, the drive for accountability will never

Table 17.2 Kohlberg's stages of moral development and external accountability

Kohlberg's stages of moral development adapted to an accountability protocol	Expected external accountability levels
Stage 1: Punishment and obedience orientation. Physical consequences	Very high
Stage 2: Instrumental relativist orientation. Right actions satisfy needs	Very high
Stage 3: The interpersonal concordance of good boy/ nice girl. Good behaviour wins approval	Very high
Stage 4: The law and order orientation. Fixed rules. Right behaviour is following rules, obeying authority	High
Stage 5: The social contract legalistic orientation. Right actions defined in terms of individual rights agreed by the whole of society	Low Earned autonomy
Stage 6: The universal ethical principle orientation. Right determined by conscience and ethical principles	Very low Earned autonomy

lessen in a political situation where education is seen as a drain on the economy, not a valuable enhancement of a country's resources.

Introducing the planning for school renewal

The Universal Five Phases of Successful sustainable change

When newly appointed school leaders arrive at their schools, instinctively they will tend to evaluate the human and physical resources available and then with this initial assessment done they will begin planning for both the present and near-future learning and teaching. However, what has not been recognised in the educational literature, or for that matter, in leaders' performance management is that effective school leaders already have developmental sequences for such processes in their minds. We have noted that these sequences of successful change in schools follow an almost universal pattern. The stages of most school plans follow these five phases:

1 Identify a need.
2 Plan agreed actions.
3 Implement first stage of action, and win support.
4 Finesse actions to ensure changes are embedded.
5 Exit and monitor.

This Five Phase Change Model is widely used in project management and by other large organisations, as we have shown in Table 17.3, and it describes structural aspect of change.

Table 17.3 The universal phases of school and project developments

Phases	Joint Chiefs of Staff (2018)	(Werling 2014)	Project development Villanova (2019)	MacNeill & Silcox Five phases of sustainable school renewal
Phase 1	Shape	Rescue	Project initiation	Need identified
Phase 2	Clear	Clear	Project planning	Sell planned solutions
Phase 3	Hold	Shape	Project execution	Build a critical mass of implementation
Phase 4	Build	Consolidate	Monitoring, and control	Embed whole school change
Phase 5	Transition	Evaluate	Project closure	Exit and monitor

The human aspect of the Five Phase Change Model

It is easy to lose sight of the human aspect of any change model and in schools, because we are people organisations, and we, as school leaders, need to be aware of what is happening to our people. In schools, we are all aware of Maslow's Hierarchy of Needs and this model is highly relevant when we examine the human aspects of change.

The Human Agency Hierarchy of Sustainable School Renewal Model (Figure 17.1) sets the measures of human welfare that is applicable in each phase of the *Universal Phases of School and Project Developments*. For example, in Phase 3 of this model of change, the school is building up support for a change in the way that it teaches spelling and it is appropriate for the school leaders to be guided by the stages in Figure 17.1 because it informs the sensible leaders' actions.

In Chapter 1, we discussed a Case Study, "Architectural Determinism", in which open areas were given to groups of teachers so they could implement a new style of instruction and classroom management. In the case of failure, many teachers did not progress beyond Stage 1 of the Human Agency because they did not know what was required of them. As each problem was solved the next stage of the Hierarchy would present a list of problems for teachers and school leaders. In many cases the human aspect of the proposed change meant that it did not proceed beyond Phase 3 in many schools.

Sequencing of planning development

It is interesting that in education, as in most civilian enterprises and military operations physical safety is always the first objective. As we have discussed earlier an incoming school leader may be faced by overt resistance and a toxic staff culture. The sequencing of the developmental processes employed will always be required regardless of the school context. It is an activity that requires skilled leaders to apply appropriate strategies to achieve the desired outcomes of building an effective and efficient organisation.

The five key steps to sustainable renewal 209

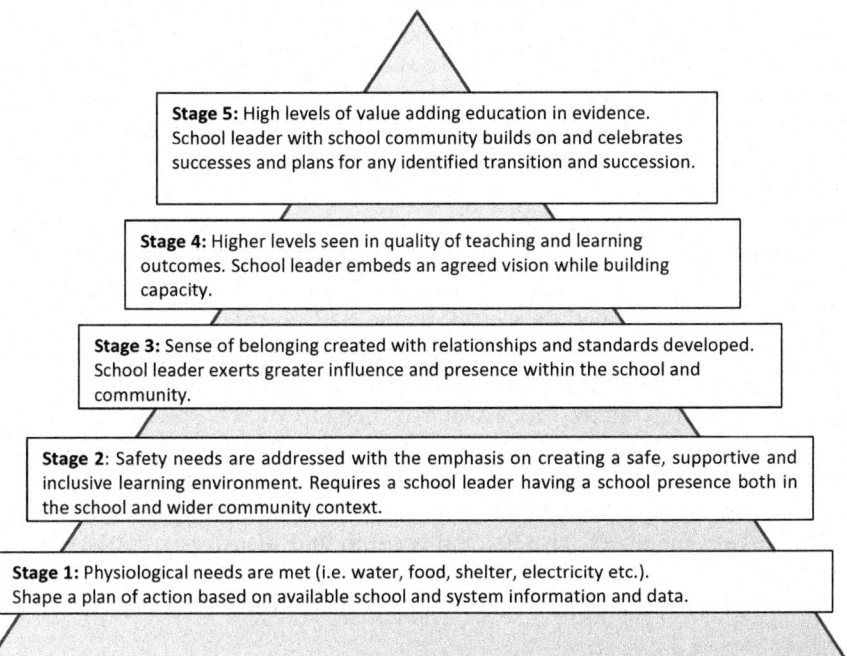

Figure 17.1 Human Agency Hierarchy of Sustainable School Renewal.

Table 17.4 The five universal stages of sustainable renewal and the leaders' roles

School renewal stages	Pedagogic leaders' roles
Stage 5 Transition/ succession planning	Review successes. Ask, "Where to next?"
Stage 4 Building capacity	Continue to build on successes and engage the media. Sell success and benefits for students.
Stage 3 Holding the line	Build on successes (Schechter, 2020). Engage with media to sell the vision. Continue to win over doubters. Hold the critical mass of the population.
Stage 2 Clearing the decks	Be able to respond according to each situation. One leadership style does not fit every situation. Show courage. Address negaholics and their influence. Win support.
Stage 1 Shape, Plan and establish by doing groundwork	Gather every bit of information that is available and make useful contacts while doing this. Complete a SWOT analysis and address each quadrant.

Adaptable, multi-skilled leadership

The ability of school leaders with limited skills to survive in complex and evolving school contexts is questionable. In the late 1950s there was a popular television Western series called Paladin. Paladin was a hired gun with the mantra; "Have gun will travel". If his mantra were adapted to education as: "Have one success, will travel," then it becomes a recipe for disaster particularly for aspirant and developing leaders. By way of example, if school leaders become infatuated with *servant leadership*, and then after a period of success in a stable, middle-class school they gain promotion to a larger, tougher schools with a battle-scarred staff such a form of leadership may not fit such a context. At this time, the servant leaders are pushed to one side as the staff operate in a teaching survival mode. We argue for a leadership *horses for courses* model, not dissimilar to the Tiger Woods analogy we outlined in Chapter 8 applied to teaching skills.

An important strategy for growing ownership of the sustainable renewal process was recognised in Schechter's (2020, p. 16) strategy of building on success: "The goal of *learning from success* is to create a learning community that investigates its own beneficial actions, a community that focuses on discovering team members' professional wisdom and identifying action-oriented knowledge." The benefits from *Learning from Success* in the Hold, Build and Transition stages of sustainable renewal are that it can:

1   reduce defensiveness and enhance motivation;
2   generate transformation;
3   enhance reflection on effective practices;
4   create positive organisational memory; and
5   generate a commitment to and an investment in learning among diverse members of a school community (Schechter, 2020, pp. 19–20).

Secondly, succession planning in the transition stage can consolidate all of the changes put into place during the renewal process. Succession planning in schools is a career and school development process effectively employed by school leaders to develop members of staff with a high aspirant leadership potential and takes a long-term view of the school's human resource needs in a school renewal context. While it has long been recognised that succession planning in an organisational context, is an important human resource activity it is only in more recent times that its application and full potential within the education area has begun to be developed.

The biggest challenge facing the school leader is ensuring that succession planning remains a dynamic process focused on identifying, assessing and supporting a school's future leadership in line with its strategic direction. Aspirant leadership programmes can be developed to enable staff to interact professionally with more experienced and perhaps more knowledgeable staff, enabling a sharing of ideas of successful teaching practice as well as enhancing their overall leadership competencies.

We have identified from our school and district experiences three key areas that are crucial to ensure successful outcomes of any aspirant leadership programme. They are:

- the use of strategic partnerships,
- the identification and use of available administrative expertise,
- championing of staff through fair and principled management.

Traditionally, leaders have tended to have an eye to developing their own replacements, but this is an approach that is often found wanting because of its ad hoc and subjective nature. Without a systematic planned approach, succession can be determined more by how skilful employees are at flattering their superiors, as was indicated in Chapter 6. Effective development of staff leadership potential calls for careful analysis of their training and development needs along with the identification of appropriate learning experiences (work assignments, special projects, formal training programmes, etc.). Consequently, it must be underpinned by an efficient performance management process, with well supported and relevant training and development programmes operating in an ethos and culture that encourages individual growth from within the school as an organisation. As staff members have varied backgrounds, training needs to be tailored to account for these individual differences.

An important component of succession planning programmes in the school setting is the emphasis on self-growth. Teachers needed to work collaboratively towards achievement of shared goals and take responsibility for innovation to enhance school performances. To achieve this aim, they need to be able to access high-quality professional learning and training programmes with links formed to performance review and future career direction.

In teaching we often talk about the hidden curriculum; the intangible things students learn in the classroom, like citizenship and tolerance. Likewise, it is also in schools when school leaders adopt a proactive approach to succession planning, they are addressing the hidden curriculum of staff management, and bringing about more positive attitudes in teachers and staff to their profession and school renewal.

References

Boyd, R., MacNeill, N., & Silcox, S.B. (2006). Relational pedagogy: Leading from the front. *Perspectives on Educational Leadership*, 5 (Australian Council for Educational Leaders). https://www.academia.edu/32027556/Relational_Pedagogy_Leading_from_the_front

Chairman, Joint Chiefs of Staff (2018, 25 April). Counterinsurgency. Joint Publication 3-24. https://www.jcs.mil/Portals/36/Documents/Doctrine/pubs/jp3_24.pdf

Dannemiller, K.D., & Jacobs, R.W. (1992). Changing the way organizations change: A revolution of common sense. *Journal of Applied Behavioural Science*, 28(4), 480–498.

Galbraith, R.E., & Jones, T.M. (1976). *Moral reasoning.* St. Paul, MN: Greenhaven Press.

Schechter, C, (2020). *The collective wisdom of practice: Leading our professional learning from success.* Thousand Oaks, CA: Corwin.

Villanova University (2019). Five phases of the project management lifecycle. https://www.villanovau.com/resources/project-management/5-phases-project-management-lifecycle/

Werling, E. (2014). Rio's pacification: Paradigm shift or paradigm maintenance. https://igarape.org.br/wp-content/uploads/2016/04/Rio%E2%80%99s-Pacification-.pdf

18 Conclusion
Positioning the future-oriented school

The ultimate measure of leaders is not where they stand in moments of comfort, but where they stand at times of challenge and controversy.

Specifically, this book has sought to highlight the important impact of a school leader's pedagogical leadership disposition on the phenomenon of school renewal as a form of cultural and curriculum change.

It is anticipated that this interactive narrative has informed, advised and added to the development of understandings for both current and aspiring school leaders to the impact that school leadership behaviours have on school renewal and associated leadership-oriented activities. Also, as experienced school leaders ourselves we have attempted to redefine the concept of school renewal within a modern global schooling context, taking into consideration aspects of school accountability, staff and school leader resilience, individual situational characteristics, the school as a learning organisation as well as exploring concepts relating to distributed leadership, collective efficacy, sustainable change modelling, and value-adding. Consequently, we hope that the work has been able to offer to the reader advice for the ongoing development of renewal approaches in their respective schools and act as an aid in the future development of school leaders.

The context for the information in this book has been distilled from experience in the real-life school setting which we believe has provided a degree of external validity to the discussions.

We hope that this work has extended previous commentary about school renewal by developing a revised conceptual model underpinned and grounded by our forty-six beliefs about schools and school leadership that highlights, and further contributes to, the knowledge about the relationship between school pedagogic, curriculum and cultural change and school leader leadership, thereby giving a clearer perspective of renewal influences in a school context.

The impact that a school leader's behaviour disposition has on the promotion of a change agenda in a school community, particularly in terms of the degree to which those behaviours significantly influence a school's renewal endeavours, has been detailed to some degree given its importance in the process.

We acknowledge and understand the fact that individual school leaders differ in their self-efficacy beliefs and that these differences have behavioural consequences. This point, added to the knowledge that school leaders' development of a greater understanding, sensitivity and empathy about the importance that perceptions of their own capabilities have in effecting and managing renewal changes in a school makes the work even more relevant to the school leader of today. The school leader has a significant role in setting a sense of purpose and direction for the school renewal agenda, and this underwrites the importance of effective communication skills in negotiating and articulating a shared vision for the process.

Furthermore, we have identified that a reciprocal relationship exists between successful implementation of a renewal agenda and its subsequent impact upon the behavioural disposition of the school leaders and, subsequently, on their willingness to initiate and implement a change agenda in their school in the future. A leader's behavioural disposition and personal sense of efficacy has a significant impact on their willingness to engage in school renewal. The presence of that impact suggested that a school leader's positive attitude towards change, demonstrated by behaviours that are strong in change agency, visioning, issue discovery, relationship building and risk willingness, and these play an important part in facilitating whole-of-school change endeavours.

We have found from experience that school leader actions are essential in promoting visioning processes and relationship building underpin successful school renewal. We believe that there is a positive relationship existing between a school leader's experience in effecting change, risk willingness and proactivity and the leadership of school renewal. Consequently, it is important that school leaders are predisposed and have the necessary efficacy beliefs to undertake the process in the first instance. Other factors such as school location, school size, school leader age and gender were not believed to affect leadership approaches; however, some situational aspects such as staff and community disposition towards change did in fact have an impact.

Leadership within a renewal context is concerned with deep-reaching whole-of-school change, with school community shifts in underlying assumptions and beliefs about learning and teaching required. Achieving ongoing school cultural change and renewal is a major challenge for today's school leaders. The implementation of a successful renewal agenda highlights the importance of leadership attributes in cultivating an unwavering moral ethic of continuous and lasting change among staff and community stakeholders, and for us this is our Never-Ending Story.

Our continued emphasis has been on identifying the individual school leader as a pedagogic leader in defining and articulating a compelling vision for the future, and engaging and inspiring staff towards the desired direction of renewal agenda including the building of alignment of stakeholders as a key ingredient of success. The school leaders' role as coach, facilitator and supporter of people is noted, as are contemporary social values such as trust, respect and diversity that they need to exhibit and exercise in building willing coalitions. As a pedagogic leader engaged with major change the school leader needs to be prepared for the element of risk and potential conflict that accompanies challenges to the status quo in a school. Therefore, the school leader's proactivity, pedagogical knowledge and credibility and risk-willing disposition are significant influences that can underpin the initiation of a successful renewal process in the school.

School renewal does not happen by decree from well-meaning school leaders. Similarly, it has been argued that there is a need for the school's leader to drive the proposed change agenda and to progressively build the necessary coalitions as it unfolds. An outcome which supports the belief that school leaders need to alter existing relationships in order to enhance the opportunity for renewal in a school's learning and teaching to eventuate.

Throughout this book we have argued that tomorrow's schools will need leaders who hold an unshakable belief in the ultimate success of their schools. Leadership research in schools continually reinforces that informed successful, future focused practice is characterised by school leaders who:

1 Articulate an exciting mission, vision, values and goals for the school within a future-oriented context.
2 Ensure that a school's education programmes are responsive to student needs by emphasising achievement and engagement for *all* students.
3 Focus attention on developing a productive school culture that encourages collaboration in learning and teaching.
4 Use appropriate targeted data to guide decision-making and continuous improvement.
5 Build on success, thus acknowledging staff engagement.
6 Take responsibility for building sustainable leadership capacity in the school.

It is known that some schools have productive cultures; others have problematic ones. To move towards a productive school culture a school leader will need to articulate within their respective learning and teaching cultures:

- If we expect all students to learn, *what* is it we expect them to learn?
- *How* will we know if they are learning it?
- And what will we do when they don't?

A *Hippocratic Oath* for school leaders could be cited as "... to help all students succeed to their potential in the global environment within which our community is an intricate and important part". To achieve this outcome school leaders will require their schools to have approaches in its pedagogy that are consistent with the value statement of the school and assessment processes that accurately reflect what students know.

The research is abundantly clear; nothing motivates a child more than success when learning is valued and high expectations are held by schools and their community working together in partnership. However, a vision without commitment and shared understanding won't give you a great school, and a vision without the right staff attitude is irrelevant.

The only way to deliver to the teachers who are achieving is to not burden them with those who are not achieving. Future-oriented school leaders will not have the time resources to micro-manage staff. The best people don't need to be micro-managed, they need to be guided and well led. As Collins (2001) indicated: "Letting the wrong people hang around is unfair to all the right people, as they inevitably find themselves compensating for the inadequacies of the wrong people. Worse, it can drive away the best people."

In order to prepare schools to cater for the challenges that schools will face in the future we need to unlock and further develop the intellectual capital among school leaders and staff, and this will in turn improve the status and standing of teaching as a profession.

Effective school leadership is predicated on the assumption that improving students' learning, through engaging pedagogy, is the purpose of schooling. To have a viable, world-class vibrant school education system, will need strong and credible leadership from leaders and teacher leadership teams in their respective educational settings. The aim must be to have empowered school leadership. School leader must see their role as a leader of leaders, not of followers.

Major educational reform in recent times has tended to be focused upon structural change and curriculum modification, unfortunately with neglect of the learning process and school pedagogical practices. Consequently, we see that government and system attempt to reform schools and schooling through the imposition of externally prescribed, pre-determined goal and outcome initiatives. Transforming schools, whether directed towards reform or school renewal, is inextricably linked to the exercise of school leadership. For school renewal to be progressed successfully there is a need for strong, ongoing pedagogical leadership from the school leaders. It is clear that in performing the role of school leader, the school leader becomes the context setter for school change and the designer of learning experiences for the school community.

Therefore, the educational leader's role must be oriented towards improving the status of the teaching profession and a personal commitment to:

- Ensure that quality learning and teaching is the central focus in every classroom.
- Ensure that a coherent, engaging, clearly articulated and sequential core curriculum is provided for teachers to follow.
- Provide a safe, secure, disciplined and quality learning environment that enables students to access a well-rounded education and also, importantly, for teachers to practise their craft and to be valued for the contribution they make.
- Support the enhanced growth of a well-qualified teaching workforce.

Undertaking school renewal is a big step for a school's staff. It isn't tinkering around the edges. It is about reaching a common agreement about making changes in the way that the school does business in terms of learning and teaching endeavour. Renewal is achieved through a process of opening up school and classroom practices and assessments to collective reflection from a range of internal and external stakeholders.

Experience would indicate that people do not make substantive changes quickly and easily. Consequently, it is important that leadership take the necessary time to decide whether this approach to school renewal aligns with the way stakeholders think the school should improve its work with students.

Today's teachers and administrators are collectively faced with the complex task of creating a sense of purpose and direction for a school – and this requires pedagogical leadership – not corporate managerialism from the school leadership. As an educationalist first, it is important for school leaders as to make a difference in the culture of the teaching and learning programmes in schools.

Having access to informed successful practice will assist school leaders embrace the student learning component of their role, and enable them to focus on pedagogical activity that will impact on what happens at the classroom level in terms of enriching student outcome achievement.

As pedagogic leaders it is the school leader's role not only to determine what should be learned but also to help create an environment that is inclusive and which will maximise each student's learning opportunities. Further, it is leadership's role to contribute to the creation of a climate in which experimentation can occur and in which mistakes can be learned from. Such a culture we believe is a prerequisite in a renewing school.

Sustainable school renewal – An ongoing, continuous improvement orientation

Renewal is a continuous journey that needs to be sustained through collaborative staff and stakeholder endeavour. It is about engaging school stakeholders in a process of striving for continuous improvement in the school's learning culture, student outcomes and greater pedagogic effectiveness and efficiency; and is seen as an ongoing pursuit of improvement in all facets of a school's pedagogic culture. Consequently, in order to facilitate and implement such a mindset, a school leader needs to have a clear understanding of what exactly renewal as a continuous change paradigm entails. The schema presented in Figure 18.1 gives a diagrammatic representation of that journey.

Understanding the concept of renewal is the first step in applying continuous improvement to the school's learning and teaching culture. This entails careful, considered planning of the renewal agenda and the identification of key aspects of the school's curriculum culture that needs to be improved. It is at this stage that the school leader gathers as much data as possible, considering what needs must be addressed (**Need Identified**).

Conclusion

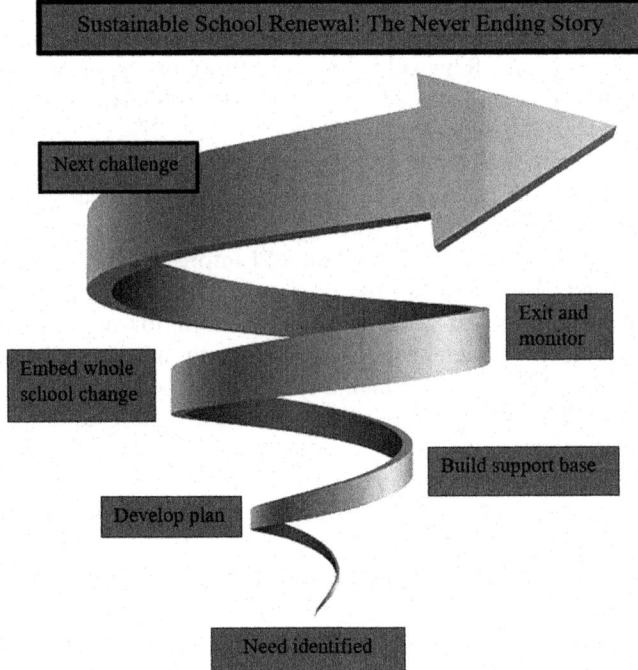

Figure 18.1 Sustainable school renewal schema.

Next, the school leader's task needs to be focused on leading the creation of a suitable plan and agenda for the proposed changes and setting out clear expectations for timelines and outcomes to be achieved (**Develop a Plan**). In the planning phase, a school leader needs to establish clear expectations, objectives and processes necessary to deliver the desired results in accordance with the change agenda goals. Setting clear expectations is a key to achieving renewal because the accuracy of the goals and their completeness is a major part of the process of improving.

Initiatives are more likely to fail unless the school leader is able to build a support base among staff and a willingness from a significant cohort of them to buy into the renewal change agenda and to be proactive in implementing it (**Build Support Base**). Staff buy-in is the first step to carrying out any identified change in a school. It is, however, never really guaranteed as we have indicated, particularly if the culture is toxic. We have found that school leaders enjoy being involved in changes that improve school outcomes, but unfortunately more often than not staff will have an initial tendency to fear and fight changes proposed as we could see in Gleicher's equation.

Third is the need to execute what has been articulated during the planning phase of the process. Once a critical mass of support for the change is achieved the school leader may need to quickly deal with smaller issues that can arise, while giving those items with potentially greater impact the care and attention they deserve. As indicated renewal is a continuous improvement process and, as the name suggests, involves constantly re-examining and improving school learning and teaching processes (**Embed Whole School Change**). It involves the school leader:

- Focusing on student outcome and curriculum improvement – Ensuring that the school has an ongoing focus on incrementally improving pedagogy, curriculum and relationships with stakeholder groups.
- Creating an attitude to and culture of continuous Improvement – Communicating that the renewal agenda is the responsibility of all staff and stakeholder groups, not just the school's leadership.
- And, importantly, publicly supporting those staff who are implementing the change, and identifying and coaching those staff members who are not up to speed.

At each stage in a sustainable renewal journey a reality check is required to ensure that what has been achieved aligns with what is expected. As renewal is an ongoing change journey data collection is important at all phases as through its analysis it is then possible to consider what has and can be improved therefore, giving direction to future change initiatives that aim to achieve greater results next time (**Exit and monitor**).

When the improvement is consolidated, the bar is raised and with an aim to even better performance next time (**Next Challenge**).

In Table 18.1 we separate the concept of renewal as a continuous school improvement journey from the concepts of a single school innovation initiative.

Table 18.1 Renewal and innovation differences in school settings

	School renewal	School innovation initiative
Effect	Is long-term, but there are no major seismic changes. Change is ongoing and embedded.	Often short-term, and likely to entail a more drastic change.
Pace	Small well considered and resourced steps.	Big steps often limited resourcing and outcome specific.
Change	Gradual, consistent and ongoing.	Often strained, hurried and unpredictable.
Participation	All stakeholders in the school community.	Only key players involved; leadership teams, teaching teams, specialists teachers, etc.
Focus of effort	Staff seen as the most valuable asset and carriers of the change agenda.	Technology often has a significant role.

A summary of our beliefs about educational renewal and change and school leader pedagogic leadership

Throughout this book we have clearly stated our beliefs about educational leadership and change. These beliefs as listed in summary form in Table 18.2 and are grounded in our collective experience as school leaders for in excess of forty years in a range of school scenarios.

Table 18.2 Our personal beliefs about education, leadership and school change

1. The sustainable re-culturing of a school requires a proven renewal paradigm of change that can be activated by the school leader.
2. The improvement of students' learning outcomes often requires a significant change in a school's pedagogical culture.
3. A leadership disposition that values and encourages fairness, openness, honesty, loyalty and integrity in relationships will facilitate the creation of a learning and teaching culture that is purposeful and empowering and subsequently renewal ready.
4. Principal efficacy is an essential factor that underwrites successful and sustainable pedagogic change.
5. Re-culturing a school requires a clearly defined and well communicated vision of an agreed future, which generates commitment, not compliance.
6. Principals' self-efficacy beliefs, in association with their personal behavioural dispositions, impact directly on school improvement, effectiveness and renewal endeavours.
7. The enabling of schools to be empowered with the authority to make decisions that reflect the needs and aspirations of the individual school and the local community will enhance community perceptions about the value of learning and teaching.
8. That one template of schooling does not fit all school situations, because there is never one right design or one structure that will suit every school in a variety of situations.
9. The professional relationships that teachers establish with their students form the bases of an inclusive pedagogy.
10. A measure of good leadership is the accommodation of the multitude of situational factors that impact significantly on school leadership strategies and decision-making.
11. A toxic school culture, if not excised by the principal, will derail any attempts to initiate school curriculum or cultural change.
12. Weak school leaders tend to create and foster a more sycophantic staff culture.
13. School change to be effective and sustainable requires demonstrated pedagogic leadership from the school principal.
14. The leadership attributes associated with initiating and leading sustainable school change and those anticipated to be required in generating school renewal, require differentiation, particularly in terms of the principals' roles and their understanding of pedagogy and curriculum implementation.
15. Where empowerment is fostered, teamwork and collaboration thrive.

Table 18.2 (Cont.)

16. Student learning will be enhanced when performance management conversations between the school leader and the teacher collegially address effectiveness, performance and improving students' learning.
17. A principal engaged in school renewal will need to possess excellent communication and people skills, and be prepared to coach and mentor staff.
18. It is better to be a leader among leaders than a leader of followers.
19. Many schools are over-managed by the principal, but under-led.
20. Delegation is not distributed leadership in schools
21. The school as a learning organisation is an organisation that is skilled at creating, acquiring, and transferring knowledge, and at modifying its teachers' behaviours to reflect new knowledge and insights.
22. Continuous school improvement and renewal requires a commitment to learning. Therefore, the first step for the school principal is to foster an environment that is conducive to that learning. Noting that not all learning comes from staff reflection and self-analysis. Sometimes the most powerful insights come from looking outside one's immediate school environment in order to gain a new perspective on teaching and learning.
23. In the absence of ongoing learning, school staff simply repeat previous practices and therefore changes remain cosmetic, and student outcome improvements are either fortuitous or at best short-lived.
24. An empowered school is one in which individuals have the knowledge, skill, desire and opportunity to personally succeed in a way that leads to improved student outcome success.
25. Empowerment within a school context is a process of enabling staff to adopt new desired pedagogic behaviours that further their individual aspirations and those of the school in general.
26. When school leaders put the priority on adding value to the schools' learning and teaching culture, improved student achievement outcomes follow.
27. Value can be added to a school in different ways, such as through changes to pedagogy, the learning environment and relationships with and between stakeholders.
28. Leadership within a school that is predicated on value-adding can best be understood as an amalgam between a value creation mindset and leadership intent with behaviours that are necessary to translate that mindset into quality learning and teaching endeavours.
29. The selection of the right people for school leadership positions is of critical importance as leaders have such a significant impact on overall teacher effectiveness and in turn the overall organisation's performance and success.
30. Improving emotional intelligence in the school workplace can have a direct and positive impact on:
    - The effectiveness of the school's leadership and management.
    - Staff morale and retention.
    - Communications and relationship building.
    - Client satisfaction and student learning outcomes.
31. Effective principals have the skills to manage their own emotions and moods, and to influence the emotions and moods of other people towards best possible outcomes.

(Continued)

Table 18.2 (Cont.)

32.	Public scrutiny of schools and the education enterprise will only increase with time, not decrease.
33.	School leaders in renewing schools will need to understand that they have a significant role in growing the intellectual and resilience capacity of all staff, including themselves.
34.	An effective school staff concentrates on their core business: the quality of its learning and teaching programmes.
35.	A principal's mantra should be that failure is not an option.
36.	Schools will increasingly have to risk manage aberrant mental health issues.
37.	Growing staff skills, by providing appropriate resources, authority, opportunities, motivation, as well as holding them responsible and accountable for outcomes of their actions, will contribute to general staff competence and satisfaction.
38.	Principals are the advocates in every school for optimising every student's learning capacity, and their catalytic teachers are the enthusiastic leaders who get this done.
39.	A principal engaged in school renewal will need to possess excellent communication and people skills, and be prepared to coach and mentor both new and existing staff.
40.	The levels of accountability required of schools are usually a measure of public trust.
41.	Accountability is recognised as a dynamic and heuristic process. It is part of what a school is, not something it does. Each school will need to identify through its planning processes its own path to improvement and then as a collaborative and inclusive exercise, it then becomes a part of everyone's responsibility.
42.	Teachers are more willing to accept the accountability demands required of them if the leader to whom they are accountable has creditability.
43.	The commitment to excellent public schooling underwrites our entrenched beliefs in democracy, equity and social mobility.
44.	In any school renewal process the sustainability of a change is often difficult to determine as embedded change becomes the accepted way of doing things over time, and it then becomes the foundational base of the next iteration of renewal.
45.	A school renewal process never has just one leader as positional power has little credibility if the renewal is going to be embedded in practice of every classroom teacher.
46.	School leaders need to forecast what values, skills and knowledge their students will need in a society thirteen years in the future. And, we all need to be cognisant of what the international testing is telling us about where we sit in what will be the new order.

We have taken care in this work to ensure that our perceptions of school leader leadership and change match the reality that will be found in today's schools. Many school leader colleagues have been consulted over the years to ensure that their perspectives on the belief statements we have presented are congruent with our own experiences as educators.

Creating an educational environment accommodating of these beliefs, trends and accountability pressures within a school renewal paradigm is the challenge for today's school leaders. It is an ongoing challenge.

Simply giving school leaders more information and more readings about renewal and the importance of pedagogic leadership is not likely in itself to improve educational outcomes in schools. Instead, we have approached this book with a view to providing very real insights and a workable guide to leading ongoing and substantial educational changes in their schools.

Often there is a disconnect between the management of a school as opposed to the educational leader with the former often resisting embarking on a renewal agenda where the later simply embraces it. Hence the sub-title of the book – *A Guide for Ground-breakers and Not Caretakers.*

We have found through our own journeys and forays into change models, that not surprisingly, managers tend to look less favourably upon large-scale curriculum, pedagogic or cultural change given their tendency to be risk averse in respect to changes. On the other hand, leaders with a strong pedagogic credibility are far more likely to engage with and to support a renewal change agenda in their schools.

Those who read our belief statements, as listed, both managers and pedagogic leaders, will we believe appreciate their truth, and applicability in the world of schools today.

We have embarked on this book with the belief that if school leaders are fully informed about the real advantages of them engaging their school in a renewal agenda then the educational outcomes of our students and the satisfaction of staff and stakeholders in general will subsequently be greatly improved.

In essence, believe that in the case of heroic, risk-taking, pedagogic school leadership: Who Dares Wins, and the students benefit.

Reference

Collins, J. (2001). *Good to great: Why some companies make the leap ... and others don't*. London: Random House Business Books.

Appendix

The pedagogic profile: Assisting teachers' professional, pedagogic learning

Principles/Level 1	Level 2	Level 3	Level 4
≫ OPPORTUNITY TO LEARN ≫ Teacher pre-programmes work. ≫ All students work on material tchr believes is interesting on material tchr believes is interesting.	≫ Teacher decides learning programme. ≫ Students motivated by tchr. and engaged in learning.	≫ Class meetings to accept tchr beliefs about student needs. ≫ Some learning processes taught. ≫ Remediation seen.	≫ Students devise meaningful investigations. ≫ Teams. ≫ Explicit models taught in context. ≫ HOTS. ≫ Metacognition and learning processes taught – wall charts.
≫ P2. CONNECTION and CHALLENGE ≫ Learning experiences do not recognise prior learning and the skills and values are taught at the same time every year.	≫ Learning experiences recognise prior learning in maths and reading. ≫ Students challenged normatively.	≫ Students work in groups building on strengths. ≫ Peer modelling. ≫ Integrated curriculum challenges.	≫ Teamwork. ≫ Negotiated challenges. ≫ Zone of proximal development. ≫ Integrated curriculum, open-ended tasks, authentic learning.
≫ P3. ACTION & REFLECTION ≫ Student sit in rows and work through exercises from photocopied material or black board.	≫ Students in rows working material provided by tchr. ≫ Some concrete experiences in maths and T&E.	≫ Students in groups, integrated curriculum, rich open-ended tasks. ≫ Negotiated outcomes. ≫ Reflection & goal-setting in portfolios.	≫ Authentic tasks which relate to life in community. ≫ Negotiated goal-setting and reflection in all learning: cognitive, affective, physical & social learning.

≫P4. MOTIVATION & PURPOSE ≫Goals set by teacher but not communicated to students. ≫Students expected to be motivated by long term-goal-employment, etc.	≫Goals set by teacher and communicated in terms of expectations. ≫Motivation external.	≫Students have some input into courses and goals. ≫Students are motivated by group dynamics.	≫Class meetings negotiate the curriculum (within parameters). ≫Rubrics collegially developed. ≫Meaningful work and class environment motivate students.
≫P5. INCLUSIVITY & DIFFERENCE ≫Teacher ensured that students' needs were accommodated in achievement groups – reading and maths.	≫Teacher has TAGs and SAER programs in place.	≫SAER and TAGs in place. ≫IEPs signed off by parents. ≫Culture of inclusion in classroom.	≫SAER, TAGs, IEPs signed off by all parties. ≫Aboriginal & ESL students welcomed. ≫Classrooms accommodate physically disabled students.
≫P6. INDEPENDENCE & COLLABORATION. ≫No independence, tchr makes all of the decisions. ≫Some teacher directed group work.	≫Some independence. ≫Some group work.	≫Some class meetings. ≫A degree of independence in decision making about the curriculum. ≫Lots of group collaborative work.	≫Class meetings. ≫Negotiated curriculum. Substantive conversations. ≫Collaboration is the norm. ≫Sophisticated group work, roles taught explicitly. ≫Strategies charted.
≫P7. SUPPORTIVE ENVIRONMENT ≫Low-level support. ≫Competitive environment. "Haves" and "Have nots". ≫Low level of student morale. ≫Yelling at students.	≫Support from teacher in a parental manner. "My Kids". ≫Traditional relationships. "Haves" and "Have nots". ≫Some yelling.	≫Support from teacher and students. ≫Supportive environment. ≫Students' roles starting to be used in groups. ≫Happy working environment.	≫High level of support. ≫Students have significant roles in class organisation. ≫Students feel included and valued by all parties. ≫Failure is seen as a learning experience. Peer feedback & debriefing.

Appendix 225

(*Continued*)

(Cont.)

Principles/Level 1	Level 2	Level 3	Level 4
≫A1 – A5 ASSESSMENT: valid, educative, etc. ≫Teacher sets tests. ≫Standardised tests used. ≫Portfolios are work samples. ≫Students ranked. ≫Failure punished.	≫Comprehensive standardised testing. ≫Portfolios have some annotations. ≫Subject based assessment.	≫Student profiles used. ≫Portfolios include annotations. ≫Some reflection & goal-setting. ≫A lot of black line masters in portfolios. ≫Learning journeys & 3 way conferences.	≫All students profiled. ≫Portfolios include annotation, reflection, goal-setting, learning journeys, 3 way conf. ≫Reporting policy negotiated with stakeholders. ≫Some S.O. levelling. ≫Rubrics negotiated with class.

Index

Accountability 186–198; accountabalism 198; link to change 13; and school planning 49; approaches to 122, 137; external 54–55, 64–66, 95, 108, 111, 140; and public confidence 155, 186–193, 205–206; cultural influence of 69; venomous 197

Barriers to change 77; situational factors 78; 84–87; staff and union resistance 77, 78; system policies and processes 80–81
Building capacity: among staff 184; through trust 23, 141; staff readiness 141

Catalytic staff: defined 179–180; characteristic of 183–184; importance in school re-culturation 19, 34, 93 181,
Catalysts for change: system reforms 62; community and stakeholder aspirations 46, 48, 50, 54, 57, 63–64, 133
Change: general xvi, 1–3, 7, 9; school renewal as a change 1–4, 7–10, 12, 15–16, 18, 23–24, 32, 45, 52, 93, 101, 141, 179, 181, 201, 212, 214, 218; and catalytic staff 179–180; and leadership 8, 10–13, 15, 19, 21, 25–26, 28–29, 33–34, 39, 42, 45, 51, 54, 85, 93, 122, 133, 149–150, 155–156, 178, 184, 190, 200–201, 203, 214; and vision 46, 50, 133; critical mass for 180; sustainable school xvi, 2, 10–13, 21–22, 25–26, 48, 59, 76, 100, 129, 133, 149, 200–201, 207–211; and learning organisation 129; and efficacy 31–33, 154; system drivers of 2, 4, 16, 63, 80, 98, 191, 195, 206; and distributed leadership 202;

cultural 13, 38, 42, 53, 83, 133, 184, 204, 212; teacher and community perspectives about 8, 13, 16, 18, 20, 33, 38–39, 41, 48, 54, 77, 84, 122, 178–179, 182; pedagogic 10, 26, 35, 58–59, 70, 95, 105, 108–109, 111, 117, 140, 165, 184, 204; barriers to 77–90
Charter Schools 63
Coaching 114, in encouraging collaboration 18; supporting staff 22; see also peer observation and mentoring
Collective efficacy xv, 40–42, 142, 183, 213

Devolution: advantages of 66–67, rhetoric associated with 69–74
Distributed leadership: defined 119–120; not delegation 123–124, links to organisational maturity 120
Drake Predictive Profiling instrument 151–152

Efficacy defined 31, 35, 38, 40
Efficacy and flow 39, 55–56
Efficacy and risk taking 32; see also leadership efficacy and change
Emotional intelligence: perspectives of 124–125; defined 153; links to leadership traits 152–154
Empowerment 64, 102, 105, 116

Flow theory 39, 55; and school leadership 56; mental 56; emotional 56–57

Hero leadership 120
High stakes testing 120, 125
Hippocratic oath for school leaders 215

Independent school movement 65, 138

228 Index

Leaders" personal commitment to change 11–12, 24–25, 44, 57, 72, 101, 151, 216, 220
Leadership behaviours xvi–xvii, 5, 18–22, 24–26, 31–34, 42, 52–54, 76, 78–80, 85–86, 137, 149–156, 181–183, 213–214, 221
Leadership disposition towards change xvii, 17–18, 20–22, 25–26, 29, 31–33, 42, 53–54, 56, 85, 93, 105, 150, 154, 165, 213–215, 220
Leadership efficacy beliefs 31–33, 38, 158; see also self-efficacy; efficacy
Leadership efficacy and change 1, 17, 21, 23, 28, 31–32, 39, 42, 50–51, 54, 76–77, 85, 149, 154–156, 180, 214, 220
Leadership of school renewal 10–11, 17, 21–23, 26, 32, 38, 50, 72, 76, 100, 116, 141, 149, 156, 181–182, 213–214
Leadership resilience 55, 161, 165, 166, 213
Learning organisations xvi, 8, 9, 127; defined 129; locus of control 128; characteristics of 130; relationship to school culture 128, 133–134; and professional capital 128; commitment to 130, 132, 146, 195, 203
Loose coupling in schools 188

Measuring value added aspect of schooling 143–145
Mental health issues 160–176; in schools 166, 167–169, 172–176, 222; growth of 170, 175
Mentoring 17, 20, 113–115, 156
Mission 45–46, 158, 203, 215
Moral leadership 39, 120; in vision setting 44, 57; in learning 60; see chapter 4

New Public Management 54, 72, 82, 98, 99–100, 136, 179, 187, 195

Organizational efficacy 11, 130, 139–140
Outcomes Based Education xv, 5

Pedagogy defined 70–71, characteristics of 95–97, 109, 117, 204; and curriculum 12, 23, 52, 84, 97, 100, 175; and student learning 10, 50, 69–70, 109–110; authentic 117; and teaching 26, 69, 87, 105, 109, 147, 165, 204, 220; school focus 26, 72, 95, 104, 115, 146–147, 150, 205, 215–216, 219; and school purpose statement 48–49, 204

Pedagogic efficacy 34–37
Pedagogic leadership 28, 44–45, 50, 52, 73, 80, 100–101, 104, 113, 141, 194, 205, 220–221
Peer observation 17, 113, 115
Performance management 113; as an accountability and feedback mechanism 113; as a conversation 113; in developing and supporting staff 114–116; of the principal 138–139, 207; and the school system 211
Planning 108, 189, 204, 208; school level 48, 138–139, 190, 193, 222; for professional development 148; succession 140, 210–211; system level 69, 138–140; workforce 138, 140, 216; teacher level 109; for school renewal 207–209, 217, 218; validation of 193, 197
Profiling leadership behaviours 149–156
Profiling teacher pedagogic awareness 71, 116–117; see also Appendix
Public Confidence in schools 186–188, 195–96
Purpose statement 45, 48, 57

Reculturing a school 1–2, 11–12, 23, 44, 52–53, 101, 184, 220; locus of control 12
Risk management 173 – 174, 195, 222
Risk willing leadership 136, 154–155, 165, 180, 200, 214–215, 223

School as learning organisation 8, 128, 130–131, 133, 213, 221: see chapter 10
School board 103–104, 139, 188; and principal performance management 138–139; and school accountability 190, 196; in independent empowered school 65–66, 137–138
School effectiveness 7, 11, 26, 28, 40, 51–52, 65, 68, 140, 144, 149, 156, 178, 203–204, 221
School Improvement xvi, 1, 8, 11, 59, 132, 135; and leadership 51, 220; and school culture 48, 100; and accountability 49, and change 59; and renewal 148, 219, 221; see also change
School planning 47, 139
School purpose statement 45, 48, 57; see also vision and mission
School reform 34, 93, 97, 99, 105; different from renewal 1–14, 22, 25, 101; characteristics of 16–17; system level 64, 77, 137, 216; see also chapter 1

School Renewal xiv–xv, 1–4, 7, 9, 12, 15–16, 19, 25, 41, 74, 79, 101, 141, 146, 149, 183, 200–202, 210, 213–214, 215–216, 220–223; differentiating from school reform 2–4, 7–8, 15, 22; influences on 18, 41, 45, 48, 77–78, 217; planning for 207–209; see leadership of school renewal
School renewal schema 217–218
School teacher leaders: see catalytic teachers
Self-promoting managers 84
Self-efficacy 34, 39, 41, 51, 55, 214; defined 31–32; and behavioural correlates 28, 33, 38–39, 42, 50–51, 54, 155, 220; and flow 39, 56; situational specific 76
Shared leadership commitment 57–60, 203, 221–222
Situational factors 76–94, 220; leadership 52–53, 76, 120; variables 36, 64, 68, 83, 116, 213–214
Staff as barrier to school re-culturation 19, 78, 84, 90, 216; risk willingness 93, 130–131, 134; readiness 174, 180
Staff commitment 12, 26, 35, 37–40, 45, 47–49, 53, 113, 115, 123, 147,167 Student -centred pedagogy 110
Staff resilience 37–38, 105, 164, 166, 168–169, 222
Stakeholders 133, 217, 223; and school vision 45, 48, 50, 59, and school relationships 72, 85, 93, 139, 145, 182, 201, 203, 214; and accountability 186; and distributed leadership 202; in renewal agenda 217, 219, 221; commitment 10, 47, 50, 141, 216
Student mental health issues 170
Sycophants; as barrier to re-culturation 84–87

Sycophantic school culture 77, 88–90, 220
Sycophantocracy 86, 88–93

Teacher efficacy 34, 36–37, 39–40, 85, 184
Teacher leaders 9, 148, 179, 216 180; characteristics of 180
The Teaching X Factor 185
Tiger Woods's golf bag 111
Toxic culture survey 87
Toxic management 82, 84–85
Toxic school cultures 83, 86, 90; intentional 82; unintentional toxicity 82; addressing the issue 86

Value adding 139; defined and contextualised 143, relevance to schools 144; measuring of 145–146; student voice in 146
Values: of school leadership xvii, 11, 24–25, 29, 33, 44, 65, 105, 158, 165, 202–203, 205, 215, 220; of staff xv, 12–13, 16, 24, 52, 179; prevailing school and community 4, 7–8, 11, 44–45, 51, 58–59, 67, 81, 116, 133, 145, 147, 179; audit of 132; impact of change on 3, 4, 7, 12, 132–133; enduring nature 7, 3
Venomous accountability 197–198; see also accountabalism
Vision as an aspiration 10, 13, 16, 47, 49, 131, 142, 158, 203
Vision characteristics 49, 51, 147
Vision defined 38, 44; shared nature of 8, 10, 12, 16, 29, 47, 50, 57, 214; leadership role in setting 11, 12, 21, 27, 33, 45–46, 49; and renewal 19, 33, 50, 209; in school re-culturation 11, 44, 133, 184, 220; as a school's compass 44
Vision horizon 203
Vision stewardship 51, 201
Visionary leadership 152, 155–157, 180